Sociological Studies 3

PROFESSIONS AND PROFESSIONALIZATION

ADVISORY EDITORIAL BOARD

SOCIOLOGICAL STUDIES 3

Professions and Professionalization

EDITED BY

J. A. JACKSON

Professor of Social Theory and
Institutions, Queen's University
Belfast

CAMBRIDGE at the University Press 1970

CAMBRIDGE UNIVERSITY PRESS
Cambridge, New York, Melbourne, Madrid, Cape Town, Singapore,
São Paulo, Delhi, Dubai, Tokyo

Cambridge University Press
The Edinburgh Building, Cambridge CB2 8RU, UK

Published in the United States of America by Cambridge University Press, New York

www.cambridge.org
Information on this title: www.cambridge.org/9780521136471

© Cambridge University Press 1970

First published 1970
This digitally printed version 2010

A catalogue record for this publication is available from the British Library

Library of Congress Catalogue Card Number: 75-123346

ISBN 978-0-521-07982-2 Hardback
ISBN 978-0-521-13647-1 Paperback

EDITOR'S PREFACE

The concept of profession and the grounds on which certain occupations claim to enjoy professional status is a highly appropriate example of the kind of conceptual area which this series aims to explore. As in the first two numbers on *Social Stratification* and *Migration* the purpose of this volume is to raise a number of questions about the adequacy of theoretical concepts used by sociologists and others to describe social phenomena. In particular the adequacy of concepts that have 'passed into the literature' needs constantly to be reassessed in terms of new research findings and varying empirical examples. The editorial aim of the series is not, however, to provide a new 'final' statement in the form of a 'reader' or a set of papers which tidy up the theoretical garden.

In the best sense it is hoped that Sociological Studies will provide *working papers* on a theme of general and continuing interest to social scientists rather than final statements. The international range covered by the contributors together with the intention that they should speculate freely on the problem produces inevitable discrepancies of viewpoint and highlights further problems yet to be resolved. Equally it is hoped that the series will continue to provide, as it has in its initial volumes, a forum for the development and furthering of contemporary theory in the social sciences as these develop from varying traditions and with differing national tendencies and interests.

Each of the papers in this volume is published for the first time. My wife has continued to provide valuable editorial assistance in preparing the volume for publication on a tight schedule which aims to bring out each annual number less than a year from the completion of the authors' manuscripts. Sociological Studies 4 will be devoted to 'Role' and will appear in 1971 and the theme of Sociological Studies 5 in 1972 will be 'Social Change'.

J.A.J.

Belfast
April 1970

CONTRIBUTORS

G. Harries-Jenkins
Staff Tutor in Social Studies, University of Hull

M. N. Hodge
Research Student, University of East Anglia

H. Jamous
Chargé de Recherche, Centre National de la Recherche Scientifique, Paris

T. Leggatt
Lecturer in Sociology, University of Sussex

V. Olesen
Associate Professor of Sociology, University of California, San Francisco

B. Peloille
Research Fellow, Centre de Sociologie de l'Innovation, Paris

C. Turner
Senior Lecturer in Sociology, University of East Anglia

E. Whittaker
Department of Anthropology, University of California, Berkeley

CONTENTS

1 Professions and Professionalization – Editorial Introduction

JOHN A. JACKSON

1

PROFESSIONS AND PROFESSIONALIZATION-EDITORIAL INTRODUCTION

JOHN A. JACKSON

The development of the study of professions and professionalization by socio-logists has been matched, at least in part, by the growth of professional conscious-ness among sociologists themselves. The last two decades have seen in both Eastern and Western Europe and in the United States the emergence of the social scientist in a role which has demanded both the authentication of his discipline (his profession) within the academic community and also, as demands increasingly have been made upon him for research and policy, in the society at large. The profession of sociology, and in particular the professional bodies of national groups of sociologists, have increasingly, and often rapidly, developed from simple associations of those 'interested in the subject' and including many journalists, social workers and school teachers, to a tight body developing at least vestigial standards of authentication and defining a code of practice and an ethical sub-committee responsible for the practice of the discipline.Students of professions and the process of professionalization have been no less subject to the broader characteristics of the process observed in longer-established professional groupings.

A recent meeting of the university teachers' section of the British Sociological Association characterized the features of development peculiarly well in the assertions that (*a*) the true professionals were those who had been trained specifically in sociology and had not originally been trained in other disciplines, (*b*) this group – all those trained since 1950 – stood in contra-distinction to those who had reached sociology by other routes, (*c*) the profession should be concerned by the wide dissemination of sociology being both taught and practised by those who had not received such training, and in (*d*) the concern expressed about the proper place of research, and finally (*e*) the specific attempt by the Association to define standard procedures for research projects and to develop in its ethical sub-committee a code of practice.

The rapid growth in the range and number of 'professions' and the intellec-tual disciplines and the *pratique* linked to them raises anew the problem of the nature of the profession as a particular kind of occupational group with charac-teristics apparently not shared by other occupational groups. As Parsons asserts 'professional men are neither 'capitalists' nor 'workers' nor are they typically governmental administrators or bureaucrats'.[1] Parsons goes on to claim that although there may be a good deal of ambiguity at the fringes there is very little doubt about the central occupational characteristics of the professional. Such an analysis, however, rests squarely on certain assumptions regarding the characteristics of professions in the West and in particular the rise of professions since the period of the industrial revolution. That this rise is principally associated with the rise of the universities is hardly accidental. The profession as we know it — and as Parsons defines it — depends on the notion of the university as the institution of the intellectual. The modern university with its emphasis on teaching and research provides both the training and the intellectual tradition itself but in some measure incorporates also the legitimating structure of authority and competence. It is in the university that intellectual traditions have become institutionalized with these combined functions — united in British and American universities, separated but both apparent in the universities and the research institutes found on the continent of Europe.

What is the nature of the intellectual disciplines which have become institutionalized within the framework of the universities? As the curriculum of the modern university has developed and diversified it has produced new areas of competence assuring the status of profession. And yet it is not simply the universities which endow them. Some of the traditional professions — such as medicine on the continent of Europe or law in England, — have not always been found within the universities; rather they have developed a guild-like structure. The professions have needed to fulfil certain conditions of their group self-interest; the best solution has not always been to harmonize the group interests within the framework of the universities. Often the extreme emphasis on rationality stressed by the intellectual discipline has been in conflict with the practical case-law and apprenticeship methods of training favoured by those classes able to define the qualifications and standards required by aspirants to professional membership. Significantly law schools, especially on the European continent, and medical schools, especially in British universities of the nineteenth century, have formed the core disciplines around which the university grew. With earlier British universities such as Oxford and Cambridge and in many universities in the United States the core discipline was usually theology, reflecting the part played by religious bodies in founding university establishments. These three core professions found in the universities a means whereby they could perpetuate the characteristics of their professional wisdom as being based on the generalized learning of humane disciplines and in close association with them rather than simply depending on 'craft' factors in the learning of techniques and skills. The setting of the training process within the environment of an academic community with primary concerns in the dispassionate

1   T. Parsons, 'Professions', *International Encyclopedia of the Social Sciences* (New York, 1968), p. 539.

profession of knowledge itself serves to extend the range of legitimation, to add lustre and supra-authority to the ideals of detachment, public rather than self-interest, service to an ideal and ethic. The universities have gained a legitimation of a utilitarian kind by the demonstrable needs which are met by those it certifies as competent — this allows the continued presence of many faculties whose contribution is demonstrably non-utilitarian in character.

It is in no sense a criterion of professionalism whether certification is incorporated within a university framework but to the extent that universities have formed the primary legitimating institutions of expertise based on the manipulation of knowledge, as distinct from craft based activities, it has been usual for aspirant professions to find incorporation within the structure of universities for their training courses (e.g. veterinaries, dentists, town-planners, social workers). Normally the university's relationship is partial in that there appears within the training programme itself a tension between the abstract intellectual training (good of and for itself in terms of the liberal humane values of education and research) and the instrumental needs of developing actual practitioners involving the awkward and necessary business of allowing the 'trained' candidate to come into contact with the object of the exercise. There is already a tension here between 'medicine' and 'the treating of the sick'.[1] The first a pursuit of objective knowledge for its own sake; the second a lesser activity which for the pursuit has its primary function in the provision of examples and data (a laboratory) rather than the much vaunted service goal of the 'professional'.

The tension that is here exhibited is equally characteristic of other professions than medicine though it has developed in different ways in different circumstances. In law, in Britain, the primary function has been practical — few students study law for itself — there is little encouragement for the study of jurisprudence — Oxford and Belfast being exceptions (the latter for the reason, among others, that it serves the need of a relatively small population and does not need to turn out many lawyers). In France by contrast the Faculté de Droit assures the basis for a general academic discipline — almost the role of the Arts Faculties in Britain.

Hughes has rightly pointed out that the significant question to ask about occupations is not whether or not they are professions but to what extent they exhibit characteristics of professionalization.[2] The most important element in the rephrasing of this question is of course the definition of the problem in dynamic terms which recognize that in relation to the range of criteria by which a profession may be denoted, there may be considerable variation at different times and under different circumstances. This leads Denzin to suggest that professions are like social movements. 'They recruit only certain types of

1 See H. Jamous and B. Peloille, 'Professions or Self-perpetuating Systems?', pp. 127—37.
2 E. C. Hughes, 'Professions', *Daedalus* (1963).

persons, they develop highly elaborate ideologies and supra-individual values, they have their own mechanisms of socialization and they often attempt to proselytize and bring new persons into the fold.'[1] Such a social movement based on occupational membership and capacity is clearly uniquely non-instrumental in the sense in which Lockwood and Goldthorpe have developed the use of this term.[2] By contrast to their Luton workers the true 'professional' is work-oriented to the highest possible degree — for him it is the basis of a social move-ment developing, the more professionalized it is; a code of ethics and ideology comprehending not merely the work situation but extending beyond this to define a status and a style of life of universal relevance, in all aspects of life. A doctor or a priest is always 'on duty' in this sense; his vocation is a twenty-four hours a day, seven days a week, lifetime commitment. His occupational role is comprehensive and the implication is that membership of the occupa-tional group confers an acceptable and comprehensive life-style. For such occupations the broader aspects of a socialization process and educational framework, which not only closely controls selection but also provides training in terms of a general tradition, is clearly particularly appropriate. A trained mind is given precedence to technical competence which it is assumed can be readily picked up once the formal education process is complete.

The idea of a scaling of professions according to the degree to which their orientation falls into a more general 'education for life' category or a specific 'education for task' category is obviously only one of a number of factors which can be used to describe a typology of professions along very similar lines to those by which one might distinguish social movements. Cults may, for instance, be distinguished from institutionalized religious churches or denominations by their highly specific individual instrumentality, whereas membership of a religious body, at least by implication, defines a wider set of assumptions — a world view— appropriate to its members as a group.[3] Professional status and recognition by the wider society, at least in part, would appear to relate to the extent to which the techniques and the generalized system of knowledge and ideology are held in tension with one another.

Two other aspects of the ideological orientation of the profession should be considered. The service ideal of the professional is usually taken to be one of the key characteristics of the profession. But although an objective disinterestedness may indeed be a necessary condition of task performance, it is important to ask from whence this really derives. There is no reason to assume that professionals are either more charitable or more interested in their fellow men than others.

1 N. K. Denzin, 'Pharmacy — Incomplete Professionalization', *Social Forces*, 46, 3 (1968), 376.
2 J. H. Goldthorpe, D. Lockwood *et al.*, *The Affluent Worker: Industrial Attitudes and Behaviour* (Cambridge, 1968).
3 J. A. Jackson and R. G. Jobling, 'Towards a Definition of the Cult', in D. Martin (ed.), *The Sociology Yearbook of Religion in Britain* (London, 1968), pp. 102–4.

What, rather, is significant, is that their occupational niche is defined around problems of universal, or at least widely experienced, social concern. In each case they encompass specialized areas of knowledge which affect all individuals but where only a few can become expert. By virtue of their character these areas of knowledge assume a mystery a quality of the sacred whereby they take on a distinct mystique which distinguishes them from more mundane matters. The professional becomes necessarily the high priest of that area of knowledge in which he is acknowledged to be competent. The normative framework of his training assumes that he will engage in activity normally taboo (the cutting up of cadavers by medical students; the drawing of nudes in a life class by the artist; the probing of inner secrets by the psychiatrist; the examination of the body by the doctor). His training thus represents an initiation into mysteries; the processes of initiation may be more or less institutionalized but one of the factors of an analysis may well need to be 'degree of contact with elements given a highly charged (sacred) place in the central value system of the society'. The church, medicine and law all embrace such religious, physical and property elements to a high degree.

If one views professions along the lines of the more cynical approach enjoined by Schumpeter it is helpful to see them in terms of their monopoly over certain resources (knowledge) which are appropriate to certain social needs.[1] The niche which they have established as the basis of their exploitation of these resources and the activities which derive from them will clearly vary in the extent to which they allow a development of the area — and one will see a tension developing between a process of *mystification* (neologisms, research, creation of knowledge, etc.) and *demythologization*. Clearly some professions are better able to exploit their monopoly in these terms than others. Normally they are those better able to exploit the legitimation of their exclusive position derived from the general propositions of their practice — ethical, scientific, sacrificing, etc. all-embracing and therefore humane. Life and death of all men is in these terms a better bet than houses (long-term concerns); general medicine than dentistry (a man can get along without teeth); writing than broadcasting, and so on.

To extend this discussion in these terms would clearly be beyond the capacity of this introduction. Several of the contributions to this volume have expressed a plea for a more central concern with the sociology of occupations rather than taking for granted assumptions implying a distinction between occupation and profession. Turner and Hodge, for instance, believe in placing their discussion of occupations and professions clearly in terms of the division of labour stating that any occupation is capable of acquiring those elements, or aspects of them which

1 J. A. Schumpeter, *Imperialism and Social Classes* (Oxford, 1951), pp. 133-221. It is also useful to note here the development of the notion of 'entrepreneurial niche' by writers such as F. Barth, 'Economic Spheres in Darfur' in R. Firth (ed.), *Themes in Economic Anthropology* (London, 1967), and *The Role of the Entrepreneur in Northern Norway* (Bergen, 1964).

we have come to associate with professions. All occupations develop a culture, a terminology, a set of rules of craft, learning modes and dispositions. Many develop protective associations or guilds, organized associations or trade unions which act to institutionalize a given position in the occupational structure and further serve to define the relationship to the wider social structure. In a recent study of qualifying associations in Britain Hickson and Thomas have indicated that the older the association the more likely it is to yield a high score on those factors which they take to characterize professions.[1] Wilensky in his important article 'The Professionalization of Everyone?' points to the phenomenon of professionalization as increasingly affecting every occupation.[2] Significantly in socialist societies in Eastern Europe the word profession is used interchangeably with occupation and the distinction is not preserved.

B. Barber distinguishes the four essential attributes of professional behaviour as: (a) generalized knowledge, (b) primary orientation to the community interest, (c) internalized code of ethics, (d) rewards which primarily symbolize work achievement.[3]

It will have been noted that what has been stated so far in this paper would lead to some questioning of the assumptions implied in this essentially functionalist account. Ben-David, it seems to me, in his discussion of professions in relation to the class system, gives a more useful emphasis. It is the only appropriate perspective for the consideration of occupational groups and the status attributes that are proper to them. In Schumpeter's terms 'the place of professions in the social stratification of modern societies becomes easily discernible. They are a group of newly-created roles, carrying out novel and most rapidly expanding social functions . . . They have taken in these respects the place of the self-made *entrepreneur,* which in its turn had replaced the nobleman-landlord and the knight as the occupational ideal of Western societies.'[4] Ben-David goes on to point out that it is a characteristic of present-day societies to find the professional assume a central place in the class system though its locus varies according to the class system of the society. He makes clear the basic point in his view that:

Even the adherence of these professional classes to the socialist policies of their post-revolutionary countries does not differ so much from the liberalism of the rising *bourgeoisie* in the last century. Certainly the socialist middle classes are not more equalitarian in practice than their liberal predecessors used to be. Their emphasis on welfare policies, such as the provision of educational and health services, scientific research or technological show-pieces, is no less a

1 D. J. Hickson and M. W. Thomas, 'Professionalization in Britain: a Preliminary Measurement', *Sociology,* 3, 1 (January 1969), 48.
2 H. L. Wilensky, 'The Professionalization of Everyone?', *American Journal of Sociology,* 70 (1964), 137-58.
3 B. Barber, 'Some Problems in the Sociology of Professions', *Daedalus,* 92, 4 (1963).
4 J. Ben-David, 'Professions in the Class System of Present-day Societies', *Current Sociology,* 12, 3 (1963-4), 296-7.

matter of self-interest for the professional person than industrial production and the distribution of consumer goods is for the *bourgeois*. Professional middle classes are interested in social conditions which are optimal for the efficient performance of their activities, just as businessmen are interested in conditions necessary for theirs.[1]

II

The association of the professions in their development through the nineteenth and twentieth centuries with the universities and higher education generally has demonstrated the relation of the professions to some branch of learning and science. It is worth developing a little further the organizational framework of the professions and their articulation with their respective publics and the world to demonstrate a further dimension.

The fields of knowledge as we have already indicated revolve around areas which we have defined as mysteries — they involve essentially sacred elements access to which is the privilege of the *cognoscenti* — the professionals. In part they acquire their power from the formal academic training — the study of the objective and descriptive elements; combined with this are the elements of socialization and initiation into the wider class ideology of the professional group. Within the framework of increasing specialization, and indoctrination into the professional mystique is a combination of experience, apprenticeship and most importantly sets of attitudes appropriate to the different audiences of laymen and other professionals, assistants and competitors. In terms of all these elements the full role-set of the professional is defined.

This assertion does not cover the further problem of how it is that this authority is recognized by the society at large — and in particular by those whom the profession 'serves'. The discussion in this volume by Harries-Jenkins on the relationship between professions and organizations demonstrates that the authority base of the profession is not derived from the legitimation of rationality implied in Weber's model of bureaucratic organizations. Nor, if we are to follow Weber, is it to be found in the ideal-type formulations of either traditional or charismatic authority. In a recent introduction to a study of town-planning and housing policy Halsey has suggested that we need to define a fourth type of legitimation for the authority of the professionals in the modern world. Professional authority is that enjoyed 'by those who have been appointed to "a sphere of competence" on the basis of qualifications attested by a profes-sional group of peers'. Halsey goes on to point out that while many of the claims of a technical nature made by professionals will not differ from those of a bureaucratic organization it is also possible for their claims to derive from what he calls 'a kind of group charisma'. In these cases the judgements of the profes-sionals 'may be quite opaque to those outside the profession. The professional, by definition, is absolved from justifying his decision; he does not need to reveal

1 *Ibid.* pp. 297-8.

his basis in theory or fact or value.'[1]

Again one is dealing with the element of mystification referred to earlier; the craft and the ideology and learning that go with it must be guarded from the uninitiated. The process of professionalization can thus be seen, in part, as a process of increasingly protective measures to define the boundaries between the sacred company of those within the walled garden and those outside. Feld, in developing a model of 'primitive' military organizations suggests that: 'By definition . . . a primitive armed force confines its activities to the body of its actual members . . . The organization regards itself as the state of nature, and the outside world as the possibility of corruption and the fall of man . . . The primitivist approach systematically includes an image of the outside world which is essentially negative in nature.'[2] Feld contrasts his primitive type of military organization with a competitively oriented model which accepts equally rational competitors in the same field located outside the organization.

To the extent that professions develop their organizational structures and their attempt to maximize access to and control over resources in a given sector of knowledge and practice, they correspond in some measure to Feld's first type. The key dimension in Feld's primitive organizational type, of course, is that distinguishing the sacred from the profane. Outsiders are irrational, dangerous and potentially corrupting to the purity of the rational *cognoscenti*. The threat of corruption is ever present, however, in the form of the competitive forces in society at large — rival organizations, sub-professions, the dissemination of hitherto reserved knowledge through mass media.

Although this sacred-profane typology cannot be carried too far in relation to the analysis of the professions it is tempting to indicate ways in which it might suggest hypotheses in relation to the status attributes of given professions and the ranking structure within as well as outside professions. In the case of the military it is notable that status tends to be distributed in direct relation to the degree to which the activity corresponds most closely to behaviour defined as purely military. Infantry and cavalry regiments have higher status *because* they have no utility at all outside the military sphere. They are at the centre of the professional circle, those others in the organization, engineers, doctors, paymasters, etc. are defined as nearer to the periphery. They are contaminated to the degree that they perform tasks which are *also* performed outside the military organization based on a rationality which is not defined *solely* by the military.

In the case of medicine one may again suggest that this analysis applies to the specialist who enjoys high status and the general practitioner whose status is relatively lower. Although primarily a technologist, the specialist's technology is defined purely in terms of the rationality of his profession. It can have no

1 A. H. Halsey, 'Introduction' to N. Dennis, *People and Planning; the sociology of housing in Sunderland* (London, 1970), p. 25.
2 M. D. Feld, 'The Military Self-image in a Technological Environment', in M. Janowitz (ed.), *The New Military* (New York, 1964), pp. 164–5.

function outside it. The general practitioner and the nursing staff enjoy lower status because firstly they must deal more directly with the profane world (patients not cases) and also because many of their healing functions differ little from those practised by non-professionals in the general domestic care of the sick. Their professional mystique is thus compromised by the contact they must make with the profane world.

In the case of teaching similar gradations can be observed. The high status enjoyed by those who teach in universities rests in part on the uniqueness of their position, in relation to facilities for research. They are high priests of the temple of learning, making some contribution to knowledge itself; in addition they enjoy the advantage of teaching only those already carefully selected (the extent will vary from country to country) as able to benefit from their wisdom. The ideal is a pure research function and this is expressed in the fact that those who tend to enjoy highest status in the universities are those who teach *only* graduate students. Prestige is distributed throughout the profession of learning according to the twin qualities of the esoteric value of what is taught and the consequent difficulties involved in attaining it *and* the audience to whom it is communicated. Lowest status is thus reserved for teachers in the primary schools to which *everyone goes* to learn *what everyone knows*.

It is not possible in this brief introduction to carry this analysis further. Much of the substance of the argument is in any case developed in the other papers in the volume. It is, however, useful to note how reforms in the more established professions have been actively resisted in terms of just such criteria of 'unique rationality' or 'group charisma' enjoyed by the professional elite. Jamous and Peloille make the point in their paper that those appointed to make proposals for change were exactly those whose self-interest inevitably led them to oppose change. 'And it was demanded of them that they change the very system which was the source of their own authority and privilege and which had given them the power to bring about reform.'[1]

The case of law has not been dissimilar. The bulk of the literature on the legal profession and the practice of law has consisted of writing by lawyers about lawyers for lawyers. Twining has noted in relation to recent deliberations in Britain about lawyers' fees: 'It would appear that neither academic lawyers nor economists were involved in the preparation of the Law Society's submission to the P.I.B. [Prices and Incomes Board] and what is more significant, this is almost certainly considered to be entirely natural.'[2]

If, as the argument of some of the papers which follow suggest, our attention should be addressed to the sociology of occupations rather than the distinction between occupations and professions, then it is probable that increasingly a

---

1 Jamous and Peloille, *op. cit.* p. 137.
2 W. L. Twining, 'Lawyers under the Microscope', quoted with permission from a Public Lecture delivered at The Queen's University, Belfast in February 1968, p. 7.

'competitive model' will become more appropriate for an analysis of the practice of professionals and this is indeed suggested by the studies of professionals in previously undefined situations by Strauss and his colleagues.[1]

III

The papers in this third volume of *Sociological Studies* can only cover a small range of the variety of conceptual and empirical issues which derive from the study of professions and professionalization. Significantly all express a certain dissatisfaction with many of the basic assumptions which have been apparent in much of the literature in this field. The authors have found, in a number of different spheres, that they are constantly forced back to more fundamental considerations of the division of labour, the nature of occupations and the relationship of occupational roles to the definition of class interest, social status and the access to power. The view of professions as class interest groups though reflecting the cynicism already referred to in Schumpeter and Ben-David's approach finds a good deal of support in specific cases and relates closely to the aims and ambitions of those occupational groups which are actively trying to become professionalized. It is clear from studies of qualifying associations and particular cases that the process may be only partial and not always either successful or complete.[2] The check list of factors used by Hickson and Thomas provides a useful gauge with which to begin an analysis.[3] For such professionalizing bodies inevitable anomalies are likely to appear; at institutional level they suffer from the gaucheries of the *nouveaux riches* and demonstrate the dynamic process which characterizes occupational groups generally. Both professionalization and de-professionalization are constant features in the maintenance of a particular structural situation and set of constraints.

The case of the cat which became a fellow of the English Association of Estate Agents and Valuers[4] can be matched by equally ludicrous examples of ticket-gaining through qualifying associations which are more concerned to increase numbers than they are to maintain standards. The final paper by Olesen and Whittaker concentrates especially on these problems but it is worth emphasizing here that the significant question must become 'what are the means by

1 A. Strauss, *et. al.*, *Psychiatric Ideologies and Institutions* (New York, 1964).
2 See especially G. Millerson, *The Qualifying Associations: a Study in Professionalization* (London, 1964); B. G. Glaser, *Organizational Scientists: their Professional Careers* (Indianapolis, 1963); M. Lieberman, *Education as a Profession* (Englewood Cliffs, 1956). For an interesting case which extends the discussion outside the range of conventionally defined professions see A. L. Stinchcombe, 'Bureaucratic and Craft Administration of Production: a Comparative Study', *Administrative Science Quarterly*, 4 (1911), 168-87.
3 Hickson and Thomas, *op. cit.*
4 *The Times*, 10 December 1967. 'The application form described Oliver Greenhalgh as a rodent operative. Questions on qualifications and experience were ignored.'... 'The impressive certificate states that he has been engaged in the work of estate agent for "the period required by this association". It adds: "He has satisfied the council as to the thoroughness of his knowledge of estate agency and valuation subjects.".'

which an occupational status becomes reified and expanded into wider social significance?' rather than 'Is occupation x or y a profession or not?' To this extent the emphasis on the developing professionalization of all occupations stressed by Wilensky has roots in those aspects of the theories of the division of labour expressed by both Spencer and Durkheim — and as Hodge and Turner point out, much neglected ever since.

In their paper an attempt is made to raise fundamental questions about the crystallization of occupations in terms of the creation, management and control of resources. As a theoretical approach this perspective questions the whole relevance of the division of labour as a dynamic process in which the interests and ideologies of particular occupational groups are developed. In their analysis, so far as industrial and post-industrial societies are concerned, they single out four main areas particularly relevant to the study of professions and professionalization. They ask what is the substantive theory and technique? what is the extent of the monopoly claimed over it? to what extent is this externally recognized? to what extent and how effectively is it organized?

The paper by Harries-Jenkins begins by elaborating a definitive list of the elements of professionalization. From six constituent elements he derives some twenty-two structural sub-elements which characterize professionalization. In particular he includes a useful typology of eight types of professional associations. This discussion develops further some of the issues raised in the previous paper and carries it forward to develop the relationship of these professional characteristics to the organizational structures in which even 'free professionals' characteristically find themselves employed. The juxtaposition of this developed professional model with the rather more fully discussed sociological concept of bureaucracy allows a number of important problem areas to be analysed and exhibited in relation to particular empirical cases such as the military. It is significant that Harries-Jenkins like the authors of the previous paper is concerned primarily with the definition of occupational activities in response to the demands of the structural situation of the occupation itself. In this case the demands of the profession of which he is a member and the organization which employs him provide both separate constraints and potentially conflicting interests but also situations in which task performances may need to be re-defined by the combination of groups of professionals, with different professional ideologies, in new organizational frameworks — a situation which Anselm Strauss has described in relation to hospital institutions as locales in which various professionals compete for and 'stake out various claims to share in the treatment process'.[1]

This relationship between organization and profession has a further dimension in the relationship of different groups within the same profession. The conflict between practice and research finds a particular focus in the institution respon-

1 Strauss, *op. cit.* p. 368.

sible for selecting, training and examining new recruits to the profession. The case of the French university-hospital illustrates this characteristic dichotomy in relation to a highly successful maintenance of power by a particular professional elite. Interestingly, the threat to the autonomy of this group and the consequent possibility of structural change within the profession is derived from amendments to the system imposed on it by external demands in the shape of the Debré reforms and their subsequent implementation. The analysis of this particular group of key professionals leads the authors to raise serious doubts about both the legal-rationality model of organizations and Parsons' idea of disinterested professionals.

The development of the medical profession in Britain contrasts sharply in some respects with that in France, especially in the strain between forces making for professional integration and for diversity on the one hand; and the impact of new organizational frameworks derived only partly from the professional ideology such as the National Health Service. As in the case of France the tension between professional self-interest and public good has maintained a bipartite system, but one increasingly modified by broader changes such as the decline of a real entrepreneurial basis for medical practice outside the hospital system and the consequent development of both hospital oriented bureaucratization and 'community' — or 'profession' — oriented medical ideology which finds its main expression in contemporary controversies over the reform of medical education.

The discussion of the medical profession is complemented by a study by Leggatt of an unsuccessful profession (teaching) in terms of its failure to achieve and sustain the status enjoyed and consolidated in monopolistic organizational frameworks by both medicine and law. A service profession, derived even more directly than the other older professions from the central authority of the medieval church, teaching in the main has failed to sustain the exclusive class interest which has characterized medicine and law. In terms of our earlier discussion along lines developed by Feld[1] teaching is the most profoundly contaminated (secularized) profession because with the rise of mass education its mystique is compromised by the fact that in general the tasks it performs are within the general competence of all who have been taught themselves and since those on whom it practices are children, many of these functions are substitutes for parental roles in any case. Leggatt also comments on the significance of larger numbers of women members in the profession and the particular characteristics of the teacher's work situation.[2]

1 Feld, *op. cit.*
2 It should be noted that increasing attention is being paid to the position of women in other professional occupations as well as teaching. See, for instance, R. K. Kelsall, *Women and Teaching* (London, 1963); V. Klein, 'The Demand for Professional Womanpower', *British Journal of Sociology*, 17, 2 (June, 1966), 183-97. Political and Economic Planning (P.E.P.) is at present preparing a report in collaboration with the Tavistock Institute of Human Relations on women's careers in higher management and the professions.

In the final paper Olesen and Whittaker have provided an extensive review of the literature that has developed around the area of professional socialization. They combine the three main areas of occupational sociology and the discussion of the nature of professions; individual change particularly as this encompasses the socialization process involving both learning and unlearning; training and the assumption of new and specific role and status definitions; lastly the study of the social institutions through which occupations are organized and the means by which they conduct recruitment and socialization processes. The authors are particularly concerned with the situation and developing consciousness of the student, drawing on their own study of student nurses as well as a number of other studies both in the U.S.A. and elsewhere. Their main concern and indeed their concluding emphasis rests on the dynamic between the process of professionalization and the means by which the process is achieved by specific individuals in particular training situations.

2 Occupations and Professions

C. TURNER and M. N. HODGE

2

OCCUPATIONS AND PROFESSIONS

C. TURNER and M. N. HODGE

INTRODUCTION

'Occupation and Profession' neither defines the area of study so labelled, nor
delimits it from other possible areas of study, but merely serves to generate
certain expectations. Studies in the field of industrial sociology have been
concerned with men at work and the work environment. The various human
relations approaches and small group approaches have been particularly in
evidence. More recently attention has been concentrated upon the structure and
functioning of work organizations, and on inter-organizational relationships.
The field of organization theory has become a focus of attention in its own
right, drawing much from industrial sociology, but broadening the scope of
coverage to non-industrial organizations. The study of trade unions, industrial
relations and labour problems has tended to be treated as a relatively distinct
sub-field of industrial sociology. Studies of occupations have tended to centre
round the analysis of professions and semi-professions, and of occupational
careers. Much interesting work is going on in the field of military sociology,
but far too few of the general ideas are utilized outside the field. All these areas
and approaches are of direct significance in the study of occupations. The
general orientation adopted in the present paper focuses upon ideas concerning
the crystallization of occupations, a part of which requires consideration of the
processes involved in the division of labour which affect the creation, management and control of resources. For purposes of convenience, the ideas developed
relate specifically to occupations and professions within the context of modern
complex societies, although in principle the analysis could be extended to cover
a much wider range of societies.

Spencer and Durkheim were very much concerned with the transformation
and development of societies, and viewed the division of labour as a critical
element in the processes involved. It is worth reviewing a selection of their
general ideas as a starting point for the present analysis. Spencer attempted to
differentiate analytically between conscious and coercive division of labour, a
basis for his ideal type 'militant society', and unintentional and non-coercive
division of labour, a basis for his ideal type 'industrial society'. Spencer was well
aware that both these strands of the division of labour were complexly inter-
twined in any actual society. It is interesting to note, however, that whereas ideas

relating to conscious and/or coercive division of labour have flourished and are prominent in contemporary stratification-oriented sociology,[1] ideas relating to unconscious and/or non-coercive division of labour have been given much less systematic attention. Spencer also emphasized that with increasing division of labour and the involvement of an expanding number of people in this process, the potential for the development of utilizable social resources expanded at a much higher rate. Nevertheless he was careful to emphasize that 'established organization is an obstacle to re-organization'. In particular he felt that 'succession by inheritance whether to class position or to occupation conduces to stability', whereas selection by ability would lead to greater efficiency.[2]

Durkheim thought of the increasing struggle for existence, which accompanied the growth of material and moral density and of social volume, as necessitating a greater division of labour. Improved productive capacity was seen as a consequence of specialization, in response to generated social needs. He was particularly clear about the tendencies of modern industry: 'it advances steadily towards powerful machines, towards great concentrations of forces and capital, and consequently to the extreme division of labour. Occupations are infinitely separated and specialized'.[3] With the increasing specialization of economic activities,

'An economic activity can be efficaciously regulated only by a group intimate enough with it to know its functioning, feel all its needs, and able to follow all their variations. The only one that could answer all these conditions is the one formed by all the agents of the same industry, united and organized into a single body. This is what is called the corporation or occupational group.'[4]

For Durkheim the nearest approach to this then existing were 'syndicates', composed of either employers or workmen, though he is careful to observe that this was only a rather formless and rudimentary beginning of occupational organization. The syndicates were private associations, without legal authority, and there was no regular contact between the distinct syndicates of employers and employees. The guilds are cited as an historical example of occupational organizations which in their time were particularly effective.[5]

Both Durkheim and Spencer were very much concerned to emphasise that the division of labour provided a basis for *cooperation* and *interdependence*, and have been subjected to serious criticism for an overemphasis on social integration generally. Nevertheless, neither ignored the analysis of conflict and competition, and both acknowledged a distinction between a minimum

[1] J. Ben-David, 'Professions in the Class Sytem of Present-day Societies. A Trend Report and Bibliography', *Current Sociology,* 12, 3 (1963), 246-330.
[2] H. Spencer, *The Principles of Sociology* (London, 1893), especially chapter X, 'Social Types and Constitutions'.
[3] E. Durkheim, translated by G. Simpson, *The Division of Labour in Society* (Glencoe, 1966), p. 39.
[4] *Ibid.* p. 5.
[5] *Ibid.* pp. 7-23.

necessary cooperation and total cooperation. Durkheim, writing particularly about occupational organizations, emphasizes that 'The number of syndicates is theoretically limitless, even in the interior of the same category; and as each of them is independent of the others, if they do not federate or unify there is nothing intrinsic in them expressing the unity of the occupation in its entirety.'[1] This is an extremely important point to bear in mind.

Spencer and Durkheim were operating in terms of what would be labelled highly abstract macro-theory by contemporary sociologists, and it is clearly necessary to develop ideas concerning the division of labour and the crystallization of occupations at a much less abstract level if they are to be applied to the analysis of current work behaviour. Caplow is one of the main contemporary writers who has developed the division of labour theme in the sociology of work.[2] He focuses upon problems of the assignment of work and the control of both allocation processes and technical skills. This leads to the obvious suggestion that the division of labour and the organization of occupational groups may be promoted by those who consider themselves likely to gain thereby, as well as for more altruistic reasons. This raises the general problem of the degree to which particular active participants in a society help to shape and mould social institutions, and the means employed in the production of such results.

Bendix's work on industrialization contains a consideration of relationships involved in the changing division of labour, and of the ideologies appertaining to such relationships. In contrasting the development of ideologies of management in Russia and England in relation to the differentiation of work activities, Bendix indicates the vital part played by the emergence of group consciousness and communication in the division of labour, and demonstrates the necessity of viewing the economic division of labour as an integral part of a more general social division of labour. He also focuses attention on the development of large scale organization and notes some of the implications of a high degree of specialization: 'The few who command must control but cannot superintend the execution of their directives...their subordinates tend to acquire power even without authority to the extent that their *expertise* removes them from the effective control of their superiors.'[3]

Occupational differentiation is one aspect of the division of labour, and in the context of industrial and post-industrial societies may be discussed in relation to what are constitutively defined as work rather than non-work activities. This does not imply that there are few links between these types of activities, but simply that for purposes of the present paper work activities constitute the central focus.

1 *Ibid.* p. 6.
2 T. Caplow, *The Sociology of Work* (Minneapolis, 1962).
3 R. Bendix, *Work and Authority in Industry* (New York, 1956). For illustration of these themes see especially chapter 4, 'The Bureaucratization of Economic Enterprises'.

Even within the sphere of work, the division of labour entails the emergence of numerous social positions each with potentially different sets of interests, and subject to various modes of organization. For example, the differentiation of social positions may occur with respect to hierarchical structuring, task speciali- zation, the patterning of organizational role-sets and the differential allocation of rights and rewards within an employing organization. In addition memberships in trade unions, qualifying associations, study associations and other forms of occupational associations may provide axes of differentiation. Over and above this there is the possibility of all sorts of informal network contacts, both within the general context of work and in the broader social context, which may provide relevant bases for the differentiation of work interests and activities. The crystallization of interest groups and the organization of the activities of such groups, therefore, is an extremely complex phenomenon, of which the degree of crystallization of occupations, and of occupational identities, and the degree of organization of occupational groups and categories is but one area.

It is possible to develop a fairly elaborate theoretical orientation dealing with the relevance of the division of labour to, and the use of it by, occupational groups and categories. From a sociologist's point of view, this could involve attempting to assess the sort of resources involved in the division of labour – i.e. the differential distribution of various forms of knowledge, manipulative skills and abilities, and tools, machinery and equipment between interested parties both within and between occupations – the ways in which such resources are controlled, and the general processes of resource transmission and use. Obviously, a vital part of the necessary data for any specific analysis would be the ideas and ideologies concerning both the definition of resources and access to and control over them, advanced by participants in the society under study. This would need to be complemented by observational data on the actual activities of the participants.

Some differentiation of occupational categories is implicit in most of the writings on work behaviour, though the bases of differentiation are not always clearly stated. For example, with such commonly used general categories as professional, semi-professional, non-professional; manual, non-manual; and skilled, semi-skilled, unskilled, it is often unclear precisely which dimensions are being used to distinguish the categories. The categories themselves often tend to serve as a guide to the sort of analysis which the sociologist attempts. Thus, for an analysis of 'skilled workers', such as shoemakers or printers,[1] an examin- ation of the skills involved, of the degree of control over the skills exercised by the craftsmen as opposed to that exercised by other interested parties, and of

---

[1] E.g. shoemakers; W. L. Warner and J. O. Low, *The Social System of the Modern Factory* (New Haven, 1947). E.g. printers; S. M. Lipset, M. A. Trow and J. S. Coleman, *Union Democracy* (Glencoe, 1956); F. C. Munson, *Labour Relations in the Lithographic Industry* (Cambridge, 1963).

the nature of the relations between the various groups involved, might commonly be expected. The development of the craft, and the various steps in the process of defining, redefining and attempting to exercise control over the emerging skill, and of consolidating claims to categories of rights would also be a relevant part of such an analysis. In contrast, an analysis of 'manual workers' or 'professionals' would normally proceed along rather different lines.[1]

PROFESSIONS, SEMI-PROFESSIONS AND PROFESSIONALIZATION

The main issues which have been debated in the study of professions and professionalization centre around the problems of distinguishing a profession from a non-profession, and of discerning processes of professionalization. With the former problem, the major task is usually thought to involve the isolation of sets of critical discriminating characteristics or variables. This approach which is well illustrated by the work of Greenwood and Millerson,[2] is primarily factorial, though it should be noted that the possibility of the emergence of new professions or the disappearance of old ones is not ruled out. In contrast, the professionalization approach commonly rests on a set of assumptions, often implicit, about the nature of a profession, while the main emphasis is placed upon the identification of some sort of developmental sequence, as, for example, in the work of Caplow or Wilensky.[3] These approaches may in fact be fused as in the classic work of Carr-Saunders and Wilson, or in the contemporary work on semi-professions.[4]

These two approaches to the study of professional occupations and professionalization constitute useful starting points for analysis, but are neither necessarily in conflict, nor necessarily complementary. The first approach, distinguishing between a profession and a non-profession, may use as its critical discriminating characteristics those which attach to an occupation once it is considered to have unequivocally approximated to a profession, i.e. a presumed special type of occupation. In other words the discriminating characteristics are likely to include at least some which are indices of the current recognition of the occupation, rather than guides to its crystallization in its present form. Barber issues an additional caveat: '... concepts like style of life, corporate solidarity socialization structures and processes, which apply to all other groups as well as

---

1   E.g. L. R. Sayles, *Behaviour of Industrial Groups* (New York, 1963); A. M. Carr-Saunders and P. A. Wilson, *The Professions* (London, 1964, 1st edition 1933).
2   E. Greenwood, 'Attributes of a Profession',*Social Work*, 2 (July 1957), 45-55; G. Millerson, *The Qualifying Associations* (London, 1964).
3   Caplow, *op. cit.* esp. pp. 139-40, but see also pp. 137-9 on other aspects of occupational change; H. L. Wilensky, 'The Professionalization of Everyone?', *American Journal of Sociology*, 70 (September 1964), 137-58.
4   Carr-Saunders and Wilson, *op. cit.;* A. Etzioni (ed.), *The Semi-Professions and their Organization* (New York, 1969).

B

to professional ones, are not the *differentia specifica*'.[1] With the second approach, in so far as studies of professionalization deal with developmental sequences, they may avoid this type of problem, but they still imply the existence of 'professions' as a distinct occupational type, towards which the occupations under consideration are moving, and it is not always obvious how the profession model is related to the processes being studied. There is also the problem raised by Abrams: 'But if professions emerge they may also recede — scribes, pharisees and alchemists are cases in point.'[2] He goes on to make a very good case for the view that the British armed services are currently undergoing a process of recession. The idea of processes of recession, however, still implies a model of profession from which an occupation is receding, although the factors influencing recession may not be the same as those involved in emergence.

It is often claimed that there is a high degree of consensus amongst sociologists on the distinguishing characteristics of professions and professionalizing occupations. Goode writes: 'If one extracts from the most commonly cited definitions all the items which characterize a profession...a commendable unanimity is disclosed: there are no contradictions and the only differences are those of omission.' He goes on to specify '... subtracting the derivative traits such as high prestige, power and income from those which are sociologically causal. The two remaining core characteristics are a prolonged specialized training in a body of abstract knowledge, and a collectivity or service orientation.'[3] Ben-David in his trend report on professions in the class system notes that writings

'provide a consistent set of observations about the distinguishing characteristics of professional organization and behaviour. These are: the existence of a vocational sub-culture which comprises explicit or implicit codes of behaviour, generates an *esprit de corps* among members of the same profession, and ensures them certain occupational advantages, such as an equalitarian rather than authoritarian type of supervision in bureaucratic structures and monopolistic privileges to perform certain types of work... It seems that professional sub-cultures and the rest of professional characteristics emerge on the basis of prolonged study and training in a certain field and can be maintained by research activity, professional literature, legislation, etc., even where professional organizations are not very prominent and do not possess official privileges.'[4]

Barber is somewhat more cautious, but notes that considerable progress has been made towards the definition of 'the professions' and lists

'four essential attributes: a high degree of generalized and systematic knowledge; primary orientation to the community interest rather than to individual

1 B. Barber, 'Some Problems in the Sociology of the Professions', *Daedalus*, 92, 4 (1963), 671.
2 P. Abrams, 'The Late Profession of Arms: Ambiguous Goals and Deteriorating Means in Britain', *Archives Européennes de Sociologie*, 6, 2 (1965), 240.
3 W. J. Goode, 'Encroachment, Charlatanism and the Emerging Professions', *American Sociological Review*, 25 (December 1960), 903.
4 Ben-David, *op. cit.* p. 251.

self-interest; a high degree of self-control of behaviour through codes of ethics internalized in the process of work socialization and through voluntary associations organized and operated by the work specialists themselves; and a system of rewards (monetary and honorary) that is primarily a set of symbols of work achievement and thus ends in themselves, not means to some end of individual self interest.'[1]

These quotations have been included not only because they indicate areas of central concern to sociologists interested in occupations and professions, but also because they illustrate the common tendency towards a unitary conceptualization of profession. Much of the writing on professionalization exhibits the same tendency.[2] This is a useful method of approach, but the time is perhaps ripe for an attempt to match theoretical models more closely with empirical findings. The models of 'professions' advanced by sociologists are nearly always acknowledged to be ideal types, and it is common to find statements that the actual professions studied deviate from the models in particular ways. Moreover a brief perusal of the literature is sufficient to establish that such deviations tend to occur in somewhat different areas, from profession to profession.

It should be possible to isolate a series of dimensions, and their associated variables, which at least merit attention in the study of professions, semi-professions and professionalization. The listing of dimensions and variables, however, is not a particularly useful exercise in itself, and it is desirable to indicate at least the general theoretical orientations in terms of which the variables might be organized into a conceptual scheme. A resource approach is the one adopted in the present paper. It has the merit of being utilizable at a sufficiently abstract level for purposes of general theorizing, yet provides a definite guide to the sort of lower level concepts and operational definitions which are required for empirical analyses in any particular field of study. With respect to professions, semi-professions and professionalization, it involves asking fundamental questions about the ways in which professions and semi-professions are defined, with special emphasis on the basic resources involved, and problems of access to and utilization of these resources. The significance of this approach is especially apparent in the consideration of ongoing processes of resource management and control. At a highly abstract level, the following questions need to be posed:

(1) What is the substantive base of any profession or semi-profession? (2) How do substantive bases of differing professions or semi-professions relate to each other? (3) What are the major categories of persons involved in the management and control of substantive resources? (4) What means of management and control are used by the different categories of interested parties?

In the context of complex industrial and post-industrial societies, a considera-

1 Barber, *op. cit.* p. 672.
2 In addition to the works cited above see the selections in H. M. Vollmer and D. L. Mills, *Professionalization* (Englewood Cliffs, 1966).

tion of four main areas of analysis seems to offer a useful means of beginning to explore the more general problems associated with studies of professions and professionalization. These four areas concern: (1) the degree of substantive theory and technique in the practising of professional or semi-professional activities; (2) the degree of monopoly over claimed professional or semi-professional activities; (3) the degree of external recognition of a profession or semi-profession; and (4) the degree of organization of a profession or semi-profession. These areas are closely interrelated and it is clearly necessary to devote detailed attention to the analysis of their interrelationships, as well as to each particular area.

Degree of Substantive Theory and Technique

An ubiquitous assumption in writing on professions appears to be that a profession has an essential underpinning of abstract principles which have been organized into a theory, set of theories, or at least a complex web of theoretical orientations. The abstract principles are not viewed as immutable, but may be subject to change as a result of a variety of pressures, not the least of which is the demand from within the profession or certain sections within it for clarification and elaboration of the basic principles. Alongside this set of basic principles are various practical techniques for the recurrent application of at least certain of the fundamental principles, though it should be noted that the relation of theory to technique is an extremely complicated matter. The theory is usually cast broad enough to include rules concerning the selection or exclusion of techniques. The canons governing the application of legal theories, medical theories and theologies, for example, provide some marked contrasts.[1] The techniques, like the principles, are themselves subject to modification and change through time. Changes of principle and technique are often interrelated, and present extremely interesting analytical problems. Insofar as the basic set of theories and techniques are significant social resources, any modifications, especially if they affect the application of techniques, are potentially highly strategic resources, both within the profession and in the wider society as well.

The degree of substantive technique and theory requisite for the carrying out of professional or semi-professional activities is a fundamental yet highly contentious aspect of occupational analysis. The question of what passes for knowledge in any society or social group at a given time, and the current means of establishing various forms of knowledge has been a perennial theme of intellectual inquiry. It is clearly not feasible for a sociologist to set about acquiring an intimate knowledge of the substantive techniques and theories of a wide range of professions and semi-professions as a preliminary to sociological analysis. Even if this approach was to be adopted, it would still be necesssary to set up criteria for comparing and evaluating the different bodies of technique and theory. In

1 These canons should be clearly distinguished from codes of ethics, which are mentioned below.

other words, the evaluation would be carried out on the basis of an explicit, or possibly implicit, schema in terms of which so-called similar properties of differing bodies of technique and theory were invidiously compared.

It seems probable, therefore, that any such schema would be developed around judgements concerning the social desirability and utility of occupational activities and the actual performance of the occupational activities and the ideological claims relating to them made by participants, rather than in terms of the substantive principles and techniques themselves. In other words the sociologist would be concerning himself with *claims* concerning the substantive theory and techniques and indices of activities which in part at least were oriented towards the substantiation of such claims. But claims to knowledge and skills are usually very closely linked with claims to some degree of monopoly over occupational activities, and both of these aspects may be intricately related to problems of the external recognition and organization of the 'profession'. For example, as sociologists have been quick to point out, a significant feature of claims to professional status by groups of self-designated professionals is that non-professionals are not fully competent to evaluate the knowledge and skills of 'professionals'. There is both a claim to uniqueness of the principles and/or techniques, and a claim to sole right of competent judgement by the 'professionals'. Alternatively the question of the degree of technique and theory involved has been tackled by attempting to obtain indices of the amount of training and induction required to produce competent practitioners. But again, this is at best an indirect approach, which requires recognizing standards of competence for practice and making evaluations concerning the quality, necessity and relevance of the induction processes and training programmes.

It is not surprising, therefore, that writers on professions and professionalization, while acknowledging the centrality of substantive theory and techniques underpinning professional occupations, have tended to grapple with problems concerning claims about such knowledge, its codification, transmission and modification rather than enter into the hazardous arena of evaluating differing and possibly overlapping bodies of technique and theory which often incorporate their own canons of 'truth'. And it may be suggested that the former areas are precisely those with which the sociologist is most competent to deal, which is of course part of the sociologist's own occupational ideology.

Degree of Monopoly

The degree of monopoly over claimed professional or semi-professional activities involves both ideological and pragmatic aspects. At the ideological level, a claim to a high degree of monopoly over 'professional activities' constitutes a charter in the Malinowskian sense of the word. It is a declaration, a bid for recognition and an attempt at justification intricately interwoven. The declaration is likely to be couched in terms of there being a complicated set of abstract principles, which are applicable to what Goode has termed 'the concrete problems of living'.[1] The bid for recognition may take the form of a claim to exclusive possession of knowledge and associated techniques, or at least to their greatly superior application. The justification is commonly advanced on many grounds, among which the possession of esoteric knowledge and high skill, the performance of tasks of high social value, the image of community service and dedication, and the denial of competitive claims may well feature. The charter of a group of professionals, to be effectively stated, clearly requires organization, and its utility to members of the profession or semi-profession depends upon the degree of recognition which it is accorded by critical sectors of the population as well as upon its exact content. The charter may also be competitive and involve pejorative accusations of encroachment and charlatanism, i.e. the emergence or existence of counter claims.[2]

The presentation of charters or of fragments of them may be specially tailored for receiving audiences. This presents extremely interesting problems regarding organizational strategies and tactics. For example, leaders attempting to form a new occupational association have to decide upon their mode of self presentation to potential members, to established associations in the field, if any, and to interested publics. A vague and ambiguous charter may facilitate particularistic appeals to each of these sectors and even to different segments within them. Furthermore, once an association is firmly established, the 'official' charter may be modified to take account of long run interests, or the interests of new elements in the leadership. The variations on this theme are potentially manifold. Selznick's work on Bolshevik strategy and tactics, and Wilensky's analysis of organizational intelligence provide illustrations of some of the complexities involved in this type of analysis.[3] Nevertheless, one of the clearest implications for the sociologist is that data on the activities carried out by associational members is essential to supplement the analysis of charters.

The analysis of charters can be approached by a form of content analysis. Some of the possible themes for the construction of a framework for analysis are indicated above. The coherency and clarity of presentation of charters is likely to vary, and in any case, problems of their interpretation, and of the possible elaboration of sub-unit ideologies need to be taken into account.[4] Codes of ethics, for example, are clearly one aspect of charter. Millerson, in his examination of over one hundred and thirty British qualifying associations, found that less than a quarter had formal written codes.[5] The remainder most probably includes at one extreme organizations which had well-developed but unwritten codes, and at the

---

1 W. J. Goode, 'The Theoretical Limits of Professionalization', in Etzioni (ed.), *op. cit.* p. 227.
2 Goode, 'Encroachment, Charlatanism and the Emerging Professions'.
3 P. Selznick, *The Organizational Weapon* (New York, 1960); H. L. Wilensky, *Organizational Intelligence* (New York, 1967).
4 P. Selznick, *T.V.A. and the Grass Roots* (New York, 1966).
5 Millerson, *op. cit.*

other organizations which had developed hardly any ethical norms, with the majority of organizations falling somewhere in between. Codes of ethics, whether written or unwritten, usually include relatively few prescriptions and/or proscriptions, thus leaving a considerable area of equivocation outside the ethical rules. Furthermore codes of ethics are notable for their relatively high levels of abstraction, which can be linked with substantial ambiguity at the level of action.

Whatever assertions are made about monopoly over occupational activities, it is extremely unlikely that any group will be able to enforce a claim to complete monopoly over the full range of activities to which it lays claim. It is also worth noting that there may be a complex division of labour within identifiable occupational groups. This applies not only to patterns of differentiation which have become formally institutionalized, such as that between solicitors and barristers[1] so that it could be said that they constitute distinct occupational groups, but also within a particular field of specialization, such as lawyers who choose to devote their attention to cases in a narrowly defined field. O'Gorman's study of New York lawyers who had taken on matrimonial cases, provides an admirable illustration of the differing degrees of specialization chosen by the lawyers in the sample with respect to matrimonial cases.[2] Smigel's study of Wall Street lawyers, when contrasted with Carlin's work on neighbourhood lawyers, opens up further perspectives on the organizational and career processess by which specialization within the law field could possibly become institutionalized.[3] Bucher and Strauss illustrate these general points with reference to the medical profession, and further indicate that in terms of what professionals *do* they may carry out activities which are closer to those of persons in allied occupations than to those of some of their co-professionals.[4]

At a more pragmatic level it is necesssary to enquire into the nature of the core techniques and applications of the claimed professional knowledge. One important avenue of investigation is the assessment of the material resources and facilities involved in the performance of occupational activities. What sort of tools and technological equipment are involved? What are a professional's requirements with respect to working space? What communication channels exist for contact with clients, with co-professionals and with other persons involved in the provision of work resources? To what extent is a professional dependent upon non-professionals either for the provision of such resources, or for access to them? Is there differential access to this type of resource between co-professionals? Such questions as these clearly imply a series of questions about the organization of professional resources, and might appropriately be

1 Carr-Saunders and Wilson, *op. cit.* pp. 7-28.
2 H. O. Gorman, *Lawyers and Matrimonial Cases* (New York, 1963).
3 E. O. Smigel, *The Wall Street Lawyer* (New York, 1964); J. E. Carlin, *Lawyers on their Own* (New Brunswick, 1962).
4 R. Bucher and A. Strauss, 'Professions in Progress', *American Journal of Sociology,* 66 (January 1961), 325-34.

investigated alongside questions about the promulgation and diffusion of professional knowledge.

Degree of External Recognition

Most writings on professions and professionalization either state or imply that public recognition is a critical aspect. But public recognition is a multi-faceted phenomenon. There are several possible publics to whom members of an occupational group may address themselves. The 'clients', whether individuals, groups, or large-scale organizations or some combination of these, constitute perhaps the most significant of these publics, but there may be several others. These include: (1) co-workers outside the occupational group, who are either necessarily or incidentally implicated because of their role in the division of labour, (2) other occupational associations, which may be either complementary or competitive, (3) employing units and employers' associations, (4) government bodies taking a direct legislative and/or administrative part in the regulation of occupational activities, (5) educational and training institutions, and (6) other individuals, groups and organizations, which collectively might be labelled the general public, but who will have sectional interests and differential knowledge. Moreover, as any detailed micro-analysis would disclose, the various categories of public listed above may be internally differentiated with respect to knowledge, opinion, and interests concerning a given occupation.

A direct method of attempting to measure degree of public recognition is to ask representative samples of persons in each of the general categories listed above both factual and attitudinal questions about the occupational fields under investigation. These questions might probe for the ways in which people classify and categorize occupations, the images they have of these occupations, their views on the value and utility of such occupations, their overall ratings of the occupations, and their experience of contact with occupational personnel. It would also be pertinent to enquire into people's sources of information concerning various occupations. In order to supplement this material it would be desirable to record the nature and type of actual encounters between members of the public and practitioners of the occupation.

Clients and potential clients constitute an extremely important category. There are always those potential clients who for various reasons, such as lack of financial resources, non-recognition of professional competence, inability to obtain a practitioner within the time available, or belief that non-professional services are at least adequate if not superior to professional services, or because of sheer ignorance of the means of access to professionals or of the services they offer, breach the claimed monopoly of professionals. Another complex aspect of relations with clients involves mediating agencies. Such mediation may be carried out by a professional colleague, by an organization employing the professional on a more or less permanent basis, or by a variety of other organizations and associations. The issue of the extent to which an employer of professionals is a client as opposed to a mediator between professional and clients of the organization is a sensitive matter of debate, especially where material and/or other resources necessary for carrying out professional tasks are provided by the employer.

Degree of Organization

Sociologists have devoted a considerable amount of attention to the organizational aspects of professions and semi-professions. Millerson has attempted to develop a typology of professional associations, and undertook a detailed examination of qualifying associations.[1] Etzioni, in his introduction to a recent collection of papers on semi-professions, indicates that organizational questions were central to the way in which the volume was conceived.[2] A review of the selections in Vollmer and Mills further confirms the importance attached to varying forms of occupational associations in the study of professionalization.[3] This concentration on organizational aspects is equally important with a resource approach, since organization is the primary means both of exercising control over and access to basic occupational resources. In addition, the context in which competition for and conflict over occupational resources occurs in industrial and post-industrial societies, is one in which large-scale organizations in business, commerce, education and government predominate.

Two general approaches to the organization of professions and professionalizing occupations have been developed, the community approach and the formal organization approach. For the most part, these different perspectives have been kept distinct, although there are some excellent studies such as those on military socialization, in which the two aspects are treated together.[4] The community approach to the study of the professions is perhaps best illustrated by the work of Goode, who lists the following characteristics of a professional community:

'(1) Its members are bound by a sense of identity. (2) Once in it, few leave it, so that it is a terminal or continuing status for the most part. (3) Its members share values in common. (4) Its role definitions *vis-à-vis* both members and non-members are agreed upon and are the same for all members. (5) Within the area of communal action there is a common language, which is understood only partially by outsiders. (6) The community has power over its members. (7) Its limits are reasonably clear, though they are not physical or geographical but social. (8) Though it does not produce the next generation biologically, it does so socially through its control over the selection of professional trainees, and

1 Millerson, *op. cit.* esp. p. 5 ff.
2 Etzioni (ed.), *op. cit.* pp. x-xvii.
3 Vollmer and Mills (eds.), *op. cit.*
4 E.g. J. P. Lovell, 'The Professional Socialization of the West Point Cadet', in M. Janowitz (ed.), *The New Military* (New York, 1964).

B*

through its training processes it sends these recruits through an adult socialization process'.[1]

The emphasis is clearly upon qualitative aspects of the relationships among a group of professionals, and between a professional community and the wider society. In particular, the themes of communication and consensus within the professional community, of socialization and control of community members, and of external evaluations of a professional community as a whole are emphasized.

The community approach tends to place less emphasis on the means by which the ends of the professional community are pursued than upon the ends themselves. This gives rise to questions concerning the extent to which such ends are part of an occupational ideology, and the degree of coherence of the ideology. Elsewhere Goode makes the valuable point that leaders within an occupation play a major role in devising occupational strategies and tactics,[2] and it may be suggested that they are likely to be attracted, whether consciously or unconsciously, to an ideology which stresses harmony and integration. It is also relevant to note that the pursuit of particular ideological ends usually has a much wider range of consequences than is indicated by ideological statements, and it is part of the sociologists' task to examine this range of consequences. In contrast, the formal organizational approach tends to concentrate the analysis upon organizational mechanisms and techniques, and upon their consequences for the pursuit of specified organizational goals.

The two approaches tend to foster differing perspectives on occupations. The community approach stresses the common interests, activities and goals of 'professionals' and the development of intricate informal social networks and feelings of solidarity among those carrying out essentially similar activities, whereas the formal organization approach fosters the development of an emphasis upon the enumeration, registration and licensing of 'competent professionals', the codification of standards of practice and conduct, and the application of formal controls over members. Community and formal organization are not incompatible, however, as an assessment of the material on guilds, such as the bakers,[3] or more generally of the 'traditional English professions', the Church, the Law and the Military, serves to illustrate. A tight formal organization and a community pattern of ideology and association can be mutually reinforcing. On the other hand, it is quite possible to envisage highly structured formal organizations lacking communal association and consensus, or alternatively well-developed communal networks and ideology without formal organization.

---

1 W. J. Goode, 'Community within a Community: the Professions', *American Sociological Review*, 22 (April 1957), 194.
2 W. J. Goode, in Etzioni (ed.), *op. cit.*
3 S. Thrupp, *A Short History of the Worshipful Company of Bakers of London* (London, 1933).

Nevertheless in contemporary industrial and post-industrial societies, at least one and usually more formal occupational associations are nearly always involved in the organization of professions and semi-professions. Such professional organizations and qualifying associations have a wide range of differing goals, of organization structures, and of strategies of operation. Rather than erect a typology of professional associations, however, as Millerson has attempted,[1] it seems reasonable to ask a set of general questions about (1) the structures of occupational organization, and (2) the occupation-related activities with which occupational associations might in theory concern themselves, with a view to devising scales for the measurement of the major variables. But immediately this raises the much more general question: Why limit the scope of the conceptual scheme to professions, professionalizing, and de-professionalizing occupations? Before attempting to outline the sorts of activities which might be considered relevant, therefore, this question needs to be squarely faced.

THE ANALYSIS OF OCCUPATIONS

In the previous section, an attempt was made to suggest ways in which a theoretical orientation for the study of professions, semi-professions and professionalization might be developed, and to indicate some of the main lines of enquiry which might be pursued in empirical research. This approach, however, while perhaps useful for heuristic purposes, seems to adhere too rigidly to certain preconceptions concerning professions. It is extremely difficult to identify *differentia specifica* of professions. Insofar as it is possible to discern *differentia specifica*, they appear to distinguish between one so-called profession and another, rather than between the categories of professional and non-professional occupations. There also appears to be fairly widespread in the literature an assumption that the fit between sociological models of professions and actual professions in operation is not too close. The basic suggestion to be advanced, therefore, is that *an attempt should be made to develop a framework for the analysis of occupations, rather than of professional occupations alone.*

The labelling of occupational categories is a complex process. For example, the occupational classification which the U.S. Bureau of Census used in 1960 'consists of 494 items, 297 of which are specific occupation categories and the remainder are sub-groupings (mainly on the basis of industry) of 13 of the occupation categories'.[2] A much more elaborate scheme has been developed by the U.S. Bureau of Employment Security: in the 1965 edition of the *Dictionary of Occupational Titles*, 'There are 21,741 separate occupations defined which are known by 13,809 additional titles, making a total of 35,550 titles defined'. It is

1 Millerson, *op. cit.*
2 United States Bureau of Census, *United States Census of Population 1960, Occupation by Industry* (1960), p. viii.

also noted that 'This edition contains 6,432 jobs new to the Dictionary.' The Registrar General's 1966 Classification of Occupations for the United Kingdom lists 210 occupation unit groups, excluding a category for inadequately des-scribed occupations.[1]

Such classifications are in fact highly generalized, when considered in relation to the actual division of labour obtaining in the United States or United Kingdom. This is well illustrated by the description of Faculty Member, College or University, listed in the most sophisticated of the above-mentioned schemes:[2]

FACULTY MEMBER, COLLEGE OR UNIVERSITY.

(education) 090.228. Conducts college or university classes for undergraduate or graduate students: Teaches one or more subjects, such as economics, chemistry, law, or medicine, within a prescribed curriculum. Prepares and delivers lectures to students. Compiles bibliographies of specialized materials for outside reading assignments. Stimulates class discussions. Compiles, administers, and grades examinations, or assigns this work to others. Directs research of other teachers or graduate students working for advanced academic degrees. Conducts research in particular field of knowledge and publishes findings in professional journals. Performs related duties, such as advising students on academic and vocational curricula, and acting as adviser to student organizations. Serves on faculty committee providing professional consulting services to government and industry. May be designated according to faculty rank in traditional hierarchy as determined by institution's estimate of scholarly maturity as ASSOCIATE PROFESSOR; PROFESSOR; or according to rank distinguished by duties assigned or amount of time devoted to academic work as RESEARCH ASSISTANT; VISITING PROFESSOR. May teach in two-year college and be designated TEACHER, JUNIOR COLLEGE; or in technical institute and be designated FACULTY MEMBER, TECHNICAL INSTITUTE.

This description gives a fair overview of an occupational ideology, and indicates the range of activities which a faculty member *might* be expected to carry out. It also indicates that a division of labour is likely to be found within the occupational category. The actual patterns of the division of labour and activities carried out by different faculty members is highly variable, as also is the range of occupational groups and associations to which they belong.

It is interesting to note, however, that the above classifications are commonly subjected to reduction and simplification by the application of macro-stratification assumptions, i.e. by the use of such categories as manual, non-manual, skilled, semi-skilled, unskilled, managerial, technical, professional, and non-professional, or by reference to occupational prestige, or by imposition of a predefined class model such as a Marxian one. These macro-stratification

[1] United States Bureau of Employment Security, *Dictionary of Occupational Titles,* vols. I and II, 3rd edition (1965), vol. 1, p. xv.
[2] General Register Office, *Classification of Occupations, 1966* (H.M.S.O., London, 1966). United States Bureau of Employment Security, *op. cit.* vol. I, p. 263.

assumptions tend to be superimposed and used as a means of dividing up what is admittedly an extensive field of study, namely that of occupations. Hence the investigations into professions, *or* manual occupations, *or* white-collar occupations, and into occupational association among professionals, *or* among manual workers, *or* among white-collar workers, etc. This raises especially difficult problems when attempts are made to 'explain' differences between white collar, manual and professional workers in terms of macro-stratification. An alternative approach, which is outlined and roughly illustrated below is to attempt to study occupational organization without imposing prior stratification boundary assumptions in this way. This is not to suggest that the stratification ideas are of no relevance. The point at issue is their prior imposition. The utility of stratification concepts may then be considered on both empirical and theoretical grounds, rather than on *a priori* grounds alone.

Occupational organization, however, should not be confused with an occupation. An occupation may be constitutively defined in terms of similarities of activities carried out within a general scheme of division of labour. Such similarities may exist regardless of whether the persons involved are aware of them and regardless of there being any social relationships between people involved. Given this sort of definition, the number of possible occupational classifications is only limited, in theory at least, by the variety of analytical distinctions which can be made concerning types of activities and the properties of activities. The approach via occupational organizations stresses one particular aspect, namely the way in which patterns of social relationships are developed, perpetuated and discontinued between networks of persons participating in similar activities in the division of labour. It also implies examining the ways in which such networks of persons set about identifying and pursuing what they consider to be their collective occupational interests. This is neither to suggest that all participants in an occupational group or association necessarily share common interests, nor that the pursuit of sectional and non-occupational interests fails to occur in occupational groups and associations. Moreover, it does not imply a unitary occupational organization concerned with all matters appertaining to an occupation.

The processes by which occupational organization emerges, is perpetuated, modified, and possibly dissolves, are but poorly understood. In most instances where formal organizations or associations are constituted, there have been pre-existing patterns of non-formal occupational association, which continue and co-exist with the more formal structures. Such patterns of non-formal organization are likely to reflect more general patterns of association, as for example in the case of an occupation which has been handed down from father to son over the generations, or in the case of shared educational experience which provides a network of future occupational contacts. In setting out to examine the crystallization and operation of occupational organization, therefore, it is necessary to consider the form of organization, the ideologies advanced, and the activities carried out, and to attempt to relate these to the wider social structure.

From a theoretical point of view a reasonable starting point is to establish at any given point in time the main axes of differentiation associated with the division of labour. At an empirical level, this involves enquiring not only into who carries out what activities and how the sets of activities carried out by different persons are inter-dependent or possibly independent, but also into the participants' images of the nature of the relationships in which they are involved. In other words, it is desirable to establish in general outline the sort of social context in which the particular occupational organizations under investigation are operating. The differences in the development of legal and medical occupations in the United States and the United Kingdom can perhaps best be understood in the light of this type of background information.

The sociologists' problems of finding a convenient starting-point for further analysis are vastly increased when no *formal* occupational organization can be identified. On what basis can a 'community' style of occupational organization be distinguished? The bases of occupational organization can be extremely varied. Among those which are commonly cited are mutual interest in theory and/or techniques related to occupational activities, carrying out activities on the same type of materials, carrying out activities with the same type of equipment, sharing a similar work situation, sharing a similar market situation, ideological claims concerning the right to carry out particular types of activity, and locational propinquity. More generally, it might be said that wherever and whenever the opportunity for social relations involving persons with similar occupational interests arises, a basis for the pursuit of occupational interest exists.

The point which is central here is that similarities of occupational interest may be based upon the carrying out of similar activities, the carrying out of distinct but complementary activities, or on some more general criterion such as the supposed existence of a common body of underlying theory, or even some vague and undefined element labelled 'tradition'. It is also extremely important to note that any one individual may belong to several occupational groups, networks, and associations at once. This becomes particularly evident when non-formal organization is treated alongside formal organization, but is common enough even when considering formal organization out of this broader context. For example, membership in the Royal College of Physicians or the Royal College of Surgeons fits alongside British Medical Association membership, and may well be combined with further memberships of medical associations. Alternatively the printer who is promoted into a lower managerial post may retain his membership in a craft union and join an enterprise staff association in addition. When the complications of both on and off the job informal contacts are taken into account, this greatly increases the patterns of association to be investigated. It is precisely the existence of this variety of avenues open for the pursuit of occupational interests which renders the analysis of occupations so tortuous.

Insofar as formal occupational associations exist, the task of identifying members becomes somewhat simpler because membership criteria are usually established. Also at least some rules and procedures for the government of the association, and for the participation of members tend to be developed. The way is also opened up for an analysis of the general charter of the association, especially as it is conceived by the more active members. It then becomes possible to compare the occupational ideology of individual members with the more general ideology of the charter, especially if there is a written charter, whereas in the absence of the formal association, much more reliance necessarily has to be placed on the analysis of the ideologies of individuals. The distinction between formal and non-formal organization, however, should not be overstressed. Arguing by analogy with Duverger's work on political parties, which in many respects are organizationally similar to occupational associations and indeed often overlap to some extent, it is possible to contend that the organization of a 'cadre party' exhibits greater similarities with Goode's professional community than with Millerson's formal qualifying association.[1]

The key to the approach which is being advanced here, however, rests with the examination of the activities which may be directly or indirectly sponsored by an occupational organization. Such activities may be considered under the following general headings:

  I. Activities relating directly to occupation
      (1)   The development of substantive theory
      (2)   The development of practical techniques
      (3)   The transmission of substantive theory
      (4)   The transmission of practical techniques
      (5)   The provision of materials and equipment
      (6)   The regulation of working conditions
      (7)   The regulation of market conditions
      (8)   The identification of practitioners and the recognition of qualifications for practice
      (9)   The promotion of standards of practice
     (10) The promotion of internal relations between members
     (11) The promotion of public recognition

  II. Ancillary activities[2]

The principle of selection of these forms of activity follows the ideas developed earlier in the paper. It is based on the notion that these are potentially critical

---

1 M. Duverger, *Political Parties,* translated by B. and R. North (London, 1967); Goode, 'Community within a Community'; Millerson, *op. cit.*

2 No schema for the investigation of ancillary activities is developed here, but such activities should not be discounted. The political activities of trade unions, for example, are an extremely relevant factor.

resource areas, and a knowledge of the agencies and processes of control involved in relation to such activities indicates not only the extent to which occupational organization has crystallized, but also where the potential for control lies. The relevance of this type of approach for the study of non-professional occupations is well illustrated by the case of the maintenance workers analysed by Crozier and by the example of workers' attempts to exert controls over their working conditions as set out in Lupton's *On the Shop Floor*.[1]

By focusing upon activities which in theory at least can be carried out in relation to any occupation, the way is opened for two rather different means of approaching the study of occupational organization, although the end results may be very similar. On the one hand, it is possible to start with any one or more identifiable occupational organizations, and to examine the activities carried out by each organization, and to relate these to the activities carried out by other groups, networks and associations operating in the same field. Alternatively it is possible to start with some occupational label such as medical practitioner, printer, bank clerk, or general labourer, and to seek answers to the question of how occupation-related activities are organized. In either case, if systematic answers are obtained to the question of who (i.e. individuals/groups/networks/ associations) carries out such activities, a general mapping of the interested parties can be achieved. Answers to the further question of the ways in which such activities are organized reveal something of the complex processes involved in occupational organization and should also open the way for the identification of the major power groups involved, if indeed there are any. To develop a fuller understanding of the crystallization of occupational organization and its relation to an occupational field, however, it is necessary to examine the ways in which both the activities and the interested parties have changed over time.

There remains the task of giving a few brief illustrations of the approach suggested, which at least indicate some of its consequences and some of its potential. For this purpose an arbitrary choice of medical practitioners, printers, bank clerks, and labourers in the context of British society has been made. The remarks which follow have been drawn from more extensive analyses, which are themselves part of work in progress.

The case of medical practitioners is instructive.[2] When the occupationally related activities are examined, there is a clear twentieth-century trend towards increasing specialization and division of labour, but it is important to note that at the beginning of the century medical practitioners constituted a well-established occupational category. There is no doubt that at present the development of techniques and the application of substantive theory are dominated by medical

1 M. Crozier, *The Bureaucratic Phenomenon* (London, 1964); T. Lupton, *On the Shop Floor* (Oxford, 1963).
2 For medical practitioners see: Carr-Saunders and P.A. Wilson, *op. cit.*; Millerson, *op. cit.*; P. Vaughan, *Doctors' Commons* (London, 1959); S. W. F. Holloway, 'Medical Education in England, 1830-1858: a Sociological Analysis', *History*, 49 (October 1964), 229-324.

practitioners themselves, albeit that in many new developments those medical men who are involved work in conjunction with electronics specialists, laboratory scientists, pharmaceutical entrepreneurs, etc. The hypothesis may be advanced, however, that the degree of control of the development of substantive theory underpinning the practice of medicine exercised by medical practitioners is decreasing. Several factors are relevant to this. An increasingly smaller proportion of medical practitioners are involved directly in the development of theory. The proportion of specialists with backgrounds in biology and biochemical theory rather than in medical practice is increasing. The funding and organization of research become more serious issues as research technique becomes more sophisticated, and the emphasis shifts towards more complex biochemical control and preventive medicine. The ability of private foundations and public authorities to influence the overall direction of research is greatly increased when they provide the necessary funds, though their decisions may well be influenced by medical practitioners, and there may be little effective control of the research once the funds have been granted.

As far as the transmission of both techniques and theory is concerned control rests mainly with medical practitioners themselves, but is not vested in any one formal institution. Throughout the relatively lengthy period of training, a student is exposed to a variety of influences, even in some cases to medical sociologists, but instruction in techniques and the majority of significant testing for the student is carried out by medical practitioners. The further period of internship also provides a high degree of exposure to the influence of medical practitioners. The whole of the training period, in fact, constitutes an opportunity for the intensive socialization of future medical practitioners, and it is pertinent to note that the socializing agents are predominantly specialist doctors and surgeons attached to universities, teaching hospitals and other hospitals. But particularly with the modification and development of theory and applications, the continuing education of medical practitioners becomes a crucial issue. Considerable attention is given to this aspect by formal associations such as the Royal College of Surgeons, the Royal College of Obstetricians and Gynaecologists, and the British Medical Association through publications, conferences and national and local meetings. They thereby lend support to the diffusion of knowledge, and play a significant role in the direction of current medical practice.

The formal registration of qualifications for medical practice has been the prerogative of a statutory instrument, the General Medical Council, since 1858. This body, which has continuously been dominated by eminent medical men, administers entry to the medical register, and is also responsible for striking off practitioners for misconduct. The two other points which should be noted are that the G.M.C. exercises general quality control over training but neither offers training nor conducts examinations itself, and that the G.M.C. is subject to the Privy Council and thus has direct means of access to this powerful organ of government. The medical register clearly provides a means of identifying legally recognized medical practitioners and distinguishing them from others, but further differentiation within the category of registered practitioners is provided by reference to the particular degrees held, universities attended, qualifications and memberships in the Royal College of Physicians, the Royal College of Surgeons, and the Royal College of Obstetricians and Gynaecologists, as well as by stage and type of medical career.

The regulation of working and market conditions provides an interesting insight into occupational processes. The general practitioner, while having a general moral obligation to render services at the time when treatment is sought and maybe at a particular place as well, is in a position to bargain with private patients over remuneration and conditions of treatment, and can be said to have a high degree of autonomy in this. But with the current situation of socialized medicine the degree of bargaining power is diminished to the extent that patients use the national health system. With agencies of government as the main paymaster, the British Medical Association assumed the extremely important role of negotiating over market conditions, not only for the general practitioner but for the medical staff of hospitals as well. The general practitioner, while losing a considerable degree of autonomy in respect of market conditions, has yet both acquired greater freedom to organize on a group practice basis, to routinize surgery hours, to employ administrative staff, to refer emergency cases to local hospitals even in advance of the occurrence of the emergency, and at the same time become more of a diagnostic specialist, acting as the front line man in contact with members of the public requiring medical services, but doing less of his own dispensing, and making wide use of pathology laboratory services, and of referrals to medical specialists for treatment.

In contrast, in the hospitals working conditions have tended to be determined by senior consultants, within the limitations imposed by the availability of resources, but there is evidence to suggest that hospital administrators as a body are becoming much more influential in the determination of resource allocation than previously. The working and market conditions of housemen, for example, have been an important issue recently, and it is instructive to note how their protest has been handled in hospitals, the B.M.A. and their own separatist associations.

These illustrations are intended to lend support to the general impression that in practically all of the areas of activity related to medicine, *medical practitioners themselves enjoy either a controlling position, or at least can exercise considerable influence.* This is not to suggest, however, that there is a single monolithic controlling institution. Quite to the contrary, there are a wide variety of formal bodies and associations supplemented by relatively strong informal networks of relationships. Control over medical practice may in fact rest mainly with medical practitioners, but the variety of associational and non-formal means of pursuing specialist or sectional interest must not be under-estimated. Particular associations attract and often promote relationships between medical practitioners with common interests, but it is equally true to say that each of the bodies mentioned above, with the exception of the G.M.C., caters for a wide range of interests or areas in addition to the areas in which it is predominant. As far as public recognition is concerned two general points are worth making. Medical practitioners have an extremely high degree of 'public visibility', which is a considerable advantage in claiming status and rewards as long as they can maintain an image of effectiveness. Biochemical researchers, by contrast, have very low visibility generally unless they commit grave errors with public repercussions, although they are currently playing an extremely important role in medical research. The other point about public recognition is that medical practitioners have direct access to the highest organs of government, not only via the Privy Council, but also as officials and advisors of the administrative and policy making sectors concerned with health and welfare, sectors which are of considerable political significance.

Despite the strong controlling position of medical practitioners in relation to current occupational activities, the trend appears to be towards a slight weakening of this control, both in terms of the intrusion of non-practitioners in research, organization and financial allocation, and in terms of the segmentation of interests and activities among medical practitioners. The present situation with respect to psychology and psychiatry in British medicine provides a good illustration of occupational problems arising over the development of new theories and techniques largely outside the control of medical practitioners, and the dilemmas of incorporation exclusion. Historically the picture was very different and it is suggested here that the emergence of 'medical practitioner' as an occupation can be understood by examining the ways in which the occupationally related activities themselves, the social characteristics of the persons carrying them out and exercising control over them, and the contemporary social context changed. This type of analysis also provides considerable insight into the current structure and organization of the various medical associations and organizations.

The case of the bank clerk contrasts markedly with that of the medical practitioner.[1] Perhaps the most striking feature is the degree of control over occupationally related activities of the bank clerk which is exercised by the employer, i.e. by the policy makers in each banking organization. In nineteenth-century banking the image that is projected is of a system of close interpersonal relationships between bank clerks and employers, with trust generated over the years. The nature of the business involving the transmission and use of money

1 For bank clerks see: D. Lockwood, *The Blackcoated Worker* (London, 1958); R. M. Blackburn, *Union Character and Social Class* (London, 1967); E. Mumford and O. Banks, *The Computer and The Clerk* (London, 1967).

and financial securities is often advanced as a justification for the control exercised by or on behalf of the employers, and this is in substantial part accepted by bank clerks themselves. The growth of banking establishments and of the volume of business in the latter part of the nineteenth and early part of the twentieth century was generally accompanied by the development of formal rules and regulations as instruments of control, but informal methods of training and of recognizing merit were retained. As banks grew in size and particularly following the amalgamations immediately after the First World War, employers fostered a policy of restricting their entry to young clerks and of promotion from within. It was easy for a bank clerk to move out of the banking system, but extremely difficult for him to move to another bank. It is also worth noting at this junction that at that period banks often attempted to regulate aspects of the private lives of their employeees, as for example in the purchasing of domestic property or by 'expecting', or even insisting, that bank clerks would not marry before their late twenties.

Employers, too exercised a strict control over the incomes of bank clerks, and as Lockwood has illustrated the incomes of bank clerks have generally speaking not kept pace with those in a whole host of other occupations. The rise of the Bank Officers Guild occurred in a context of considerable uncertainty for the bank clerk. The post-1918 amalgamations in the banking world accompanied by attempts at more efficient organization led to changes of working conditions and threats to many bank clerks prospects for promotion, and advancement. In this case therefore, one might suggest that the formation of an occupational association was in part at least a response to uncertainty created by the actions of the employer, as well as to deteriorating market conditions. The B.O.G. started off in a relatively weak position, and in many banks the employers deliberately fostered internal staff associations, at the same time as refusing offical recognition to B.O.G. At the present time the National Union of Bank Employees (a transformation of B.O.G.) has achieved some measure of recognition and of influence, as witnessed by the major part it claims to have played in the recent decision to change banking hours and institute Saturday closing, though it should not be overlooked that the staff associations also appear to have played a part in this.

An indication of the strong position of employers *vis-à-vis* bank clerks has been given, but it is not intended to suggest that the employers' control was total or systematically exercised. The question arises of how N.U.B.E. has attained its present position despite considerable employer opposition. There is no doubting the employers' dominance in many areas of activity. Recruitment is a process in which personal integrity is considered to be of great importance, alongside a certain degree of numeracy and literacy. The actual process of learning banking business is primarily carried out by the age-old process of 'sitting next to Nellie'. Such on the job training is an aid to employer control of methods of work and of working conditions generally. Some employees, it is true, take the external courses and examinations of the Institute of Bankers or of one of the accountancy qualifying associations, but while this may be used as an index of industry and aspiration by the employer, it is the daily demonstration of meticulous attention to the details of practical banking, and of dependability which are the major hallmarks of merit, and pave the way for career success. 'Qualification' is thus a continuous process, achieved by the consistent demonstration of 'merit'. Nevertheless there have been significant changes in the composition of the labour force, in career patterns, and more recently in technology.

From the late 1920s to the early 1940s recruitment of male bank clerks was severely curtailed, although it is relevant to note that even at the height of the Depression, job security remained a conspicuous feature of the bank clerk's situation. Promotion opportunities, however, were fairly severely blocked, especially for younger bank clerks, recruited after the First World War. The policy of admitting female bank clerks was generally established during the manpower shortage years of World War II, and has now become a general policy for almost all banks. There has also been gradual mechanization of what were once hand procedures, such as posting, which have generally fitted well with the employment of young females, the majority of whom will have left bank employment by their mid-twenties at the latest. Perhaps the most powerful changes are those which are currently occuring with the application of computers and computer techniques in banking. These changes are occurring at a time when the promotion situation of male bank clerks has altered radically. Because of the low rate of recruitment from the late 1920s to the early 1940s, and of the retirement of those recruited before that period, those recruited after World War II, now in their thirties and early forties, have been receiving rapid promotion. The situation of the male clerks who have not yet been promoted to senior positions is one of considerable uncertainty. In addition to the possibility of blocked promotion relative to their immediate elders, and the career anxieties caused by the advent of computers in branch affairs, there are the uncertainties caused by amalgamations, and by the introduction of schemes for graduate entry.

An analysis of the position of both clerks and their union also serves to illustrate the importance of recognition to both employee associations and to employers, and the effect of competing associations, although the combination of these factors in any situation is likely to vary.[1] Blackburn discusses the effects of recognition and it would appear to be reasonable to talk of degrees of non-recognition as well as of recognition.[2] Acknowledging that recognition in itself does not necessarily lead to higher 'completeness', Blackburn nevertheless argues

---

1 Blackburn, *op. cit.*
2 For a discussion of employer recognition see also, G. S. Bain, 'Trade Union Growth and Recognition', *Royal Commission on Trade Unions and Employers' Associations, Research Paper* 6 (H.M.S.O., London, 1967).

that if the union had been recognized its 'completeness' would have been appreciably higher. Some evidence for this is provided by the membership figures for the various banks. National recognition by the Trustee Savings Banks gave the union a strong position, whilst recognition by Barclay's Bank of both the staff association and the union, the only bank to do so then, resulted in the only case of the union's 'completeness' being greater than that of the staff association.

Blackburn also provides an outline of possible developments, and the position and interests of both employers and staff associations in terms of the bargaining structure. Agreement amongst the major clearing banks as to their policies has led to two apparently interdependent processes; an interest in national negotiating machinery, on the part of employers, as a defence against the effects of arbitration on agreed joint policy in the formal context of institutional negotiations, and a questioning of the justification, logic and appeal of staff associations internal to each bank in this situation. The effect of national negotiating machinery on the recognition position of the union can be seen in the setting up in 1968 of the Banking Staff Council, representing both the union and the staff associations. The consequence has been that only one major clearing bank now refrains from recognizing the union at the time of writing. In the light of the above discussion it should be noted that there is now a division between items subject to national negotiations, and those reserved for internal negotiation in each bank.

The union has also attempted to argue comparability of work between types of banks on the basis of the necessity of a professional qualification for career advancement beyond a certain stage.[1] The possible contribution of a professional body, the Institute of Bankers, to the aspects generally considered relevant to occupational organization is by no means clear. Its activities might foster a sense of occupational identity, although research into the precise nature of such an identity and the extent of its acceptance would be necessary. Informal contact amongst bank employees, the existence of common journals, and the possible effects of geographical mobility could also be of importance, although no simple outline of the effects of these factors on the situation in banking and its development can be offered.

Printers present an even more complex case than either medical practitioners or bank clerks.[2] There is a very definite problem of whom to include under the

---

1 O. Robinson, 'White-collar Bargaining − a Case Study in the Private Sector', *Scottish Journal of Political Economy*, 14 (November 1967).

2 For printers see: G. Unwin, *Industrial Organization in the Sixteenth and Seventeenth Centuries* (Oxford, 1904); G. Unwin, *The Gilds and Companies of London* (London, 1963, 1st edn 1908); E. Howe (ed.), *The London Compositor, 1785-1900* (London, 1947); E. Howe and H. E. Waite, *The London Society of Compositors* (London, 1948); A. J. M. Sykes, 'Trade-Union Workshop Organization in the Printing Industry − the Chapel', *Human Relations*, 13 (February 1960), 49-65; A. J. M. Sykes, 'Unity and Restrictive Practices in the British Printing Industry', *Sociological Review*, 8 (December 1960), 239-54; H. A. Clegg, A. Fox and A. F. Thompson, *A History of British Trade Unions*

label of 'printers' at different points in time. But this, of course, is one of the general problems arising when an attempt is made to discuss occupational crystallization. The number and variety of both formal and informal asssociations involved has been large, and the category of employers has been extremely heterogeneous, ranging from the self-employed printer who might occasionally take on casual skilled labour, through the master printer with several journeymen, to the family printing or publishing firm and the mass circulation newspaper empires and publishing houses.

In 1583 Christopher Barker wrote that 'In the time of Henry VIII there were but few Printers and those of good credit and competent wealth', but

'In King Edward the Sixth dayes Printers and Printing began greatly to increase; but the provision of letter and many other things belonging to printing was so exceeding chargeable that most of those Printers were driven through necessitye to compound before with the Booksellers at so lowe value as the Printers themselves were most tymes small gayners and often losers.'[1]

The Stationers' Company, which had a few wealthy printers among its leaders, came to control many journeymen and master printers in London at least. At various times in the sixteenth and seventeenth centuries, there was direct government intervention, at times to support the Stationers' Company, at times to grant or rescind printing patents, and at times to restrict access to printers' work and to protect compositors.

By the nineteenth century, however, with the introduction first of power presses and later of mechanized typesetting, the printing combinations proved powerful enough to gain control over access to these new techniques, though not without struggles, especially in the latter case. The existence of a highly developed system of 'tramping' facilitated communication between local associations. Sykes argues that the printing unions developed from the workshop organization, which from its earliest days attempted to enforce the recognized customs of the trade, was a mutual benefit society, and in cases of dispute negotiated with the employer. Its origin is traced to a common interest association within the workshop, dealing only with the employer in each particular workshop. The growth of wider associations followed the expansion in size of printing shops, the mobility of labour between them, and the pursuit of collective interests *vis-à-vis* the employers. Chapels became part of wider trade union associations, but also perpetuated their existence as self-governing associations within the workshop. Control over internal relations by the chapels extended to cover such matters as night shifts and overtime. The principles on which the chapel operated were equality of views and observance of majority decisions. Such principles were generally unwritten, but entries in the chapel rule books were made to underscore old principles or create new ones. The chapel was thus

since 1889, Volume I 1889-1910 (Oxford, 1964).
1 Quoted in Unwin, *Industrial Organization*, pp. 108-9.

acting in its capacity as part of a wider association to reinforce its own operation.

As early as 1834, the London Union of Compositors held that craftsmen should regulate 'what we alone have a right to regulate, the value of our labour', and they argued against prior consultation with employers on the grounds that extensions of the principle 'will ultimately lead us into the argument that the masters have the right to regulate (piece) prices'.[1] By the end of the nineteenth century the unions, including those in printing, were attempting to impose craft customs/rules on employers. Control over both entry and content of apprenticeships and thus over the qualification process, however, is only one aspect. Little was to be gained

'by insistence on qualification unless certain types of work were reserved for a qualified worker. Here again the societies built on custom to delimit a preserve of craftsman's work, defined sometimes by the material, sometimes by the tools and machinery and sometimes by the product; and this preserve was then defended against the unqualified, against changes in the techniques or organization of production and against encroachment by other crafts.'[2]

In printing the employers were spurred into organizing to meet the unions. The unions were concerned to control the development of mechanical typesetting, and of those who manned the new machines. This was achieved by setting high piece rates and restricting output, and by entering into negotiations with employers.

Some employers held out against recognizing the rights of craft societies in the machine shop, but by 1898 a national agreement had been signed with the Typographical Association giving them the right to organize linotype operators. The demand for mass printing of standard works was another important factor. On the one hand it encouraged attempts at subdivision of tasks, and the use of new machinery, but on the other it made particular employers sensitive to withdrawal or the threat of withdrawal of labour. Some division of labour occurred, but from 1907 onwards the unions were organizing allied 'craftsmen', such as readers and machine-men, including platen and rotary minders, for 'machine-men had now come to be highly skilled men occupying a key position in the trade'. This was acceptable, whereas 'Any proposal to admit semi-skilled or unskilled groups whose existence was to some extent a threat to the dominant craftsmen of the society would have met fierce resistance.'[3]

The occupational label 'general labourer' is much more difficult to deal with in terms of the occupationally related activities schema. Hobsbawm, in his discussion of General Labour Unions points out that the idea that labourers possessed 'merely the general value of their labour' was far too simplistic. He writes perceptively of the General Unions;

1 J. Child, *A History of Industrial Relations in the British Printing Industry* (D.Phil. Thesis, Oxford, 1953), quoted in Clegg, Fox and Thompson, *op. cit.* p. 5.
2 Clegg, Fox and Thompson, *op. cit.* p. 5.
3 *Ibid.* pp. 444-5.

'As *"class"* unions they have attempted to unite all workers against all employers, generally under socialist or revolutionary inspiration. As *"labourers"* unions, they have attempted to provide effective organization for workers incapable of, or excluded from, orthodox craft unionism. As *"residual"* unions, lastly, they have organized any body of workers not effectively covered by other unions (and some that were).'[1]

The labourers were not occupationally undifferentiated: 'it was clear by 1910-14 that the union of all "unskilled" workers ... would not be one of a mass of individual floating labourers, but one of a great many local job monopolies and closed shops, whose special interests had to be safeguarded, if they were to give up their independence'.[2] The contention may be advanced, therefore, that in terms of occupational activities, as opposed to political ideology or merely convenient social categorization, there is insufficient in common between persons labelled 'general labourers' for a distinguishable occupation to have crystallized.

Gas workers in the late nineteenth and early twentieth century, however, provide a good example of occupational crystallization amongst a category of workers traditionally regarded as unskilled or of low skill. On closer examination, it becomes evident that the gas stokers and firemen occupied a strategic position. Although they were in theory 'easily replaceable', in practice they held a technological balance of power in the late 1880s. Over the preceeding two decades productivity had been increased but the old gas production equipment had been retained and at particular times of the day in the winter season was being used to capacity in many areas. The experienced stokers and firemen monopolized the knowledge of how to use the equipment to meet the exigencies of demand at peak periods. The technological balance of power was clearly an important factor in the rapid organization of gas workers in the late 1880s, but only one of many facilitating factors. The gas stokers and firemen had enjoyed a high measure of job security and relatively high wages, even during the Great Depression. There were statutory requirements concerning gas production, and local gas monopolies, many of them municipally owned and controlled, had come into being, which served to heighten political sensitivity to 'trouble' in the gas industry. The experienced gas stokers and firemen were in a sufficiently strategic position to try to establish a union along craft lines, but in fact they combined with other gas workers to unionize. This is undoubtedly linked to the traditional image of the gas workers as unskilled, to the pattern of regular mobility between the 'top' gas stoker positions and work in the yard due to seasonal fluctuations, to the fact that the threat of replacement of stokers and firemen was in practice greatest from those immediately below them in the reward hierarchy or the gas industry, as well as to the existence of socialist activists among their numbers. The organization, once created and proved effective, managed to retain its influence despite

1 E. J. Hobsbawm, *Labouring Men* (London, 1964), p. 179.
2 *Ibid.* p. 190.

the gradual introduction by the employers of new production technology which eliminated the stokers' possession of a technological balance of power.[1]

Without suggesting that the case of the gas workers is in any sense typical, it does seem to indicate that the occupationally related activities schema is useful as a means of approaching what are generally termed unskilled occupations, at a more narrowly focused level than that of the general labourer or the general union. Nevertheless, in so far as workers are organized, and through their organization attempt to affect both market and working conditions, the relevance of such organization to the study of occupations is undeniable, even if the organization in question is a general union. Organization itself is an important resource, but to be effective in occupational bargaining requires control over other resources as well. It is not without significance that so-called general unions represent a congeries of occupational groups, and because of this there are usually severe limitations on the scope of collective action in such unions. General unions have been most effective where they have been able to form strong political lobbies at local and national government levels, and thus to utilize governmental processes and structures to influence their occupational demands. Once again this illustrates the necessity of relating occupational activities to the wider social context of which they are part.

These illustrations, approached through occupational labels, give some indication of the sort of mapping of interested parties, and identification of critical resources and resource controllers which can be achieved via this approach. They also serve to demonstrate the importance of placing any one occupational association in both its general occupational and wider social contexts and to highlight the importance of Stinchcombe's ideas concerning 'the nesting of power' for this type of analysis.[2] If the illustrations had been approached in terms of particular associations, such as the British Medical Association, the National Union of Bank Employees, and the Typographical Association, this would have led to the delineation of the occupationally related activities in which each association showed an interest, those over which it attained some measure of control, and an examination of changes in such interests and control over time. Having identified and related the activities of the particular association, or at least its policy-making groups, to the wider occupational and social contexts, it would have been possible to consider, along the lines set out in the previous section of the paper, the degree of monopoly claimed over occupationally related activities by particular associations, the degree of organization of occupationally related activies, and the degree of external recognition of an occupation or occupational association. The illustrations, though brief and general, give some idea of the possibilities in this direction.

1 *Ibid.* chapter 9, pp. 158-78, for gas workers.
2 A. L. Stinchcombe, *Constructing Social Theories* (New York, 1968).

CONCLUSION

In the short space available in this paper, it has not been possible to develop a detailed application of the ideas which have been advanced. This must be the task of future publications. The essential argument which has been stated, following a review of the literature on professions, semi-professions and professionalization — a literature which in fact is heavily dominated by the writings of American and American-oriented sociologists — is that attention should be focused upon the analysis of occupations rather than upon professions or professionalizing occupations alone. Such an approach serves to emphasize the differences as well as the similarities between occupations by treating them in terms of a common analytic framework.

The problem of what constitutes an occupation is a highly contentious matter. The key to the approach advanced here lies in the attempt to conceptualize activities which in principle are relevant to the organization of all occupations. It may be objected that this implies an underlying model of what an occupation is. In a very general sense it does, and the conception of an occupation as based upon similarities of activities carried out within the general pattern of the division of labour is intended to indicate the sort of underlying model adopted. The main concern, however, is to focus upon those aspects of occupational analysis which are peculiarly susceptible to sociological investigation, namely the manifestation of occupational organization and the processes of the social recognition and categorization of occupational associations.

In particular, the claim may be advanced that the analysis of any occupational organization or of categories of persons denoted by any one occupational label, can be usefully approached by attempting to identify both the parties (individuals, groups, networks and formal organizations) involved in the carrying out of occupationally related activities, and the properties of the activities themselves. Analysis of the changing degree of control exercised over these activities by various parties and of the relation of these parties to one another can provide a significant contribution to understanding the way in which occupations crystallize, continue to operate, and change. It is necessary, however, to relate occupational activities to the wider social structure before they can be meaningfully interpreted. This is where the idea of division of labour is doubly significant. It is not only the patterning of the division of labour and the processes by which patterns are perpetuated and changed in relation to occupational activities which are important, but also the way in which these are related to the overall patterns and processes involved. The illustrations cited indicate this aspect particularly well.

Finally it should be noted that this paper has been concerned with theoretical orientations. The resource approach requires the mapping of both potential resources and those which are actually used, and the investigation of the processes of resource creation, management and control. The occupationally related activities schema provides one way of approaching such a mapping in the study of occupations. Despite its apparent simplicity, the schema can be used to generate an extremely complex picture of occupational structure by attempting to delineate the parties involved in such activities, their inter-relationships, and the varying degrees of control which each asserts over specific activities through time. It also forces the researcher to take account of the question of the changing social structures and contexts in which occupations develop and change. This type of theoretical orientation provides only a starting point, but we submit that it exhibits great promise for sociologists interested in understanding occupational organizations and their behaviour.

3 Professionals in Organizations

G. HARRIES-JENKINS

3

PROFESSIONALS IN ORGANIZATIONS

G. HARRIES-JENKINS

In modern societies, an increasing number of professionals are employed in large-scale organizations. No longer can it be assumed that the 'ideal-type' professional, if such a man ever existed, is the independent free practitioner who practises his calling in a purely entrepreneurial role. The professional of today is often a salaried employee, performing his activities within the structural framework of a bureaucratic hierarchy, in occupations as diverse as teaching, government, social welfare, medicine and industrial management. In the majority of cases, the individual in these bureaucracies, retains a distinctive frame of reference,[1] so that, as a professional, he participates in two distinct, irreconcilable systems. He is a member of two institutions – the profession and the organization. Each of these attempts to control his occupational activities, and the manner in which the former establishes standards and norms for the conduct of professional activities, contrasts with the way in which the latter specifies task objectives, and controls the means whereby these objectives are realized.

To examine the activities of professions in these systems, is to examine, as Kornhauser comments, 'the relation between two institutions, not merely between organizations and individuals'.[2] The analytical tools which are used, are frequently based on the traditional concepts of 'profession' and 'organization' as they have been formulated in separate models. Variables are based on the position of the profession as an autonomous community of shared interests, and on the position of the organization as a rational structure which must be insulated from its surrounding institutional environment. Both demonstrate certain common characteristics. In each model we find universal standards, specific expertise and affective neutrality. Yet, paradoxically, points of convergence also demonstrate the extent to which professional and bureaucratic principles provide contrasting approaches to the organization of complex tasks.[3] The con-

---

1 See R.K. Merton, 'Patterns of Influence: Local and Cosmopolitan Influentials', *Social Theory and Social Structure* (Glencoe, 1957), pp. 387-420. Alvin W. Gouldner; 'Cosmopolitans and Locals: Toward an Analysis of Latent Social Roles', *Administrative Science Quarterly*, 2 (1957-8), 281-306 and 444-80.
2 W. Kornhauser, *Scientists in Industry: Conflict and Accommodation* (Berkeley, 1962), p. 8.
3 These contrasting or alternative approaches are considered further in R. G. Francis and R. C. Stone, *Service and Procedure in Bureaucracy: A Case Study* (Minneapolis, 1956), and in A. L. Stinchcombe, 'Bureaucratic and Craft Administration of Production: A Comparative Study', *Administrative Science Quarterly*, 4 (September 1959), 168-87.

trast is essentially one between the 'vertical' structure of the bureaucratic organization and the 'horizontal' structure of the profession, and, since professionals
are employed in an environment which rests on principles of organization fundamentally different from those of their profession, these divergent principles
generate conflicts between professionals and their employers in a number of
specific problem areas.

The significance of these problem areas has not failed to attract the attention
of the researcher and the theorist. Studies have examined at length such specific
problems as the presence of role-incongruity among professionals, the role-strain
and incongruent status associated with their operational activities, the evaluation
of professional behaviour, and the manner in which professional client relationships are modified in an organization environment.[1] The basis of this research,
however, depends upon a particular concept of 'profession' which is derived
from the traditional model of the professional as an independent free practitioner
and a number of methodological problems arise when we examine the activities
of those individuals whose actions can only be performed within a particular
organization. In this instance, the concepts of 'Profession', 'Professional', Professionalization' or 'Professionalism', which we usually accept, can no longer be
used with ease, for the particular role of the work practitioner is the 'direct
result of his active membership and assigned position in a special organization.'[2]
The latter is 'special', because the fusion of the profession and organization is so
complete that the employing environment is a closed community in which
professional life and organizational life have completely intermingled. In this
community, the individual has become a participant in a unique single system,
in which his 'profession' cannot always be clearly distinguished from his
occupation. Accordingly, we cannot use Kornhauser's profession/organization
dichotomy as a means of analysis, and we are forced to re-examine hitherto
accepted concepts, associated with 'profession', if we are to evaluate the performance of individuals in these organizations.

In this paper, therefore, we are concerned with the methodological problems
which occur when we examine the activities of individuals in an environment
in which professional and organizational life have completely intermingled.

1 See, *inter alia*, Peter M. Blau and W. Richard Scott, *Formal Organization – A Comparative
   Approach* (San Francisco, 1962), pp. 64-74; Harold L. Wilensky, 'The Professionalization
   of Everyone?' *The American Journal of Sociology*, 70 (1964), 146-58; Amitai Etzioni,
   A Comparative Analysis of Complex Organizations (New York, 1961), pp. 257-61; W.
   Richard Scott, 'Professionals in Bureaucracies – Areas of Conflict', in Howard M. Vollmer
   and Donald M. Mills (eds.), *Professionalization* (Englewood Cliffs, 1966), pp. 265-75; J.
   Ben-David, 'The Professional Role of the Physician in Bureaucratized Medicine. A Study
   in Role Conflict', *Human Relations*, 11 (1958), 255-74; D. G. Moore and R. Renck, 'The
   Professional Employee in Industry', *Journal of Business*, 28 (January 1955), 58-66; J. K.
   Galbraith, *The New Industrial State* (London, 1967), chapter XI, 'The General Theory
   of Motiviation', and chapter XII, 'Motivation in Perspective', pp. 128-48.
2 M. D. Feld, 'Professionalism, Nationalism, and the Alienation of the Military', in Jacques
   Van Doorn (ed.), *Armed Forces and Society* The Hague, 1968), p. 56.

There are a number of problem areas, the first of which is one of terminology, for we wish to differentiate these particular individuals from those other professionals who may work either in a large scale organization or as independent practitioners. The accompanying danger, is that this wish to distinguish a particular group, limits our analysis to a re-examination of the question 'What is a profession', or leads us to over-emphasize evaluative attributes of occupational performance, such as the external status of the occupation.[1] This problem, however, can be overcome if Feld's term, 'ascriptive professional'[2] is used as a means of differentiation. The characteristics of this term can be deduced from the contrast between two sets of work practitioners, such as the Chartered Municipal Treasurer and the Chartered Accountant, whose activities are carried out in similar, but not identical, fields. In this instance, both are members of professional institutes, both have undergone a lengthy period of formal training, and both have taken comparable examinations. The contrast is that the former can only be employed in the finance department of a local or public authority, whereas the latter may work either as an independent free practitioner, or as the employee of a bureaucratic organization. An *ascriptive professional* can thus be defined as a work practitioner, whose task commitment is performed in a monopolistic organization which determines his status, evaluates his ability according to organizational requirements, and delineates, through a process of selection and designation, the precise area within which he will carry out his activities.

By accepting that individuals employed in these special organizations can be categorized as *ascriptive professionals,* we can escape from the professional/non-professional dichotomy which dominates so much of the literature in this field, and move on to consider the more important problem of the means whereby these activities can be evaluated. We know that these employees, among whom we can number bank clerks, Administrative Class civil servants, clergymen, military officers and so on, lay claim to professional status, but if we reject the validity of the model of the free professional as a means of comparative analysis, we are forced to consider some other attributes as an analytical tool.

In this context, our difficulties are accentuated by the presence of two subsidiary problems. Firstly, if we accept the premise that the employment of professionals in large-scale organizations is the basis of certain dysfunctional consequences, we must consider whether the strain which is similarly evident where the ascriptive professional is employed in a special organization, is derived from a similar base. This may be a minor problem of no consequence if we accept the argument that the believed distinction between 'professional' behaviour and 'bureaucratic' behaviour can be extended in meaning, so that 'professional' includes 'ascriptive professional'. Conversely, we may be faced with a major

1 See the comments of Michael D. King, 'Science and the Professional Dilemma', in Julius Gould (ed.), *Penguin Social Sciences Survey, 1968* (London, 1968), p. 39.
2 Feld, *op. cit.* p. 56.

C

problem if we conclude that the actions of the latter are neither wholly professional nor wholly bureaucratic, for then we are forced to recognize that we have
introduced a third element into the professional bureaucrat dichotomy.

Additionally, it is evident that there are, in many special organizations, individuals who could, in theory, work as independent practitioners. Many organizations, particularly public service organizations, such as the Home Civil Service
and the Military, employ a large number of individuals who have qualified in a
wide variety of 'professional' occupations. Thus the Military, for example, commissions doctors, dentists, clergymen, engineers and accountants, among others.
Yet, while some of these carry out activities which enable them to be differentiated from ascriptive professionals, in terms of the primary occupational role,[1]
others cannot be easily distinguished from the wider group of commissioned
officers, for their role function is the direct result of their membership of a
particular military regiment or branch. The problem in evaluating the actions
and behaviour of the latter as 'professionals', is that they have a dual skill whereby, in addition to their external qualifications, they possess a special body of
military knowledge and skill, and a second set of standards and norms, which
they have acquired through a complex socialization process. In summary, the
problem is whether they are to be considered as *ascriptive professionals*, that is,
as members of the officer corps, or whether they should be evaluated in
common with the larger and more widely orientated group of proressionals
who are employed in other large-scale organizations.

There are several methods whereby these problems can be overcome. Firstly,
we can conclude that the individual who is employed in a special organization
is a 'generalist' and not a 'professional', arguing that successful implementation
of his role activities is dependent on the knowledge and experience gained within
the organization, and not on the professionalism or specialism acquired by recognized training outside the employing organization. Such an argument is also
based on the narrow definition of 'profession' which is derived from characteristics peculiar to the independent practitioner, such as the professional/client
relationship, the fiduciary client relationship, the necessity for peer evaluation,
and the existence of a community sanction. If we accept this argument, we then
limit our analysis to a study of the individual work practitioner in his role as a
bureaucrat. In such a study, 'expertise', normally subsumed as a criterion of
professionalism,[2] is interpreted to mean the technical competence which Max
Weber concluded was the basis of bureaucratic efficiency,[3] since bureaucratic

1 The doctor, dentist and clergyman, for example, may also be distinguished from other
   ascriptive professionals by different military ranks or by uniforms which vary from the
   normal military pattern.
2 Kornhauser, *op. cit.* p. 1. 'Expertise' was also accepted by George Strauss as one of the
   'values' associated with professionalism. See Strauss, 'Professionalism and Occupational
   Associations', *Industrial Relations, 2*, 3 (May 1963), 8-9.
3 Max Weber, *The Theory of Social and Economic Organization* (translated by A. M.

administration is seen to be 'essentially control by means of knowledge'.[1] Because a study of this type rejects the significance of 'profession' as a sociological category, any noted evidence of role conflict or status incongruity, usually attributable to the individual's membership of the two separate institutions of profession and organization, is interpreted as one of the dysfunctional consequences of bureaucratization.[2]

Alternatively, we can, in recognizing that the concept of the 'profession' is only applicable to an abstract model of occupational behaviour, use the concept of *professionalization* as an analytical tool. This enables us to examine the essential attributes of professional behaviour, and makes it possible for us to consider the dynamic process whereby the special organization changes certain crucial characteristics in the direction of the abstract model. The evaluation of the organization in these terms also enables us to obtain answers to the question: 'How professionalized is the occupational group in various identifiable respects?' Additionally, if a continuum of professionalization is constructed in terms of common essential attributes, it is possible to compare the special organization under study with other organizations, by measuring both quantitatively and qualitatively, the extent to which professionalization has affected different forms of occupational performance.

For these reasons, it is preferable to measure the activities of the *ascriptive professional* in the special organization, in terms of the professionalization of the group. By adopting this approach, we can escape from the professional/non-professional dichotomy, and we can attain a wider appreciation of the role of the individual, than if we restrict analysis to a consideration of his bureaucratic activities. Concomitantly, any dysfunctional consequences which we note, can be related to the overall effects of professionalization, rather than be attributed to any 'third element', for the effects of professionalization are of general rather than specific applicability, since they are not peculiar to the ascriptive professional.

THE ELEMENTS OF PROFESSIONALIZATION

Unlike the concept of bureaucratization which has been extensively analysed as part of the larger sociological concept of 'bureaucracy', professionalization has largely escaped definition.[3] In part, this failure to achieve an adequate analysis of the term is the result of the concomitant failure to define 'professional' or to

1   Henderson and Talcott Parsons), (New York, 1966), p. 335.
    Ibid. p. 337.
2   See Ralph H. Turner, 'The Navy Disbursing Officer as a Bureaucrat', *American Sociological Review*, 12 (1947), 342-8.
3   A recent attempt to establish the characteristics of professionalization, is D. J. Hickson and M. W. Thomas: 'Professionalization in Britain: A Preliminary Measurement', *Sociology*, 3, 1 (January 1969), 37-53.

delineate 'profession'. The reasons for this failure are numerous, and outside the
scope of this study, but from definitions collected by such writers as Barber,[1]
Goode and Mary Huntington,[2] Cogan[3] and Millerson,[4] and from criteria
deduced from a preliminary survey of various occupational groups and organizations, we can assemble a set of constitutive definitions of professional characteristics. These can be considered further, to suggest that the variable of professionalization can be defined in terms of six constituent elements: *structural,
contextual, activity, ideological, educational* and *behavioural.* Each of these can
be further differentiated, as is shown in Table 1, to produce a list of twenty-one
sub-elements.

Table 1. *The Elements of Professionalization*

1   *Structural element*
    (a) *Specialization*: the exclusive nature of group activity
    (b) *Centralization*: the locus of the authority-sanctions mechanism
    (c) *Standardization*: the control of non-occupational behaviour

2   *Contextual element*
    (*a*) Spatio-temporal dimension
    (*b*) Size of the occupational group
    (*c*) Resources of the occupational group
    (*d*) Group relationships

3   *Activity element*
    (*a*) The goals of the occupational group
    (*b*) The role of individual members

4   *Educational elements*
    (*a*) Occupational intelligence requirements
    (*b*) Basis of systematic theory
    (*c*) Institutionalized educational process
    (*d*) Length of training
    (*e*) Cost of training

5   *Ideological element*
    (*a*) Personality involvement
    (*b*) Sense of group identity
    (*c*) Group culture
    (*d*) Status
    (*e*) Socialization process

1 B. Barber, 'Some Problems in the Sociology of the Professions', *Daedalus,* 92 (1963), 669-88.
2 William J. Goode and Mary Huntington, 'Professions in American Society', unpublished manuscript quoted in Goode, 'The Librarian; From Occupation to Profession', in Vollmer and Mills (eds.); *op cit.* pp. 34-43.
3 Morris L. Cogan, 'Towards a Definition of Profession', *Harvard Educational Review* 23 (1953), 33-50.
4 Geoffrey Millerson, *The Qualifying Associations: a Study in Professionalization* (London, 1964), table 1.1.

6   *Behavioural element*
     (*a*)   Code of conduct
     (*b*)   Evaluation of merit

Before these elements are analysed, it is necessary to anticipate the results of
the study of the *activity element* to note that since the goal of a special organization, such as the Military, is not primarily entrepreneurial, certain non-discrimi-
nating characteristics have been excluded from Table 1. These characteristics are
derived from the limitations which have been placed on the economic self-interest
of the independent free practitioner, so that they are irrelevant in the study of
typical motives of persons acting in a special organization. They include such
items as a ban on advertising, a scale of recommended charges or fees, both of
which are indicative of a particular form of professional/client relationship, and
the explicit ban on members undercutting one another.[1]

The Structural Sub-Elements

These are closely linked with the professional Associations which have been established for many occupational groups. It is these Associations which, through
their attempts to ensure the exclusiveness of group activity, have become, in
many cases, the locus of the sanctions mechanism and the centre of authority.
Additionally, the Association may attempt to attain control over some aspects
of non-occupational behaviour. The extent, however, to which these aims will be
actualized, varies in relation to the objects and form of the established Association, and a basic typology suggests that there are seven such bodies whose
activities are relevant in the general analysis of occupational groups. The eighth,
which can be termed the Prestige Association, is of limited direct value. Membership of such a body is believed to bestow a particular honour on the individual,
and a rigorous selection of potential group members ensures the exclusive nature
of the Association. The aims of this type of Association are expressed in very
general terms which are not directly related to occupational activities. The aims
of the Royal Society, founded in 1660, are, for example, 'Improving Natural
Knowledge'. Since potential members cannot apply to be elected, but must wait
to be selected because of their pre-eminence in their subject or in the public
service, the Prestige Association occupies a position which is unique among the
other occupational Associations.[2]

The remaining seven Associations differ in their objectives. Two of them are

---

1   These limitations form part of such professional codes as the 'Canons of Ethics for
     Engineers', *The Annals of the American Academy of Political and Social Science,* 297
     (January 1955), 56-8. Twenty-eight sections amplify such headings as 'Professional Life',
     'Relations with the Public', 'Relations with Clients and Employers', and 'Relations with
     Engineers'.
2   Other Prestige Associations include the Royal Academy, founded in 1768 and the
     British Academy, founded in 1901.

only of limited value in the evaluation of professionalization, for the structural sub-elements are not evidenced through the activities of the Association. The Coordinating Association is thus a collectivity of qualified persons working in a narrow field of study. It coordinates the work activities of its members without employing extensive negotiating machinery, or the application of industrial pressure techniques, to improve the working conditions or the remuneration of its members. The Association primarily exists for specialists to discuss operational and occupational problems within a narrow context, but it has no sanctions authority mechanism, and it does not seek to bestow a qualification on its members through an examination process.[1]

Similarly, the Protective Association, although its objects differ from those of the Coordinating Association, is only remotely connected with the professionalization of the occupational group. The Association exists to provide an organized means of exerting pressure on outsiders to protect the working conditions and remuneration of individual group members. Some of the objectives of this type of Association are thus comparable with those of a trade union, for in their negotiations over salary and working conditions, the Association has adopted industrial bargaining techniques. This is particularly noticeable in the activities of the British Medical Association (B.M.A.) and the British Airlines Pilots Association (B.A.L.P.A.). In the former case, for example, a ministerial decision which reduced the pay lead which Military doctors had enjoyed since 1962 over the National Health Service general practitioner, led the B.M.A. to withdraw their cooperation from the Ministry of Defence's recruiting programme. Since 1966, therefore, there have been almost no new entries of medical cadets who were in training and committed to enter, before the British Medical Association blacklisted the Service career.[2] In this respect, therefore, the undeniable authority which the Association has attained over medical affairs, enables it to offer direct economic benefits to its members comparable with those offered by a trade union. At the same time, however, we must note that other, no less important, objectives of a national medical association are clearly distinguishable from the aims of a trade union, for these are services which the former renders to society as a whole, by protecting individual clients and the public at large, from injury or exploitation.[3] Nevertheless, a noticeable development in the history of this type of Association, is that some bodies, notwithstanding their

1 A typical Coordinating Association is the Society of Town Clerks, founded in 1928. Since these town clerks are almost wholly, if not exclusively, qualified solicitors or barristers, they will also be members of other professional associations, such as the Law Society or the Inns of Court. It is the latter which are the locus of the group sanctions mechanism, and the centre of occupational authority.
2 National Board for Prices and Incomes, *Standing Reference on the Pay of the Armed Forces*, Second Report, Cmnd 4079 (London, 1969), p. 35.
3 For an analysis of the activities and objectives of a national Medical Association, see Editors of the Yale Law Journal, 'The American Medical Association: Power, Purpose and Politics in Organized Medicine', *The Yale Law Journal*, 63, 7 (May 1954), 938-47.

claim to 'professional' status have considered affiliation with the national Trades Union Congress.[1]

A further set of three Associations are more closely linked with the professionalization of an occupational group, for their objectives can be equated with the claim that the major functions of any established professional Association are 'educative in character'.[2] Yet, while this may be a valid assessment of the primary functions of three Associations — the Study Association, the Qualifying Association and the Post-Graduate Association, there are subtle variations in their respective purposes. The Study Association comprises a group of individuals who have no more than a dilettante interest in the particular subject. Additionally, some Study Associations admit group members, such as schools and libraries, to corporate membership of the Association, as well as junior members and honorary members. Some Associations consist almost entirely of specialists;[3] others have a more general membership.[4]

Although the Study Association may confer on its members the right to use designatory letters, such as F.R.G.S. (Fellow of the Royal Geographical Society), these are not, in themselves, indicative of any particular educational qualification or professional skill. In contrast, the remaining Associations of this set, have established as one of their principle functions, the object of *examining* and *qualifying* persons who wish to become practitioners in the field with which they are concerned. The principle requirement for admission to membership is thus the knowledge and ability to pass the examinations of the Association, although the charter or articles of incorporation of the particular Association, may, in an attempt to ensure the exclusiveness of the group, insist that potential members satisfy other criteria.[5]

In a number of studies, the existence within an occupational group of the Qualifying or Post-Graduate Association, has been taken to be one of the more reliable indicators of the level of attained group professionalization. It has thus been argued that the starting point in a regular sequence of professionalization,

1 At the 1968 Annual Conference of the Institution of Professional Civil Servants, a typical Protective Association, motion 112 called for 'consideration to be given to the question of affiliation to the Trades Union Congress'. See *State Service* (August 1968), p. 190. Similar motions have been considered by the National Association of Local Government Officers, and the National Union of Teachers.
2 F. T. Chapman, 'The Implication of Membership of a Professional Body — Education', *The British Management Review*, 2, 1 (1952), 159.
3 The Chemical Society and the Royal Statistical Society for example.
4 These include the Royal Geographical Society, the Zoological Society of London, and the Royal Horticultural Society.
5 These criteria include: (*a*) the requirement that potential members will have served a period of articles with a senior member of the Institution, (*b*) the need for potential members to have recognized work experience between the completion of their examination and their admission to full membership of the Institution, (*c*) the need for potential members to be sponsored by colleagues who are already full members of the Institution, (*d*) the provision by the potential member of satisfactory character references, and (*e*) enquiries by the Institution into the practical experience of the applicant.

is the creation of the Qualifying Association.[1] This chronological emphasis has also been interpreted to suggest that, since professionalization entails both conformity and the sanctioning of a specific norm, the establishment of a normative pattern is dependent on the formation of this type of Association.[2] Alternatively, it has been postulated that, since a degree of professionalization can be related to the type of Assocation which is established for an occupational group, the existence of an Association which seeks to examine members is indicative of a higher level of group professionalization than in those occupations where the relevant Association can be classified as a Study, Protective or Co-ordinating Association.[3]

A number of methodological problems, however, remain unsolved. Apart from the difficulty of classification which occurs in those instances where the group may be represented by more than one type of Association,[4] the relative status, and the value to society, of the conferred qualifications vary considerably. Thus, while the common characteristics of Qualifying Associations can be used in a Guttman scalogram to demonstrate such unidimensional variables as 'length of training', it is difficult to move from this quantitative interpretation of professionalization to a qualitative assessment. Some indication of possible differentials, which might be indicative of a related degree of professionalization, can be inferred from the contrast between the objectives of the Qualifying Association and the Post-Graduate Association. The former is designed to bestow a primary qualification on group members; the latter awards a second qualification to work practitioners who are already recognized as fully qualified. Such a distinction, however, does not resolve the problem of evaluating the contribution made by a particular Qualifying Association to the development of occupational professionalization. An additional complication is that a Post-Graduate Association may also award a primary qualification. This complication can be seen in the example of the Royal College of Surgeons of England. Potential Fellows of the College must have been qualified as medical practitioners for at least four years, and to have had six months' experience in resident appointments in general surgery, before they can sit the F.R.C.S. examination. In contrast, the grade of Member is part of the conjoint qualification L.R.C.P., M.R.C.S.[5] conferred by the conjoint examining board of the Royal College of Physicians and the Royal College of Surgeons. This qualification is recognized by the Medical Act, 1956, section 11, as one of the primary degrees or diplomas entitling the holder to

1 Theodore Caplow, *Sociology of Work* (Minnesota, 1954), p. 139.
2 Millerson, *op. cit.* p. 10.
3 W. J. Reader, *Professional Men: the Rise of the Professional Classes in Nineteenth-century England* (London, 1966), p. 163: 'An occupation's rise to professional standing can be pretty accurately charted by reference to the progress of its professional institute or association.'
4 This is particularly noticeable in the medical profession.
5 Licentiate of the Royal College of Physicians and Member of the Royal College of Surgeons.

provisional registration with the General Medical Council.

If, however, we can differentiate between the objectives of the Qualifying Association and the Post-Graduate Association, particularly where the latter only awards a second qualification,[1] then an evaluation of the contribution made by a specific Qualifying Association to the development of occupational professionalization, must be closely linked with the extent to which the Association demonstrates evidence of centralization and standardization. Where the performance of occupational activity is controlled by the Qualifying Association, to the extent that non-members cannot carry out the work function, or where the Association has developed an effective sanctions mechanism to control occupational and non-occupational behaviour, the contribution made to the development of professionalization tends to be high. Conversely, if the Association, in encouraging an increase in the size of its membership, is 'open' to a large number of aspirants, or if the Association is not interested in enforcing rules and regulations which govern occupational behaviour, the contribution tends to be low.

It is possible, therefore, to use the presence or absence of this type of Association as an elementary indicator of the extent to which the relevant occupation has been professionalized, but there are certain dangers associated with this. Not every group which is generally believed to demonstrate a high degree of professionalization, has developed such an Association. There is also evidence that groups striving for external recognition as 'professions' tend not only to depend on this form of Association for their socialization and their institutionalization, but also to over-estimate the effectiveness of their sanctions mechanism. In this situation, it is necessary to evaluate effectively and objectively the purposes of the Association, and to analyse its sanctions mechanism. The concomitant difficulties are such, that it may be impossible to reach a valid conclusion, but it is probable that a high degree of professionalization will be apparent in those Associations where the pattern of standardization, centralization, and specialization will be similar to that which can be found in the Registering Association.

The characteristics of this pattern can be deduced from the Registering Associations which control occupational activity for eleven occupational groups in England.[2] For these groups, there is a statutory requirement that members are

1 Post-Graduate Associations which confer nothing other than second qualifications, include the College of Pathologists (F.C.Path. and M.C.Path.) and the Royal College of Obstetricians and Gynaecologists (F.R.C.O.G., M.R.C.O.G., and the Diploma in Obstetrics, D.Obst.R.C.O.G.).

2 These eleven occupational groups are: Solicitors (first controlled in 1729, and now governed by the provisions of the Solicitors Act, 1957), Pharmacists (1852; now the Medical Act, 1956), Medical Practitioners (1858; now the Medical Act, 1956), Dentists (1878; now the Dentists Act 1956), Veterinary Surgeons (1881; now the Veterinary Surgeons Act, 1948), Patent Agents (1888; now the Patents Act, 1949), Midwives (1902; now the Midwives Act, 1918), Nurses (1919; now the Nurses Act, 1957), Architects (controlled by the Architects Registration Act, 1931), Opticians (Opticians Act, 1958) and Medical Auxiliaries (Professions Supplementary to Medicines Act, 1960). Occupations in Scotland are controlled by similar or identical legislation. A

C*

'registered', so that performance of group activity is restricted to those individuals whose name is included in a currently valid register. While other Associations, noticeably those of the Qualifying and Post-Graduate type, also maintain a 'register' of members, there is a fundamental functional difference. When the Registering Association expels a member, he is no longer able to practise his occupation. Expulsion from the other Associations, does not necessarily prevent the individual from continuing to exercise his occupational role, although his opportunities for securing employment may be reduced.[1] The difference can be seen in the contrasting effects which follow from removing a doctor from the register, and from expelling, for example, a member from the Town Planning Institute.[2] The doctor is legally barred from practice; the planner, in contrast, can continue to exercise his occupational role, and although employers may be reluctant to accept him in their organization, there is no legal bar to his employment.

So that the Registering Association can exercise this extreme form of control over group members, the enabling statute, whereby the Association is established, normally specifies the composition of the Statutory Committee which controls associated disciplinary committees. Indeed, the statute may go further to outline the methods of procedure for, and the powers of, the sanctions authority. The statute thus creates an organization with its own structure[3] since membership of the Committee is not restricted to individuals who belong to the occupational group. Yet, paradoxically, it is the creation of this type of Committee, despite its inclusion of 'non-professional' members, which can be taken as an elementary indicator of the high level of group professionalization.[4]

development peculiar to Scotland is the recent move to ensure that all members of the teaching profession are 'registered' with the General Teaching Council. Teachers who have not registered are no longer regarded as 'qualified' and they are barred from carrying out their occupation in Scottish schools.

1   The position of expelled role practitioners in certain occupations is complicated by external legislative requirements. Company law and Inland Revenue regulations, for example, demand that accounts are prepared only by 'qualified' accountants. The expelled practitioner in these circumstances, may find that he cannot find employment, because he is no longer able to exercise fully the whole range of his occupational activities.

2   Membership of this Institute, incorporated in 1959, is the recognized technical qualification for Town Planning appointments in public and private offices in the United Kingdom and overseas.

3   See D. Lloyd, 'The Disciplinary Powers of Professional Bodies', *The Modern Law Review*, 13 (1950), 281-306.

4   It is necessary to take the existence of the Committee, not the legal power it wields, as the index of professionalization. Other occupational groups are similarly controlled through the exercise of legal powers and, in a number of instances, entry to the group is restricted to those work practitioners whose competence is statutorily recognized. Merchant Navy officers, for example, are certified by the Ministry of Transport; Mine Managers, and Weights and Measures Inspectors are certificated by the Board of Trade. Withdrawal of this certification by the appropriate authority imposes, in the same way as does expulsion from the register of a Registering Association, a ban on the practice of the occupational role. The distinction is that the relevant Association, such as the Institute of Weights and Measures Administration, is of minimal importance in the

The problem which is associated with this use of a single indicator of profes-sionalization, is that, once again, there are a number of recognized professions which do not possess a Registering Association. Indeed, there is a group of occu-pations which have been generally accepted from 'time immemorial' to be profes-sions, that do not belong to any of the foregoing types of Associations. In Great Britain, there are three major, and one minor, occupational groups whose professional status is beyond question, even to the extent that they are accepted as 'ideal-types', which lack any of the more usual form of Association. The Bar, the Established Church, the Military, and the lesser known group of Notaries, each evolved as a distinct occupational collectivity prior to the major develop-ments of the nineteenth century. Each was thus outside the main stream of the evolution of the professions, and all refused to form the more common type of Association. The organizational structure of each of them is unique. The Bar, in contrast with the incorporated Qualifying Association, is a voluntary society which is unincorporated. Yet the Bar, like the Qualifying Association examines its members, and, like the Registering Association, can prevent an expelled member from carrying out his occupational role. The Military and the Established Church are closed occupational groups with rigid selection criteria to control recruitment. Each wields an extreme control over the functions of group mem-bers, and, to ensure supervision of both occupational and non-occupational behaviour, implements in special and exclusive courts, a sanctions mechanism based on a particularistic legal code. Notaries, in contrast, are essentially a legacy from the past, for the Scriveners' Company which has a monopoly of practice in London, is known to have been in existence in 1357, long before its mono-poly was confirmed by the Public Notaries Act of 1801.[1]

There are considerable differences of organizational forms. While two of these groups are essentially collectivities of independent free practitioners, to the extent that neither barristers nor notaries form partnerships, two — the Church and the Military — are examples of special organizations in which there has been a complete fusion of profession and organization. Indeed, the officer corps is an excellent and possibly unique example of the process of integration[2] so that 'Officership is a public bureaucratized profession; the officer corps is both a

---

control of the occupation. Centralization and standardization are thus associated with the appropriate government department, and not with the occupational Association, so that the contrast is between bureaucratic control and professional control. It was the fear that control of the occupation would be through the bureaucratic process, and not through the exercise of collegial authority, which led some Scottish teachers to oppose the creation and the monopoly of the General Teaching Council. See *The Times Educational Supple-ment*, 18 July 1969.

1 The jurisdiction of the Scriveners' Company is derived from the provisions of Ecclesias-tical Law, since practice of the occupation is restricted to those members who possess a licence or 'faculty' which is nominally granted by the Archbishop of Canterbury.

2 See Jacques Van Doorn 'The Officer Corps: A Fusion of Profession and Organization', *European Archives of Sociology*, 6 (1965), 262-82.

bureaucratic profession and a bureaucratic organization'.[1]

The common factor which links these four occupational groups, is that their existence depends upon members exercising their individual roles by prerogative, that is by derived permission. For the Military and the Bar, this can be traced back to the position of the Sovereign as the Head of the Armed Forces and Head of the Judiciary. Individual officers and judges still receive a Queen's Commission directing them to perform a function, and, since the Commission can be terminated, withdrawal of this royal prerogative means the expulsion of the individual from the occupational group. For the Established Church and the Notaries, the prerogative is that of the ecclesiastical head of the Church, but, even in this case, we can see the significance of the position of the Sovereign as the Head of the Established Church.

The Associations which have been developed for these four occupational groups can be termed Prerogative Associations, but it is evident that their form differs considerably. The Scriveners' Company retains the form of the medieval guild; the Bar has developed the collectivity of the Inns of Court, without incorporating therein the rules of Victorian professionalism. For the Church, the Association, based on a hierarchical structure, is organized on regional patterns. In the Military, an officer corps, differentiated from the rank and file by variations in the system of coercive organizational control, is linked with a complex pattern of formal and informal Associations which have been developed on the base of the individual regiment, ship or flying squadron.

Despite the difficulties which can arise if the existence of an occupational Association, *per se,* is used as an indicator of professionalization, some of the characteristics of these bodies emphasize the nature of the structural sub-elements. The importance of an authority sanctions mechanism is clearly brought out. A low level of professionalization seems to be more likely in those occupations which are linked only to a Coordinating Association: conversely, a high degree of professionalization will be usually linked with those occupations in which the group is controlled by an elaborate sanctions mechanism, to ensure a degree of insulation against outside intervention. Similarly, some Associations demonstrate the importance, as an indicator of professionalization, of the sub-element of *control of non-occupational behaviour.* Two contrasting examples of this can be noted. On the one hand, there are associations in which there is a complete absence of control over this form of behaviour, so that individual members are under no form of restriction. In contrast, in a lesser number of Associations, the rigid control which is formulated over the behaviour of members, is reinforced by the provisions of legal sanctions. The latter are both general and specific in their purpose. Individual offences against the normal pattern of behaviour may be specified in detail, and punishment may be linked to the commission of a particular type of offence. Alternatively, there may be more

1 S. P. Huntington, *The Soldier and the State* (Cambridge, Mass., 1959), p. 16.

general offences which are of a wider character, so that, in the Military, for
example, an individual can be accused of 'conduct unbecoming an officer and a
gentleman'.[1]

This control of non-occupational behaviour, can be differentiated from the
occupational code of ethics. The normative base of both is similar, but the
principle of the structural variable is related to the need to ensure public
acquiescence in differential privileges. Control of non-occupational behaviour
legitimizes the expectation that the higher the status and the greater the degree
of professionalization, the greater the obligations and the severer the punishment
for failing to meet those obligations.

Quantitative variations in the effects of these structural sub-elements on professionalization, can also be related to the differences which are revealed when the
contextual and *activity* elements are applied in a study of occupational groups.
It is evident that the variations which occur in space and time are of special
significance. Historical considerations readily demonstrate that, since professionalization is a dynamic process, the viable criteria of the process, and the nature
of occupational groups, may display varying characteristics over time.[2] A major
problem, in attempting to establish concepts of professionalization, which are
of universal applicability, is that it is difficult to identify the space and time
dimensions of these concepts, and difficult to deny that some have a limited
historical applicability. Attempts which have been made to overcome this problem by using the idea of paired concepts.[3] produce the concomitant difficulty
that this encourages the creation of inappropriate dichotomous classifications,
such as professional/non-professional or autonomous/integrated, both of which
are classifications which we have been at pains to avoid. Accordingly, it is necessary to restrict analysis to a multivariate consideration of the effects of time and
space in conjunction with the other elements under study. Initially, the spatio-

1 See, for example Air Force Act, 1955, s. 64: 'Every officer... who behaves in a
scandalous manner unbecoming the character of an officer and a gentleman, shall, on
conviction by court-martial, be cashiered.' The scandalous behaviour may be either of a
service or a social character. The specimen charge laid down in HMSO, *Manual of Air Force
Law*, vol. 1 (London, 1964), p. 366 specifies 'offensive language' and behaving in a
'drunken and riotous manner'.
2 An example of the changes which may occur over time is given by F. H. Newell, 'Ethics
of the Engineering Profession', *The Annals of the American Academy of Political and
Social Science*, 101, 190 (1922), 76. He has shown that, in the United States, prior to
the general formulation of comprehensive codes of conduct, one of the national
engineering societies 'decided that no gentleman needed a code of ethics and that no
code of ethics would make a gentleman out of a crook'. The position has now altered, as
group practitioners accept that 'a code of ethics becomes necessary not only to assist the
mechanical engineer in his conduct, but to acquaint the world with what it may expect
from a professional man'. See C. W. Rice, 'The Ethics of the Mechanical Engineer', *The
Annals of the American Academy of Political and Social Science*, 101, 190 (1922), 73.
3 See Reinhard Bendix and Bennet Berger, 'Images of Society and Problems of Concept
Formation in Sociology', in Llewellyn Gross (ed.), *Symposium on Sociological Theory*
(New York, 1959), pp. 92-118.

temporal sub-elements can be considered in association with the other contextual sub-elements; subsequently, it is possible to extend this to include the examination of the remaining sub-elements. By this method, it is expected that we can reconcile the effects of historical precedent with the evidence of contemporary situations, so that we can avoid the criticism that analysis takes place in an historical vacuum.

The Activity Sub-Elements

We have already noted that, in the examination of a special organization in terms of its activity sub-elements, the scope of our analysis is limited by the non-entrepreneurial goals of the organization. These exclude the use of traditional models of professionalization, which are based on the concept of the work practitioner as an independent free 'professional', and on the idea of the organization as a collectivity orientated towards an economic goal. Multivariate analysis necessitates a further examination of the goal of the individual organization, and the role of the individual members. Since, however, the organization is, by definition, a fusion of profession and organization, the problem area is common to both these goals and roles, for essentially, it is a problem of defining the division of labour and the differentiation of occupations.

The evaluation of a degree of professionalization is directly related to the type of work which is carried out within the organization, and to the claim of work practitioners that the tasks to be performed are such as to require specialized skills and knowledge, and that only certain persons have such competence and qualifications. The problem which arises, is that certain occupational groups have succeeded in defining as the area of their work, such a large expanse that non-occupational members are unable to evaluate the nature of the task carried out. This is particularly noticeable in those occupations in which the task to be performed necessitates the possession by work practitioners of a body of specialized knowledge. Here, the external observer is forced to accept not only the group's evaluation of the type of work to be carried out, but also their definition of the particular position in the organization, either hierarchical or neoteric, for the person possessing this specialized knowledge. Accordingly, there is a tendency in many instances to equate 'specialization' with 'professionalization', since the group's freedom of action, decision making functions, and ability to initiate policy suggest that the group can be differentiated, on the grounds of their 'professional' competence, from other groups in which task practitioners are controlled by non-occupational members.

To overcome this problem, it is necessary to consider all the elements necessary for the performance of any activity and to note their distribution. It can be expected that there will be differences in the nature of group activity and the role of individual members, as it is conceptualized by occupational group members and as it is evaluated by external analysts.[1] Nevertheless, an analysis of group activity which pays particular attention to the level of knowledge and techniques demanded from group members, can serve as a basis of inter-group comparison, and as a basis for the study of multi-directional relationships within the group.

Educational Elements

The need to consider, in the analysis of group activity, the level of knowledge and techniques demanded from group members, demands a study of the educational elements which have long been held to be among the most significant of the core traits of a profession.[2] A formally organized educational process not only leads to the acquisition of that high degree of skill and knowledge demanded from a 'professional', but also contributes to the maintenance of the traditions of the occupational group.[3] This dualism is a dynamic process. Firmly established professional groups are able to consolidate their existing educational requirements, but groups which aspire to recognition as a 'profession', continually change educational standards as they try to improve their position on the continuum of professionalization. Initially, such groups demand the minimum standard compatible with the performance of the group's activity. Subsequently, these standards which were set at a technical rather than a technological level,[4] are raised substantially. This is for a variety of reasons, most of which are related to the claim that increasingly specialized intellectual techniques are demanded of group members: 'Managers must understand them all (i.e. financial and commercial ventures, technical enterprises, communities of people at work,) and their education for this task, if it could be provided at an institution for higher learn-

1 The validity of this inference is confirmed by the conclusions reached by the Management Consultancy Group which analysed the work and practice of the British Civil Service. See HMSO, *The Civil Service*, vol 2: 'Report of a Management Consultancy Group' (London, 1968).
2 A. M. Carr-Saunders and P. A. Wilson, *The Professions* (Oxford, 1933), p. 491.
3 See Talcott Parsons, 'A Sociologist Looks at the Legal Profession', in Parsons, *Essays in Sociological Theory* (New York, 1964), p. 372.
4 The change in the level of the educational standard required from aspirant group members is clearly seen in the British engineering profession. Originally group membership demanded that candidates should possess at least a *Higher National Certificate in Engineering*. This qualification could be gained by 'part-time' attendance at a technical college, and the HNC, the standard of which approximated to that attained at the end of first-year course for a university pass degree, gave complete or partial exemption from the qualifying examinations of the various engineering institutions. Although as J. E. Gerstl and S. P. Hutton show in *Engineers: the Anatomy of a Profession* (London, 1966) at p. 43, 65 per cent of the new associate members of the Institution of Mechanical Engineers qualified for membership via the Higher National Certificate route, this method of entry has now been withdrawn. After the formation in 1965 of the Council of the Engineering Institutions, the Council decided that from 1970, all aspirant members should possess a university degree in engineering or pass the Council's examinations, the standard of which were to be set at pass degree level. The Higher National Certificate is now regarded as a *technician* qualification, and subsidiary low-status institutions have been established to

ing, would make many existing courses look trivial.'[1]

These claims by aspiring professional groups emphasize the significance of the educational elements as a viable index of group professionalization. The subjective statements made by these groups cannot, however, be taken at their face value, and it is necessary to look for objective methods of assessment. One of these is attained through the use of an *index of occupational intelligence requirements,* for this will indicate the true educational standard required in a specific occupational group. Such an index has been formulated in a number of American studies, such as those of Goodenough and Anderson,[2] or Fryer,[3] but the usefulness of this index as an indicator of professionalization is frequently limited by the absence of a known intelligence quotient for a specific occupational group. In this situation, we have to rely on the educational standard criteria which are adopted by a group to categorize aspirants. These criteria have a double significance. Initially, they are used as a backing for other non-educational criteria which are used to ensure that potential group members possess a certain character standard. In Great Britain, this is a traditional use of a standard of education as a measurement of acculturation.[4] Secondly, educational selection criteria are used in a more objective manner to ensure that group members are capable of the subsequent study of the body of systematic theory which underlies the skills of a profession.[5]

The relationship between educational selection criteria and entry into group membership is a complex one. A basic dichotomized classification distinguishes between graduate and non-graduate entry, but each of these can be further differentiated. *Exclusive* graduate entry has been established in some occupational groups, particularly in those allied to the practice of medicine and teaching. For doctors, dentists, veterinary surgeons and university teachers, among others, group membership is limited to those aspirants who possess a university degree or an external qualification of comparable standing. In some cases, however, noticeably where the occupational group does not specify the subject matter of

cater for the certificate holders, who are now excluded from the status of a professional chartered engineer.

1   J. Munro Fraser, 'What I Think of Management', *The Manager* (September 1953), p. 520.
2   F. L. Goodenough and J. E. Anderson, *Experimental Child Study* (New York, 1931). (*The Minnesota Occupational Scale.*)
3   D. Fryer, 'Occupational-Intelligence Standards', *School and Society,* 16 (1922). See also, Albert J. Reiss, 'Occupational Mobility of Professional Workers', *American Sociological Review,* 20, 6 (1955), 693-700. J. P. Guildford, 'Three Faces of Intellect', *American Psychologist,* 14 (1959), 469-79. T. Weisenburg, A. Roe and K. E. McBride, *Adult Intelligence: A Psychological Study of Test Performance* (New York, 1936) and D. O. Hebb, *The Organization of Behaviour* (New York, 1949), esp. chapter 11.
4   See, for example, B. Jackson and D. Marsden, *Education and the Working Class* (London, 1962). Olive Banks, *Sociology of Education* (London, 1968), esp. chapters 4 and 5 and their references. Steven Box and Julienne Ford, 'Commitment to Sciences: A Solution to Student Marginality', *Sociology,* 1, 3 (1967), 225-38.
5   Ernest Greenwood, 'Attributes of a Profession', *Social Work,* 2, 3 (1957), 44.

the degree, this requirement is modified to the extent that exclusive graduate entry applies only to certain aspirants. Thus, a large number of teachers in primary and secondary schools in England are non-graduates. In the Church of England, the requirement that candidates for ordination should possess a university degree, the subject matter of which is unspecified, or a particular theological diploma, is applicable only to the candidate who is aged under twenty-five, and concessions are made to the mature entrant. In the military, the proposal by the Royal Air Force that all future officers are to be graduates, is qualified by regulations which make this applicable only to direct entrants from civilian life who are selected for a full career. The organization is still able to recruit lesser qualified officers for restricted careers, or to transfer officers already in the service to a full career commission, irrespective of their lack of a graduate qualification.

The characteristics of a policy of *exclusive* graduate entry can, therefore, be modified to widen the area of choice from which aspirants to the occupational group may be selected. Modifying factors, such as the differentiation of skill required (teachers), maturity of the applicant (Church of England) or experience of the aspirant (military officers), do not, however, eliminate the differences between this category of required educational standards and the *concessional* graduate entry. The latter is applicable to a larger number of occupational groups than is the former, but it is equally subject to considerable modification. In general terms, the possession by the aspirant of a degree, usually with a specific subject content, exempts him from the examinations which the group conducts as an occupational association. The variation, which can be noted, refers to the degree of exemption, for the latter may be *total* (Town Planning Institute), *total*, subject to the aspirant gaining a pass in the supplementary examination in professional practice (Architects Registration Council) or *partial*. Partial exemption may excuse the aspirant from one part of the group's final examination (Inns of Court), from the intermediate examination (Institute of Chartered Accountants) or from specific individual subjects (Institute of Bankers).

For both of these types of graduate entry into an occupational group, it is possible to supplement the distinction between *exclusive* and *concessional* entry as an indicator of a degree of professionalization by a consideration of university faculty entrance requirements. With increasing competition from over 100,000 sixth-form students each year for some 56,000 university places, universities are able to offer a candidate a place conditional on his success in the General Certificate of Education at Advanced level, specifying what subjects they require and at what grade. The latter have been quantified by the Universities Central Council on Admissions (U.C.C.A.), which has been able to establish minimum points scores for entry into university. In the clearing operation which U.C.C.A. undertakes every September to match applicants still in search of a university place to the vacancies still available, candidates who obtained less than these minimum scores are not usually referred to universities. The score is derived from the five grades, A to E, at which Advanced level passes are awarded, and is based on a ranking which gives an 'A' five points, a 'B' four points, and so on. To merit consideration for entry into a Faculty of Medicine, the aspirant needs to score twelve points, for Law and Arts ten points, and for Science between five (Biology) and three (Chemistry). Since four out of five successful candidates in the GCE at Advanced level, pass in three subjects, it is possible to conclude that the aspirant to a medical career must come from the 10 per cent of candidates who obtain a grade 'A' pass, or from the 15 per cent who obtain a grade 'B' pass. Conversely, a much lower level of passes ensures entry into a science or technology department.

This trend is confirmed by statistics published by the Department of Education and Science, which show that 58 per cent of the candidates scoring less than nine points on the U.C.C.A. scale, in science subjects, obtain a university place, compared with the 12 per cent of candidates with a comparable score in social science subjects.[1] These scores, however, only suggest trends within the overall pattern of *exclusive* and *concessional* graduate entry into occupational group membership. There are many methodological problems which are unresolved, for the U.C.C.A. scale is affected by such external variables as, the popularity of a subject, the number of places available in a faculty, the validity of the General Certificate of Education as an objective measurement of educational standards or individual ability and so on, which limit its viability. Nevertheless, these trends, although they cannot be used in isolation as a measurement of professionalization within an occupational group, are additional evidence of the relationship between educational selection criteria and the development of occupational professionalization.

This relationship can also be seen in the alternative classification of *nongraduate entry* into an occupational group. This method of entry applies to a wide range of occupations, and, although there is no common standard of prescribed educational selection criteria, the latter follow a general pattern. Entry to the majority of occupational associations is limited to those aspirants who possess a specified number of passes in the General Certificate of Education at Ordinary level. Some associations retain their own Preliminary Examination, which is said to be of a comparable standard; others have demanded that some of the offered subjects are passed at Advanced level (Institute of Municipal Treasurers and Accountants), but these exceptions do not reduce the validity of the general pattern.

The aspirant, accepted as a registered student of the occupational association on the basis of his possessing a number of GCE passes, usually four or five but as high as seven (Institute of Chartered Accountants of Scotland), sites the intermediate and final examination of the association. In theory, it is the standard of these examinations, rather than the number of GCEs which are demanded from

1 *The Times,* 9 July 1969, p. 15.

occupational aspirants, which is indicative of the level of the educational criteria associated with the occupation. In practice, however, it is extremely difficult to arrive at an objective assessment of this standard. While some occupational associations state that their final examinations are set at a specific standard, often that of the pass degree (Corporation of Secretaries), external evaluation can only consider the level of those exempting examinations which confer concessions on the aspirant. In this context, we can differentiate between the *concessional* graduate entry to an occupational association and the *non-graduate* entry. The former is applicable only to graduates; in the latter, concessions are granted to graduates, but similar concessions are also granted to occupational students who are in possession of other external qualifications of a lower standard. A partial exemption from the intermediate examinations of the occupational association may thus be granted to aspirants who possess GCE subject passes at 'A' level (Building Societies Institute), or a technical qualification, such as the Ordinary National Certificate (Chartered Institute of Secretaries) or the Higher National Certificate (Institution of Gas Engineers). In a limited number of cases, complete exemption from the examination of the occupational association is granted to holders of these qualifications (Institute of Book-Keepers Ltd).

Although the establishment of a set educational standard demanded from aspirants, in this case the General Certificate of Education at Advanced level, and the establishment of a triple examination stage, that is, preliminary — intermediate — final, have been used as 'scale items' in a final data matrix designed to evaluate occupational group professionalization,[1] the complexity of the exemption pattern and the multiplicity of methods of entry are such[2] that it is that it is difficult to quantify these educational selection criteria. We can, however, use them to signify trends in professionalization. It can be suggested that, in terms of these criteria, a high level of professionalization is associated with those groups which are limited to *exclusive* graduate entry. Conversely, a low level of professionalization is linked to those groups which, in accepting non-graduate entry, are prepared to grant substantial exemptions from intermediate, and, more particularly, from final examinations. The majority of occupational associations, however, follow a policy which lies mid-way between these two extremes, and to evaluate the significance of the educational elements, or, indeed, to examine more fully the characteristics of all occupational groups, it is necessary to consider the importance, as an indicator of professionalization, of the remaining educational sub-elements.

One of the most important of these is the body of systematic *theory* which underlies the skills of a profession:

'The skills that characterise a profession flow from and are supported by a

1 Hickson and Thomas, *op. cit.* p. 44.
2 These were categorized by Carr-Saunders and Wilson, *op. cit.* p. 369 as 'Uniportal', 'Intermediate' and 'Multiportal'.

fund of knowledge that has been organized into an internally consistent system, called a body of theory. A profession's body of theory is a system of abstract propositions that describes in general terms the classes of phenomena comprising the profession's focus of interest. Theory serves as a base in terms of which the professional rationalizes his operations in concrete situations.'[1]

It is this linking of the professional skill with the prior or coincidental mastery of the underlying theory, that is the true difference between the skills demanded from members of a highly professionalized group, and other, less professionalized, groups. In the latter instance, there is considerable evidence of a high order of particular skill, and, indeed, some 'non-professional' occupations involve the exercise of a higher degree of skill than many professional ones.[2] Such practice of skill, however, can exist independently of any body of theory, so that role practitioners are categorized as 'craftsmen' rather than 'professionals'. The form of the educational process which is undertaken by a group member, thus reflects the extent to which the exercise of the occupational skill demands knowledge of the underlying theory, and the form is thus an indicator of the level of group professionalization.

The form of this educational process is continually changing. Traditionally, the basic method of professional education was the apprenticeship method, that is, 'learning by doing', or 'on the job training'. This differed to a very limited extent from the method of education and training which was adopted for the acquisition of craft skills. Subsequently, examinations were introduced as a test of professional competence, although a typical pattern of development was one in which these examinations supplemented, rather than replaced, the principle of apprenticeship. The realization that such tests, carried out in the atmosphere of part-time study, were an inadequate assessment of the amount of theory which the member had acquired, has led occupational groups to recognize the importance of a full-time educational process. The typical pattern of education and training for a professionalized occupational group today, is thus one in which the required body of systematic theory is obtained by individuals in a formal academic environment.[3]

To achieve this pattern, groups can adopt one of two methods. Some insist that their members undergo a full-time period of study in an institute of tertiary education; others establish their own academies in which the educational process is combined with a complex socialization and assimilation programme.[4] In both

1 Ernest Greenwood, op. cit. p. 45.
2 An often quoted example of the high degree of skill which is demanded from a craftsman, is the case of the diamond cutter. Additionally, the length of training which is required as a prerequisite to the practice of the occupational role, is longer than that demanded in many 'professions'.
3 For a descriptive account of the changes which have taken place in the English professional educational process, see Reader, op. cit. chapter 8, 'Professional Men Apprenticed' and chapter 9, 'Apprentice into Student'.
4 The most notable example of academies which have been established to educate and train

cases, this insistence on formal training can be used as an elementary index of the level of professionalization within occupational groups, but the usefulness of such an index is complicated by a number of factors. There are still to be found occupational groups which claim professional status, but which adhere to the nineteenth-century idea that 'the study required for the examination would be fitted into the interstices of work in the office or workshop'.[1] Other groups striving for recognition as 'professions' are aware of the link between the established form of the educational pattern and the postulated level of occupational professionalization. They may develop their own 'academies' in which provision is made for the teaching of a greater amount of systematic theory than was hitherto possible. Alternatively, they may insist that all potential members undergo a full-time educational course, although in neither case is there evidence that this insistence is paralleled by an increase in the standard of the theory which is being taught. A valid index of professionalization can only be constructed on this basis, if it is possible to determine impartially the nature of the theory which is prescribed for group members. This may be possible if the group relies on external examinations as a means whereby aspirants may be tested, but if the group rejects these in favour of its own subjective examinations, it is unlikely that a valid index can be constructed.

The limiting effect of these factors can be partly overcome if we adopt an extended scale which takes into account the extent to which an occupational group encourages research into its work activities. Such research is designed to produce valid new theories to serve as the basis of improved operational techniques, and it is encouraged by, and, through a process of feedback, develops the element of rationality.[2] Since this rationalism is the antithesis of traditionalism, the development of critical attitudes towards the existing theoretical system suggests the concomitant development of a high degree of professionalization. The latter therefore implies a willingness on the part of the occupational group to introduce a revised system of theory. The limitation to this relationship, however, is that rationality also encourages the development of deviancy within the group, as members react against the established theoretical system, and a consequential result can be the formation of sub-system specializations. The cohesive occupational group then seems to disappear, with the result that analysis is directed towards segmented group activity, and not the whole of occupational activity.

These two characteristics of professionalization — the study of a systematic body of theory and the degree of research carried on into group activity — can

aspirants, are the Military Colleges, which in many cases now train their graduates to a degree level. Other examples in Great Britain include the College of Estate Management, now part of the University of Reading.

1   Reader, *op. cit.* p. 117.
2   See Talcott Parsons, 'The Professions and Social Structure', *Social Forces,* 17 (1939), 457-67.

be considered in association with the *length of training* which is demanded from group members. This varies from occupation to occupation, and a scale constructed on the basis of the number of years of education undertaken after the age of eighteen, can be used as an elementary index of the degree of professionalization which may be present in a particular occupational group. The effectiveness of even an elementary scale is limited, however, by three factors. The effect of the legacy in Great Britain of a system of part-time professional education and training, and the extent to which it may be accepted by an occupational group as an adequate basis for further study has already been noted. In addition, the situation is complicated by the persistent notion that the 'content of higher education...should be stratified according to class'.[1] The length of study which the aspirant group member undertakes, consequently varies in relation to the demands of the varying institutions of higher education rather than in relation to the specific requirements of different occupational groups. With the exception of the recently established technological universities, English universities have retained an historical orientation towards 'co-operating with leisurely confidence in the task of preserving and transmitting a cultured way of life.'[2] They are thus non-vocational in character, so that it is only after following the traditional university course, that the aspirant to the occupational group studies for a specialized technical competence in business or the professions. The course of study is thus lengthened for the university graduate, irrespective of the specific requirements laid down by the occupational group. Additionally, the use which can be made of this elementary index is limited by the noted multiplicity of ways in which entrance to an occupational group, in terms of its educational requirements, can be achieved. The length of undertaken training thus varies in relation to the method of study adopted by the occupational aspirant, so that in groups other than those which insist on exclusive graduate entry, there is a continuing contrast between the length of study undertaken by the articled pupil and that undertaken by the graduate.

Similar complications can also be noted when the sub-element of the *cost of training* is used as an index of professionalization. The quantitative assessment which is possible, encourages the construction of a scale, but the true cost is blurred by the existence of an extensive grants system and subsidized training programme within the British educational system. Even so, it may be possible to construct a scale to measure the relative financial deprivation suffered by students in occupational groups before they attain full group membership, in comparison with other workers who do not undergo a training programme before exercising their roles. In such a scale, it may be expected that a high

1 Sir Eric Ashby, 'The Educational Framework of an Industrial Society', *Research*, 10, 12 (1957), 22.
2 A. H. Halsey, 'University Expansion and the Collegiate Ideal' *Universities Quarterly*, 16, 1 (1961), 55.

degree of occupational professionalization will be indicated by a high level of student deprivation, and that, conversely, a low level of financial deprivation will be indicative of a low degree of occupational professionalization.

Ideological Elements

One of the purposes of this educational training programme for members of an occupational group, is the encouragement of the cultural and professional socialization of the individual. The extent to which this has been successfully carried out can be measured through the employment of the *ideological elements* of the variable. These elements not only denote the extent to which the occupational group believes that it has achieved professional status, but also specify the means whereby such a belief can be encouraged and maintained. The sub-element of *personality involvement* thus illustrates the extent to which the individual accepts the collective demands of the occupational group, so that he works within the behavioural ambit of the profession, and the extent to which he accepts its ideologies. In a polar situation, a group member may identify himself so closely with these ideologies that he comes to believe that the specific goal of the occupation is the only occupational goal of importance. Indeed, other occupational groups are rejected:

'The physiology students feel themselves part of a larger group, devoted to building the edifice of science, and pride themselves on their participation in this endeavour and on the ultimate value of their work to society in the cure and prevention of disease...They feel that they make the important scientific discoveries on which medical practice is based, medicine itself being more empirical and superficial.'[1]

Such involvement is not limited to those occupations which believe themselves to be professions, for it can be noted in a wide variety of occupational roles particularly in those in which an element of risk is associated with the performance of the task.[2] Yet, in an occupational group which demonstrates a high degree of professionalization, the sense of personality may be greater than in less professionalized groups, because of the concomitant feeling of *group identity*. The recognition that group members have roughly similar educational and socio-economic backgrounds, and that they are united by common professional bonds and participation in the same specialist associations, contributes to the development of this sense of a common identity. Ideally, the all-pervading influence of this sense results in the complete personal involvement of the individual with the occupational group, so that the latter becomes a total social environment developing special social and political attitudes, consumption

---

1 Howard S. Becker and James Carper, 'The Elements of Identification with an Occupation', *American Sociological Review*, 21, 3 (1956), 342.
2 See L.S. Cottrell, *The Railroader* (Stanford, 1941). For the effect of 'risk' in an illegitimate occupation, see Edwin H. Sutherland, *The Professional Thief* (Chicago, 1937).

patterns and leisure activities.[1]

When we make use, however, of these two sub-elements of group identity and personality involvement in an analysis of an occupational group, we are forced to take into consideration certain subsidiary factors. It is clear that in situations where individuals are employed in large scale organizations, personality involvement will be affected by the status of the employment environment. Hastings has shown that for Chartered Accountants employed in industry, they are less likely to be attached to the concept of professional exclusiveness where the Finance/Accounting function in a firm enjoys a high status, for in this situation they look to the employing organization rather than to the professional Association for their source of status.[2] Empirical studies, such as those of Becker and Geer,[3] suggest that the extent to which an individual identifies himself with the occupational group is continually changing. Initially, the new recruit to the group displays an idealism which enables him to accept without question the group ideology. Subsequently, this idealism is substantially modified, and, for some individuals, it is replaced by an artificially induced acceptance of group identity. In these circumstances, the individual pretends to identify himself with the group, by playing a role in which his true attitude is concealed. For other group members, acceptance of the group ideology is replaced by an attitude of cynicism. When this is a collective phenomenon, it may do no more than set aside the idealistic approach to the ideology of the group for a limited period, the length of this corresponding to the length of stay in the constant environment. If this cynicism is an individual phenomenon, however, the individual again denies his role function, and accepts only a role-playing position within the organization. In this latter case, there may be a withdrawal from the sense of group identity, and, in extreme cases, an antagonism toward the occupational ideology is developed, particularly in extra-occupational situations.

Within the single occupational group, therefore, it will be possible to determine and delineate different identities, values and interests. Indeed, any occupational group can be conceptualized as a 'loose amalgamation of segments which are in movement',[4] in which the group displays both integrative and divisive potentialities. Among the cohesive factors which ensure the continuance of the occupation as a group collectivity, one of the most significant as an indicator of professionalization, will be the *group culture*. Such a culture is not unique, nor is it restricted to professionalized occupational groups, for all occupations are characterized by formal and informal groupings which generate through the

1 See William F. Whyte, *The Organization Man* (New York, 1956).
2 Anthony Hastings, 'A Sociologist Looks at Chartered Accountants', *Accountancy* (May 1969), p. 330.
3 Howard S. Becker and Blanche Geer, 'The Fate of Idealism in Medical School', *American Sociological Review*, 23, 1 (1958), 53.
4 Rue Bucher and Anselm Strauss, 'Professions in Progress', *The American Journal of Sociology*, 66, 4 (1961), 326.

interaction of social roles, a group culture. A significant distinction between professional culture and non-professional culture, however, is that the latter is the result of a behavioural interaction, whereas the source of the former is the ideological values of the occupational group. These social values are the basic and fundamental beliefs of the group, the 'unquestioned premises upon which its very existence rests'.[1] A high degree of professionalization is associated with the belief of the group that the service it renders to the remainder of society is for the good of the whole, and that withdrawal of the service would cause immeasurable harm. It is this concept of group culture which is specifically developed in the assimilating institutions which some occupational groups have established for the indoctrination of aspiring group members. Indeed, the significance of certain institutions – the Inns of Court, the Military Academies – is that they create a highly developed sense of group culture through emphasizing the ideal type of participation in the social structure. In the absence of these institutions, other occupational groups are forced to rely on the development of regional associations or 'local societies' as a means whereby a group culture may be developed. Since, however, the latter are a less effective means of indoctrination, a scale of professionalization can be inferred from the presence or absence of an assimilating institution, at which the attendance of occupational aspirants is compulsory.

This concept of group culture is also closely associated with the professional's belief in the altruism of his approach to the performance of the occupational task. Individuals contend that they practise the occupation, not for the reward which they receive, but for the sense of satisfaction which is derived from a belief that the occupation is 'of use' to the community. Group members can thus oppose any scheme which involves payment by salary[2] or in situations where, as a member of a special organization, they receive a fixed reward, be unaware of the precise amount of that payment.[3] Parsons has pointed out that this insistence on altruism may be fallacious, on the grounds that it may be impossible in practice to distinguish between business and professional activities in terms of egoistic and altruistic motivation.[4] Nevertheless, a persistent characteristic of certain occupational groups, which by its constancy, may be interpreted as an indicator of a high degree of professionalization, is the concept of *service* which is derived from the occupational group culture.

1 Greenwood, *op.cit.* p. 50.
2 One of the reasons for the opposition by members of the British medical profession to the implementation of those features of the Beveridge report which advocated socialized medicine, was their refusal to accept payment by salary. This opposition is still current, twenty years after the passing of the enabling statute.
3 In an Attitude Survey of serving officers and other ranks, carried out by the National Board for Prices and Incomes, only 49 per cent of a total sample of 3,309 estimated their income within 10 per cent of the actual amount received. *National Board for Prices and Incomes, Report No. 116, op. cit.* table 7, p. 82.
4 Parsons, 'The Professions and Social Structure', *op.cit.* p. 467.

Closely linked to this self-evaluation of the value of the service rendered to the community by a professionalized occupational group, although it can be differentiated from it, is the concept of occupational *status*. The prestige hierarchy of occupations has been described as one of the best studied aspects of the stratification systems of modern society.[1] In a number of countries, extensive empirical investigations have been carried out, from the results of which it would appear that there is a positive correlation between particular occupations and a ranked status.[2] In a more limited number of studies, attempts have been made to isolate the specific 'status' characteristics of occupations, and to consider these as factors which affect occupational prestige scores.[3] External appreciation of a group's prestige does not, however, necessarily reflect the extent to which the occupation has been professionalized. Lay appreciation tends to emphasize the status of those occupational groups with which the individual rarely comes into direct contact, or of those groups which assume a 'life or death significance in social behaviour.[4] Conversely, familiarity tends to be associated with a lower occupational prestige rating, as does a lay inability to differentiate between the generalist and the specialist who both carry out their activities within the same organization. Moreover, the methodological imperfections of many studies complicates this appreciation, since they do not distinguish between specific offices and generic descriptions of role activity, or between variations of rank in the comparison of specific offices.[5] Thus despite the employment of quantitative assessments in these studies, it is only possible to accept their findings as general statements of occupational status. From these, it can be concluded that those occupational groups with high external prestige

1   Robert W. Hodge *et al.* 'Occupational Prestige in the United States, 1925-1963', *American Journal of Sociology*, 70 (1964), 286.
2   A comprehensive bibliography is given in Hodge *et al, op cit.*, and in Hodge *et al.*, 'A Comparative Study of Occupational Prestige' in Bendix and Lipset (eds.), *op. cit.* pp. 313 and 316. See for Great Britain, C. A. Moser and John Hall, 'The Social Grading of Occupations', in D. V. Glass (ed.); *Social Mobility in Britain* (London, 1954), pp. 29-50.
3   See Otis Dudley Duncan, 'A Socio-economic Index for all Occupations', in Albert J. Reiss *et al, Occupations and Social Status, op cit.* pp. 114-28.
4   Among those occupational groups with which the public rarely comes into contact, can be included, for example, barristers. Their status tends to be rated more highly than those solicitors with whom the public may have had some dealings. It can also be argued that the reduced status of the military officer in comparison with his pre-War counterpart, is partly the result of conscription whereby the majority of the male population of a country has come into close contact with the hitherto 'remote' military officer. Medical practitioners are an example of a group which assumes a 'life or death' importance for the public. The high status which is afforded to them can be contrasted with that lesser status ascribed to the dentist.
5   The combined effect of methodological imperfections, the degree of public contact and the significance of the 'life or death' concept, can be used as a partial explanation of intra-occupational differences of prestige ratings within the medical profession. The more remote specialist and consultant within a hospital, identified by his specific rank, is graded more highly than the general practitioner. At the same time, the high status of the former contributes to a *transferred prestige* for the latter.

ratings, will be more professionalized than those at the lower end of the ranking scale. At the same time, we can see that there exists between these two extreme points, a wide indeterminate area in which prestige ratings show little correlation with any postulated degree of occupational professionalization.

An alternative method of evaluating occupational status, is to consider the self-evaluation of a professional group. Since the latter wishes to ensure its security, its work satisfaction and its social value, it emphasizes the uniqueness of the occupational task. When this is successfully achieved, the concept of status encourages organizational effectiveness, and inhibits an excessive turn-over of group members by reinforcing the process of group identity. Acceptance of the postulated status by group members, tends to reduce intra-group tension and conflict, with the result that a minimum of external controls are imposed by society on the means whereby the occupational task is performed. These factors contribute towards the maintenance of group consensus, although, conversely, they take into account the strong desire for autonomy which characterizes the highly professionalized occupational group.[1] The result of self-evaluation of status is indicative of the extent to which the group has been professionalized, to the extent that belief in high status is a reflection of an achieved high level of professionalization. Conversely, the view that the status of the group is low, is more likely to be found in those instances where there has been very little group professionalization.

At the same time, however, we must note that over-preoccupation with the concept of status is a characteristic both of groups which are striving for recognition as professions, and of groups in which there has been a decrease in the degree of differentiation in the stratified system. In the former case, the journals of a large number of occupational groups exhibit evidence of the extent to which group members are over-concerned with the status of the collectivity. In this context, there is a significant difference between the contents of the learned journals which are primarily devoted to the publication of material designed to further the systematic base of occupational theory, and those journals which are less didactic in their purpose. An analysis of the latter to distinguish types of content, shows that within the generic categories of 'Broad Professional', 'Narrow Professional' and 'Human Interest', articles which can be classified under the heading of 'Broad Professional' are oriented overmuch toward morale building rather than towards applied professional strategy. From this, it can be inferred that a concern with fundamental group values, as it is evidenced by the number and type of journal articles, is a characteristic of groups which are striving for external recognition as 'professions'. In contrast, groups which demonstrate a high degree of professionalization, use their sponsored journals as a secondary means of ensuring organizational control over group members, since publication

---

1 See John H. Goldthorpe, 'Social Stratification in Industrial Society', in Paul Halmos (ed.), *The Sociological Review, Monograph No. 8* (1964), pp. 97-122.

enables the organization to appraise and reward the activities of professional peers.

The over-preoccupation with the concept of status, which is a result of a decrease in the degree of differentiation in the stratified system, is derived from a process of relative homogenization which reduces the differences between positions at the top and bottom of the occupational scale. In the absence of an income or power differential, members of those occupational groups which form the middle part of such a scale, overemphasize the importance of the status differential which they believe to be still present. Such groups then exhibit extreme status sensitivity, as increasing industrialization produces a movement toward social equilibration. This evaluation of group status is, however, no longer based on characteristics of professionalization, for a deprivation attitude becomes apparent, and groups tend to stress their past comparative status, rather than accept their contemporary status. This form of status sensitivity is not thus directly related to the professionalization of the group, and it must be distinguished, if status sensitivity is to be used as an indicator of group professionalization, from the type of over-preoccupation with status which is associated with the group striving for external recognition as a profession.

The ideology which characterizes a particular occupational group, is induced in new members through a process of *socialization,* as a result of which the student is assimilated into the occupational group. The process includes the years of formal professional training and education, when the stereotyped images of the occupation are replaced by a complex and sometimes ambiguous perception of the professional role. It also includes the subsidiary process of induction into the norms, codes and rules which govern occupational behaviour, as well as the development, to which we have previously referred, of a group culture. To a large extent, studies which have examined the operation of these processes have concentrated on one of two extremes. They have emphasized, to the exclusion of a consideration of other factors, the importance of the mechanics of group cohesiveness, or they have concentrated on the dysfunctional aspects of the process of socialization. A contemporary problem which remains unsolved, is the extent of the differences of interest among professionals who are employed in special organizations, and the effects of these differences on changes in the occupational structure. An additional problem which is faced by organizations employing a large number of ascriptive professionals, is that the widening of the basis of recruitment to the organization, is altering the often traditional socio-economic attitude of group members towards the obligations of organizational membership. Aspirants are less committed to the collectivity, so that assimilitating institutions, whether they be universities, academies or occupational colleges which have hitherto faced little opposition to their definition of the ideology of the occupational group, are now facing new problems. As potential group members become more representative of society as a whole, the effectiveness of the traditional socializing process cannot be taken for granted. An emphasis on the unending stability of the professionalized occupation, is being replaced by the recognition that segmental ideologies are both a cause and effect of change within the group. The result is, that the mere existence of a process of socialization is no longer as viable an index of professionalization as it once was. To accommodate these new members, occupational groups are faced with a choice. They can either accept a greater amount of deviancy from the norms of the group, and thereby reduce the significance of the relationship between the process of socialization and the development of group professionalization, or they can take more positive measures. Here, the occupational group faces the problem that an insistence on members accepting the traditional form of the socializing process, may lead to the group's splintering into a number of segments. Paradoxically, it would appear that there is a trend for groups which enjoy a high level of professionalization to accept deviancy. Conversely, groups which are associated with a low degree of professionalization insist on retaining the traditional type of socialization process. In neither case, however, can the existence of the process be related directly to the degree of professionalization which is present within the group.

The Behavioural Elements

The use of the ideological elements as an index of the level of professionalization which is characteristic of an occupational group, can be supplemented by a use of the *behavioural elements*. Both categories are interrelated, but neither is reducible to the other. The *ideological* elements reflect the beliefs of the occupational group; the *behavioural* elements refer to the way in which the group reacts to external and internal stimuli which influence the method of task performance. The extent to which the group demands that a common standard of behaviour be adopted in relation to the task, is thus, in itself, an embryonic index of varying levels of professionalization. The orientation of group members to an inner reference point, which is derived from this occupational standard, encourages group acceptance of formal occupational controls. In their most highly developed form, such controls are verbalized in the particular *codes of conduct* adopted by the group, and different codes of various professionalized occupational groups represent the 'deliberate application of a generally accepted standard to particular spheres of conduct'.[1]

Emile Durkheim has demonstrated the manner in which such a standard is associated with the appropriate form of moral discipline which every social activity requires.[1] In general terms, the continuing existence of any group

---

1 Robert MacIver, 'Social Significance of Professional Ethics', *The Annals of the American Academy of Political and Social Science,* 297, (1955), 118-24.

depends on the individual member behaving as part of the whole group. If the behaviour of this individual becomes of no further consequence to the remainder of the group, the latter eventually disintegrates, for there is no longer any incentive for an individual to seek out other individuals with whom to associate. The code which lays down the required social standard thus helps to ensure the existence of the occupational group as a formal association of work practitioners. The extent, however, to which a designated code is essential for the maintenance of the collectivity as a formal association varies from group to group. It will differ according to the precise occupational situation, the structural elements of which will reflect the type of practice carried out, the techniques involved, and the responsibilities of the practitioner to his client. The latter, in turn, varies according to the autonomous or integrative setting in which the task is performed. Where the individual member of the occupational group works alone in a non-institutional environment, that is, as the traditional 'free' practitioner, society may insist that a narrowly defined code of conduct is a requirement for, and a prerequisite of, task performance. Conversely, a code may not be of such importance for the individual working with colleagues in an institutional environment. In this situation, which is characteristic of the ascriptive professional, the professional code of conduct can be subordinate in importance to the organizational code of regulations. The former is 'accepted' by the individual; the latter is 'imposed' upon him. The possibility of introducing the code of external origin for the ascriptive professional then depends upon the structural and functional elements of the employing environment. It is more probable that such a code can be introduced in those groups where there is a unanimity of purpose, for it reinforces, in these circumstances, the prescriptions of the employing authority. Conversely, it is unlikely that a true professional code can be introduced, or that, if introduced, it will be adhered to, in groups which manifest an occupational diversity which is the result of sub-specializations within the collectivity.

The codes which are adopted by an occupational group may be either written or unwritten, although as a group strives to demonstrate its professional status, one of its first acts is often to draw up a written code which is to be observed by, and, if necessary, be enforced upon group members. Yet the creation of a written code is not, in itself, a critical factor in the process of professionalization, and it is noticeable that the older associations (for example, the legal and medical collectivities) lack a written code, probably because they can rely on historical precedent or on conventions which possess the force of prescription. Self-regulative codes can also be noted in a number of occupational groups which do not aspire to the status of a profession. The essential distinguishing feature in these circumstances, is not only that the code of a professionalized group is believed to be

1   Emile Durkheim, *Professional Ethics and Civic Morals* (New York, 1957), pp. 5-9.

more explicit, more systematic and more binding on group members than other codes, or that it contains altruistic overtones, but that in the professionalized group, the written code is usually supplemented by an informal and unwritten code of conduct. The latter has often evolved over a lengthy period. It is the result of extensive group interaction, and, in certain circumstances, the unwritten code is enforced by unofficial disciplinary bodies.[1] Consequently, a highly professionalized occupational group is often governed by two codes, and the effect of this is that a possible 'dual-standard of behaviour' is avoided. The written code regulates the relationship between the professional and his client (external standards), while the body of unwritten rules controls relationships within the group (internal standards). The two rules frequently demonstrate the extent to which informal and formal conduct norms coincide, and it can be hypothesized that the aspiring professional group which lacks a body of unwritten rules, will, in formulating a written code, try to include in the latter not only the formal norms governing external relationships, but also the informal norms governing intra-group relationships.[2] The extent to which this process can be used as an index of professionalization is limited, however, because codification may be simply a logical sequence in a system of development which emphasizes the general inevitability of a codification of all the norms which are derived from group activity. It remains significant, nevertheless, that the more recently created codes of groups striving for external recognition of their professional status, do include providions specifically designed to control these intra-group relationships.[3]

As a viable index of professionalization, the absence or presence of a code of conduct for an occupational group, can be supplemented by an assessment of the effectiveness of group control mechanisms. Here, the behavioural elements subsumed in a code can be related back to the structural elements of the authority sanction. Thus the constitutive definition of a 'code of conduct' can be operationalized as the existence of a distinct *recognized* code, whereby a

1 This is no new phenomonen. In the British Army of the nineteenth century, the unwritten body of regulations which had evolved over a lengthy period of time were enforced in the unofficial 'subalterns' court martial' in which the deviationist who refused to conform to the regimental code of behaviour was 'tried', and, if found guilty, was punished. The severity of the punishment, which took the form of *hazing*, received considerable press attention, particularly in *The Times* which was one of the severest critics of these unofficial disciplinary bodies.

2 The results of this process can be seen, for example, in sections 19 to 28 of the 'Canons of Ethics for Engineers' adopted by the American Engineers' Council for Professional Development on 25 November 1947. In those sections which deal with *Relations with Engineers*, section 23 states that 'He will not directly or indirectly injure the professional reputation, prospects or practice of another engineer'.

3 The Code of the Institute of Industrial Administration (now part of the British Institute of Management) stated, for example, in Article Six that 'Avoidance of the abuse of executive power for personal gain, advantage or prestige' was one of the six main principles of the code.

degree of professionalization is related to the quantitative evaluation by group members of the existence of a code which can be effectively enforced by a central body of control. The problem which arises, however, is that for the ascriptive professional, group control mechanisms may be of bureaucratic, rather than professional, origin, for the accepted code of ethics is *imposed* upon group members by the client in the latter's own interests.

A similar distinction between the position of the 'free' practitioner and that of the ascriptive professional can be noticed when the sub-element of *evaluation of merit* is considered as an indicator of occupational professionalization. A characteristic of the concept of the 'profession', is that whereas work evaluation is common to all occupational groups, it is only in the professions that the criteria of evaluation have been so widened in scope that what is evaluated is a form of skill which is broadly defined to include the personality of the practitioner, his attitudes and his social contacts.[1] Role performance, occupational ability and the observation of specific norms are therefore not in themselves adequate criteria of evaluation, and additional factors, such as non-occupational behaviour, are frequently items of major importance.

For the 'free' professional, two contrasting models can be conceptualized as representative of different situations. In the first model, the individual is trained and educated in all the basic skills required to perform a task, although these educational factors are modified by the behavioural elements of professionalization. The work performed is carried out within the structural framework of a professionalized occupation, in which the individual performs his entire task independently of external controls, although he remains subject to peer evaluation. The standards of performance are internalized, and the evaluator is a colleague who has undergone a similar training and socializing process. In the second model, in contrast, the individual is trained only to perform a specific and limited part of the operational task, and other workers are recruited to carry out the remaining parts. In the absence of internal self-regulating controls, a system of rules is drawn up to specify the required standards and norms of performance, both of which can be evaluated from without the performance area. The evaluator tends to be a hierarchical superior who, to carry out the evaluation of merit need not be trained in the limited amount of skill which the worker possesses, for the task of evaluation is primarily that of assessing the extent to which the worker has coordinated his efforts with those of his fellows.

The distinction is between internalized evaluation of complete skills, and external evaluation of partial skills. In this situation, the independent free professional believes that any other combination of skills and evaluation is impossible, for two fundamental characteristics of 'professional' work are that skills should be completely acquired, and that external evaluation of skill by a non-member of the group is incompatible with the definition of 'professional'. On this basis,

1 Caplow, *op cit.* p. 111.

the free practitioner believes that only the first model is indicative of occupations which demonstrate a high level of professionalization, and he totally rejects the validity of the second model.

For the ascriptive professional, this distinction is far from absolute. As we have seen, the ascriptive professional, by definition, is a member of a large-scale complex organization in which the hierarchical system of control ensures that the individual is assessed by a nominal superior, who may, or who may not, belong to the same professional association. At the same time, the superior is evaluating broadly defined complete skills and is considering criteria other than role performance or occupational ability, so that, for the ascriptive professional, assessment is an external evaluation of complete skills. Such a system suggests that a third model can be conceptualized, in which an internalized standard of performance reflects norms derived from the organizational code of regulations, rather than from an external 'professional' code. The evaluator is a hierarchical colleague who has undergone, within the organization, a training and socialization process similar to that of the assessed individual, although he may not have been fully trained in the skill of the individual whom he is evaluating.

One of the effects of this third model, is that it can create organizational strain, the degree of which will be a reflection of the extent to which the assessed individual attempts to resist hierarchical evaluation of his merit. This is one of the classic areas of conflict in a bureaucratic organization, and although the latter can partly overcome this by making structural adjustments, the contrast between the viability of the first and third model suggests that this sub-element of evaluation of merit is of limited use in the assessment of ascriptive professionalization. A similar criticism is also applicable to the use of other *single* elements or sub-elements of professionalization, so that we can infer that only a multivariate approach will enable us to examine more critically the nature and form of this ascriptive professionalization. To test this inference, we can examine the activities of ascriptive professionals within a specific organization, and for several reasons, the military, and more particularly the Royal Air Force, is a suitable subject for analysis.

As we have noted the officer corps is a classic example of complete integration, as a result of which there has been a complete fusion of profession and organization. Concomitantly, the organization recruits not only potential *ascriptive* professionals, but also *achievement* professionals, who, having received an extra-organizational professional education and having undergone an external socialization process, are then assimilated into the organization. It may follow, therefore, that variations in the level of occupational professionalization will reflect this distinction between officers with only predominantly military skills (ascriptive professionals) and those with non-military skills (achievement professionals). Conclusions in this context will also be relevant to the analysis of other special organizations where individuals can be separated into those possessing predomi-

D

nantly organizational skills, and those trained outside the organization in skills of a more universal applicability. Moreover, the Military is of interest as an example of group professionalization, because although it is an 'ideal-type' with regard to certain characteristics of professionalization, it exhibits very little evidence of the development or presence of this process in certain areas which have hitherto been regarded as fundamental criteria by which occupation may be distinguished from profession. This contrast again emphasizes the merits of multivariate analysis, and it is on this basis that we can examine the Royal Air Force as an exemplar of the nature and form of group professionalization.

THE PROFESSIONALIZATION OF AN ORGANIZATION

In terms of the structural element of professionalization, the Royal Air Force is characterized by its *specialization,* that is, by the exclusive nature of group activity. Although there is a general narrowing of the skill differential between military and civilian occupational roles, to the extent that certain Air Force activity is now broadly comparable with performance in a civilian organization, the Air Force retains a particular, well-integrated body of exclusive knowledge and skill. There are a limited number of examples in which the dimensions of activity within the military organization and in the civilian world are similar, but, more frequently, the Air Force requires all group members to possess certain basic military skills which are exclusive to the organization. Additionally, the Air Force, in common with other military organizations demands from its members a greater versatility and a wider mix of skills than is required from members of the civilian organization. These differentials, particularly in the sphere of supervisory content, are applicable to both ascriptive and achievement professionals within the Royal Air Force, so that for the latter, their work differs in content and in organization from that of their civilian counterparts.[1]

The exclusive nature of this group activity is ensured through a well developed *centralization,* in which the locus of the authority-sanctions mechanism is rigidly defined. In almost every country of the world, with the possible exception of those few states in which military power is associated with the proto-dynastic origin of civil power, the military is superior in the development of this process of centralization, and in the derived cohesiveness, to its civilian counterpart. The Royal Air Force is no exception. It derives its occupational solidarity from the way in which centralization ensures that group members are subject to the general directives of a single controlling body, which supervises the manner in which they implement functional activities. Although in practice, much of the

1 A survey of the job content and conditions of work of doctors in the Armed Forces and the National Health Service, carried out by the National Board for Prices and Incomes, concluded that the work of Service doctors differed in content and in organization quite substantially from that in civilian practice. See Report of the National Board for Prices and Incomes, *op. cit.* p. 112.

day-to-day control exercised over group performance is delegated to subordinate bodies outside the central structure, the very nature of the hierarchical authority pattern ensures that the periphery responds to the advice and instructions of the centre. The obligations of instant response to these central directives are legitimized through a complex pattern of regulations and convention, and the superiority of the central authority is ensured by an elaborate sanctions mechanism. It is enhanced by the bureaucratic depersonalization of individual group members, and extraneous considerations, such as relative status, which might limit the effectiveness of a central authority in other occupational groups, are subordinated to, and are replaced by, the response to superior authorities whose legitimacy is recognized by their rank in the military organization.

To ensure that group members respond to this central authority sanctions mechanism, the bureaucratic organizational structure is supplemented by an elaborate communications network. Authority is exercised whenever a communicated directive is accepted, either when the communication itself governs the action of the individual group member, or when the individual, as the recipient of the instruction, contributes to the exercise of authority by deciding the nature of his response. Indeed, in this highly developed communications system, the channels of communication themselves often become lines of authority, so that they too contribute to the development of centralization. An activity solidarity created through this network concomitantly emphasizes the signifi cance of the exclusive nature of group activity.

The question which arises, is the extent to which this well developed, centralized sanctions mechanism is indicative of a high level of group professionalization, and the extent to which it is a corollary of a high degree of organizational bureaucratization. Analysis is complicated because the fusion of organization and profession ensures that administrative and professional skill, bureaucratic and professional authority coincide in many spheres. Nevertheless, analysis suggests that two distinct lines of authority exist within the Air Force organization. At each level, the individual receives orders, instructions and advice from a superior in his area of specialization; concomitantly, he is controlled by the immediate supervisor (line manager) for whom he works. The first line of authority is indicative of a *collegial* model of organizational behaviour, since the centralized sanctions mechanism acts as an integrating power, and not as an autocratic power. Its primary functions are to coordinate the diverse activities of work practitioners in the field of their specializations, by encouraging the flexible use of prof· essional skills, and to develop a sense of mutual contribution among participants in the organization. The response of individuals to the central sanctions mechanism reflects the emergence of such motivating factors as achievement, work fulfilment and recognition, all of which are indicative of the growth of a high level of group professionalization.

Conversely, the second line of authority is less easily identifiable. Some of its characteristics, noticeably the extent to which it recognizes the vestigial power of the central sanctions mechanism, are representative of the *autocratic* model of organizational behaviour. Others, particularly the way in which the relationship between the individual and his line superior exhibits evidence of paternalism and organizational dependency, suggest that the pattern of behaviour, in this instance, approximates to that of the *custodial* model. Concomitantly, attempts made by the organization to move away from the traditional military form of authority, based on coercion, to a form based on managerial persuasion, indicate that the ideal relationship between the individual and his immediate superior should be characterized by the criteria of the *supportive* model.[1] In the latter, power is subordinated to leadership, and organizational dependency is replaced by a sense of individual responsibility, so that, in theory, the creation of the supportive model abolishes any remaining characteristics of the autocratic and custodials. Not only is it doubtful if this model has occurred in practice, but it is also questionable if the creation of the supportive model encourages the development of group professionalization. Although acceptance of the model may lead to organizational effectiveness, one of the essential criteria of the model is that the individual is motivated towards organizational objectives, as a means of achieving his own goals. Additionally, the essence of supportive leadership is the manner in which the sanctions authority mechanism is oriented towards the central maintenance of these objectives. We can thus infer that this insistence on the organizational motivation of individual work practitioners encourages the perpetuation of a low level of group professionalization.

While it is apparent that the level of ascriptive professionalization will depend on which of these two lines of authority is dominant, either generally or in a given situation, our analysis of the Royal Air Force as a special organization, is complicated by the effects of the interaction of this central authority sanctions mechanism with the structural sub-element of *control of non-occupational behaviour,* and with the *activity* elements of the variable of professionalization. In the first instance, the contrast between the two lines of authority, which can be discerned in the structure of the sanctions mechanism, is reconciled in their common insistence on the need to control non-occupational behaviour. For both lines of authority, it is clear that, notwithstanding the comparatively recent establishment of the Royal Air Force as a separate organization, their attitude is derived from a single historical source, in that each has adapted a traditional concept of military behaviour which can be traced back to the artificial association of the 'officer' and the 'gentleman'. Since this association has persisted over time, irrespective of changes in the socio-economic background of entrants

---

1   The characteristics of these models of organizational behaviour are based on Keith Davis, *Human Relations at Work: The Dynamics of Organizational Behaviour* (New York, 1967), p. 480, and on Davis, 'Evolving Models of Organizational Behaviour', *The Academy of Management Journal* (March 1968), 25-35.

to the officer corps, each form of authority, that is, both 'staff' and 'line', has evolved an ideal-type pattern of behaviour, neither of which is clearly distinguishable from the other. Both exhibit evidence of their common characteristics, and this is most noticeable in the manner in which both forms of authority attempt, through the control of non-occupational behaviour, to make the individual aware of his personal responsibilities. The contrast between them, however, is indicative of the peculiar position of the ascriptive professional. The pattern established by the 'line' authority, for example, is primarily concerned with organizational needs, which, in this context, means the individual's sense of responsibility to the organization. In contrast, 'staff' authority is less inhibited by the organizational framework, so that it is chiefly concerned with the responsibility of the individual to a less tangible sense of profession. Organizational commitment can therefore be contrasted with occupational commitment, to the extent that duty, character and morality, as criteria of organizational conformity, can be compared with the qualities of independence, intelligence and initiative, which are subsumed as the characteristics of the behaviour of the ascriptive professional.

The power to control non-occupational behaviour is not a singularly military phenomenon, so that if this power is believed to be common to the majority of qualifying associations, it cannot be used as a discriminating characteristic of professionalization. The particular feature of the use of this power in a military environment is the manner in which the level of ascriptive professionalization is indicated by the *degree* of control which is exercised. Military insistence on the right to control non-occupational behaviour reflects the insistence which is placed on the relationship between status and obligations. It is emphasized by the degree of punishment which is awarded for a failure to meet these obligations, particularly where the latter are associated with an ascribed position. The severity of the punishment awarded in the Royal Air Force for breach of the ideal pattern of non-occupational behaviour, is indicative of the wish of the officer corps to ensure occupational cohesiveness. Additionally, the strict control of non-occupational behaviour, in ensuring a normative solidarity, encourages the development of a community sanction which recognizes the monopolistic claim of the officer corps.[1]

Concomitantly, the contemporary increase in the degree of this control is indicative of an internal appreciation of the need to raise the level of group

---

1 An indication of a change in the external appreciation of the level of professionalization can be seen in the development of this community sanction. In the nineteenth century, when external observers recognized the low level of group professionalization, critics continually argued that there was nothing done by the regular Army which could not be better and more efficiently carried out by reserve forces. This refusal to recognize the claim of the group to an occupational monopoly, can be contrasted with the contemporary appreciation that military activities can now be performed only by an all-Regular highly trained and professionalized armed force.

professionalization. This need is a recognition of the changing nature of occupational goals, for the limitations imposed by new technological innovations, fresh appraisals of the strategic force of world power blocs, the effective threat of the nuclear deterrent and the fear of total war, tend towards a position where the main purpose of the profession of arms is not to win wars but to avoid them. The social results of inadequacy in the management and control of violence in two world wars have been so considerable, that, today, the officer corps is fully aware of the need to amend traditional orientations which permitted such inadequacy. By encouraging the development of a high level of military professionalization, the personal attitudes of members of the officer corps can be changed. No longer can they be conceptualized as an ascriptive elite whose members are selected on the basis of character rather than intellect. Now, it is believed that they are members of a highly professionalized group, subject like other employees of the state, to the political control of the organs of a democratically elected government. The ethics of a 'professional man' guarantee, it is argued, in the same way as do parliamentary institutions, the political supremacy of the civil power.

The possible dysfunctional consequences of such an amendment to traditional military attitudes are believed to be minimized by the strict control which is exercised over all military behaviour, as part of the process of professionalization. At the same time, however, the Royal Air Force recognizes that the more effective method of counteracting these dysfunctional consequences, is to alter the basis of recruitment to the occupational group, and to exclude from membership the traditional ascriptive aspirant. Consequently, the pattern of recruitment into the Royal Air Force College at Cranwell has changed, although the middle class domination of the officer corps has been criticized, on the grounds that it still excludes from group membership, aspirants who come from working-class backgrounds.[1] To a very large extent, this is not the result of the military employing the ascriptive barriers of the nineteenth century[2] as means of excluding aspirants. Rather, it follows as a result of the educational barriers which have been raised to ensure that all successful applicants to the officer corps, possess the requisite level of previous educational achievement. Research into Higher Education in Great Britain has established that there is a high degree of correlation between membership of the middle-class and education at a Grammar School.[3] Since it is only the latter school, or a comparable fee-paying school, which

---

1 This is not a new criticism. See Minutes of Winston Churchill as First Lord of the Admiralty to the Naval Secretary, 8 and 25 February 1940. Churchill, *The Second World War* (London, 1948), vol. 1, p. 690.
2 See Colonel Lord West, *Remarks on the Want of Special Training of Candidates for First Commission in the Army* (London, 1859).
3 See John Westergaard and Alan Little, 'Educational Opportunity and Social Selection in England and Wales: Trends and Policy', in *Social Objectives in Educational Planning* (Paris, 1967), pp. 215-32.

provides an educational process which leads to the acquisition of the academic standards which are demanded by the Military, it follows that the majority of aspirants will come from this particular class.[1] In this context, there is a similar pattern of entry into the universities and into the officer corps, for, since both organizations insist on a comparable standard of entry qualifications, the aspirant from the working class will be in the minority in both cases.[2]

The domination of the Grammar school in this field can be seen in Table 2, which summarises the previous educational experience of graduates from the Royal Air Force College, Cranwell at a specific date. We might expect that in this branch of the Military, where the nature of occupational activities engenders a particular need for a technical, rather than purely academic pre-entry training, a large number of aspirants would have enjoyed a technical education. This, however, is not confirmed from the findings of Table 2, although, conversely few entrants attended the major public schools, the traditional source of officer recruitment. Irrespective of the branches of the Royal Air Force in which they will carry out occupational activities, the majority of candidates enjoyed a conventional pre-entry educational experience, the standard of which can be equated with that demanded from the entrant to University or to the other professions. We can also note, although this is not revealed in Table 2, that a very small number of the officers graduating from Cranwell had been educated outside England. One candidate had been at school in Wales, two in Scotland, one in Northern Ireland and one in an overseas school.

Although the level of educational achievement which is demanded from aspirants to the officer corps is similar to that demanded from aspirants to a wider range of occupational activities, an evaluation of military professionalization which uses previous educational experience as a discriminating characteristic, encounters several difficulties. Acceptance of the need to move from a recruitment policy based on ascriptive criteria to one based on achievement, is indicative of the extent to which the officer corps is aware of the relationship between the development of group professionalization and the educational variables. The problem which the officer corps faces, however, is that the needs of organizational recruitment can conflict with the demands of occupational professionalization. Future Air Force policy for recruiting full career officers, for example, is based on the concept of exclusive graduate entry. This entails a raising of entry standards, so that, to the extent that this mirrors the policy adopted in a small number of occupational groups thought to be highly professionalized, a type of entry which is limited by the demands of a specific educational attainment, is an indicator of a potentially high level of group professionalization. The

1 In a sample check of one hundred serving Royal Air Force officers, less than one-eighth had been educated outside the Grammar Schools. Of these, only 3 per cent had attended a fee-paying school.
2 See HMSO, *Higher Education – Report of the Committee on Higher Education* (The 'Robbins Report'), (London, 1963), appendix 1, table 3, p. 42.

realization of this quantitative potential is, however, hindered by a number of factors.

Table 2. *Previous Educational Experience of Cranwell Graduates: March, 1969*

Activity	N	Major Public	Minor Public	Direct Grant	Grammar	Comp	Tech
Pilot	44	–	8	6	24	4	2
Navigator	7	1	–	1	4	1	–
Engineer	23	–	2	3	15	–	3
Equipment	3	–	1	–	1	1	–
Regiment	1	–	–	–	1	–	–
	78	1	11	10	45	6	5

Major public: A public school as defined in the Report of the Clarendon Commission.

Minor public: A fee-paying school, the headmaster of which is a member of the Headmasters' Conference.

Direct grant: A fee-paying school which receives State aid in the form of a direct grant from the Department of Education and Science.

Comp: A state school, in which courses are provided for pupils of all abilities.

Tech: A state school, in which courses are provided in technical subjects.

Source: *The Times,* 21 March 1969.

No single *index of occupational intelligence standards* can be readily formulated for a large-scale organization in which diverse occupational activities necessitate the adoption of varying standards to meet specific task requirements. The Royal Air Force comprises a large number of branches which are organized on the basis of their functional specialization, so that different sub-groups within the collectivity demand different occupational intelligence standards from aspirants. An appreciation of a level of professionalization which is based on this index will therefore reflect variations derived from the particular analytical categories which are adopted.

Moreover, although the military organization has attempted to eliminate future intra-organizational variations by accepting the policy of exclusive graduate entry, organizational and functional demands in the group are such, that there is a persistent requirement for the recruitment of young aspirants. These members are not committed to a full career within the organization. They are needed to fill appointments for a short time, and they are neither required in senior positions, nor are they required at a mature age. At the same time, the dysfunctional consequences associated with the recruitment of graduates for a limited career, suggest that, to obtain these officers, the organization is better served by adopting a more liberal entry policy. At any one time, therefore the younger members of the officer corps comprise both graduates and non-graduates, all of whom are initially recruited on the basis of a differentiated career. To reduce potential intra-group strain, and to introduce a system of adequate reward, the officer corps, however, is subsequently forced to offer to some of these academically less well qualified group members, the opportunity to transfer to a full career. Over time, such officers may reach senior rank levels, may be completely assimilated into the officer corps, and may be barely distinguishable in their role activities within the organization from officers who were recruited on the basis of an exclusive graduate entry.

This modification to the apparently preferred policy of recruitment can, therefore, be interpreted as an indication of a low level of group professionalization, for it suggests that the true level of required occupational intelligence and educational attainment is lower in standard than the level associated with a policy of exclusive graduate entry. In this situation, the possession by the aspirant of an educational qualification of a standard greater than the minimum demanded, is a *desirable* quality for successful role implementation, but it is not an *essential* quality. This also appears to be confirmed by a further amendment to this policy of exclusive graduate entry. The organization needs men of experience in a wide number of junior managerial functions, and, for these activities, a viable job specification is based on individual practical experience within the collectivity, and not on specific educational attainment. Aspirants to these appointments are selected from the experienced non-commissioned officers who were initially recruited to carry out a narrow range of occupational tasks which can be clearly differentiated from those appertaining to the officer corps. These aspirants are required to possess a specific educational qualification, and this is used, in conjunction with an assessment of their trade skill, as the indicator of an acceptable occupational intelligence standard. The latter is, however, in no way comparable with that demanded from the graduate entrant, nor is the experience gained in the performance of occupational tasks commensurate with that acquired by the non-graduate limited career officer. On commissioning, these officers form a distinct group within the collectivity, and, in general terms, they can be differentiated from the full career officer.

As long as this separate sub-group of officers whose participation in occupational activities is limited by their role in the organization, can be readily identified, their existence does not complicate an evaluation of the level of professionalization attained by full career officers. To reduce intra-group strain, however, and to enable the organization to reward loyalty, some degree of promotion to more general appointments or the opportunity to transfer to a full career must be offered to members of this sub-group. Whenever either eventuality occurs, these officers are no longer restricted to the performance of the limited range of activities for which they were initially selected, nor is their occupational role different from that of other members of the officer corps. Over time, moreover, such men are fully assimilated into the corps through a complex process of formal and informal socialization, and their wish to conform to established concepts of military professionalism, such as the maintenance of group norms, is no different from that of other officers. Additionally, the success achieved by these officers in the performance of occupational activities again suggests that the level of educational attainment associated with a policy of exclusive graduate entry, is not necessarily a prerequisite of effective task performance.

The analytical problems which are derived from the presence within the organization of three types of full career officers, who, although they can be differentiated on the basis of their initial recruitment, are almost indistinguishable in terms of occupational activity, are accentuated by the extent to which the military organization is forced to recognize external occupational requirements. The officer corps in common with other special organizations includes not only ascriptive professionals, but also work practitioners who, in addition to their organizational professionalism, are also achievement professionals because of their initial training. As we have noted, the military organization employs, among others, doctors, dentists, clergymen, teachers, lawyers and master mariners, all of whom are recruited on the basis of their status as members of a specific non-military occupational group. In addition, the organization employs engineers and administrators who may be recruited on the basis of their civilian status, but who may be also recruited on the understanding that they will be trained within the organization to a standard equivalent to that reached through an external educational and training programme.

The level of achievement which is demanded from these work practitioners primarily relates to the standard which is required for membership of the external occupational group, so that, if the latter insists on a policy of exclusive graduate entry, the military organization is forced to accept this policy as a precondition of recruitment. The number of these achievement professionals is small in comparison with the total of ascriptive professionals, but an evaluation of professionalization which only takes into account the principle of exclusive graduate entry as a discriminating characteristic, does not consider the influence which these achievement professionals exert over the remaining members of the officer corps. This is particularly noticeable where both types of group members interact in the performance of a similar activity, for, here, there is a tendency for ascriptive professionals to adopt, through a deliberately cultivated policy of imitation, the norms already inculcated in the achievement professionals. Conversely, dysfunctional strains which threaten the development of a high level of total group professionalization, often arises from the potential conflict between the ascriptive professional who has been trained within the organization, and the achievement professional who has been trained in an external institution. Neither type fully understands or accepts the interpretation which the other places on the meaning of 'profession' or 'professionalism', and there is a particular tendency for the ascriptive professional to reject the need for *the study of the under-*

lying systematic theory, although this requirement is a fundamental characteristic of professionalization in the eyes of the achievement professional.

It is with regard to this need to study theory as an integral part of the programme of professional training and assimilation, that the use of the educational sub-elements of the variable most clearly suggests that the military is characterized by a low level of occupational professionalization. There are a number of reasons for the rejection by the officer corps of the validity of this concept. Some are traditional in origin, for they can be traced back to the nineteenth-century belief, derived from the continuing existence of a neo-feudal military elite, that educational and technical knowledge were not the only qualities desired in the ideal-type officer, and that qualities such as perseverance, presence of mind, accuracy of judgement, punctuality and proper behaviour were of greater importance. Others reflect an historical dichotomy in England, in which 'education', oriented towards status realization by awakening charisma in the student, can be distinguished from 'training' oriented towards role realization by imparting specialized expert knowledge. In the military organization, this distinction is distorted by a traditional preference for officers of character rather than officers of intellect. 'Education' is therefore interpreted to mean the process whereby the individual is conditioned to accept the behavioural norms of the officer corps, with their emphasis on concepts of honour, loyalty, fealty and public service. Concomitantly, 'training' is equated with a process in which the individual officer acquires a limited range of skills which are sufficient for the adequate, if not the expert performance of a specific occupational activity.

In neither instance, does the occupational group readily acknowledge the significance of the part played by the study of systematic theory in the development of group professionalization. In the case of military education, the study of theory is discouraged because its aims of developing a critical faculty are thought to conflict with the need to ensure the homogeneous nature of the collectivity. In the development of a military training programme, the study of theory can only be justified if the efficacy of the results is measurable in terms of cost effectiveness.

A further reason for the rejection by the officer corps of the importance of this educational sub-element in the development of group professionalization, is more pragmatic. An analysis of the pattern of military promotion suggests that in constructing a model based on the qualities needed from candidates for promotion, educational achievement in general and a competent mastery of theory in particular, are, at best, *desirable* rather than *critical* criteria. It appears that there is a continuing preference for the generalist, that is, for the well-rounded officer who can accept any occupational commitment by relying on the training he has received in a narrow range of skills, tempered by experience acquired through frequent changes in role activities.

As a special organization, the officers corps is not alone in meeting this professional/generalist dichotomy, for the Report of the Committee on the Civil Service (the Fulton Report) stresses that the Civil Service is based too much on the philosophy of the amateur, generalist or all-rounder, particular in the policy-making Administrative Class.[1] The remedies which the Fulton Committee suggested are moreover, equally applicable to the Royal Air Force, for they emphasize the need to master, in depth, a body of knowledge specifically related to task performance in a single area of occupational activity, and the concomitant requirement to acquire an understanding of the theory underlying the processes of staff work and management skills. These remedies were summed up in the Fulton Report as the need for a greater degree of 'professionalism', and in this context, we can see the significance of the contribution which is made by a study of the theory underlying occupational activities, to the development of a high level of group professionalization.

The problem which the Royal Air Force continues to meet, is that since entry into the officer corps is multi-portal, attempts which are made to raise the level of group professionalization through an institutionalized educational process, only apply to a limited percentage of all group members. Only a small number of the officer corps have passed through the Air Force College at Cranwell; an even smaller percentage has undergone a year's training at the Royal Air Force Staff College. One result of this is that the encouragement of the cultural and professional socialization of the officer corps, as a whole, is inadequate, so that an analysis of the occupational group through a use of the ideological sub-elements of the variable, suggests that there are considerable intra-group variations in the attitudes of members. The extent to which the individual accepts the collective demands of the occupational group by identifying himself with its ideologies varies according to his method of entry into the officer corps. It can be suggested that a high level of ideological commitment is associated with attendance at the *institutionalized educational process* carried out at the Royal Air Force College, and that conversely, a lower level is associated with attendance at the much shorter course of the Officer Cadet Training Unit (OCTU). This relationship, however, is complicated by the marked schism which exists between the ascriptive professional who possesses only military skills, and the achievement professional who, although he may be employed in an ascriptive role, retains non-military skills. From the interaction of these variables, a ranking of ideological commitment can be constructed, in which, as is shown in the paradigm at Table 3, there are noticeable intra-group differences:

---

1 HMSO, *The Civil Service*, vol. 1, *Report of the Committee, 1966-1968* (London, 1968), p. 11

Table 3. *Military Ideological Commitment*

Professional training

		Ascriptive	Achievement
Military Training	College	1	3
	OCTU	2	4

In the Table, the greatest intra-group differences are shown by the diagonals 1 to 4, and 3 to 2. The aspirant to the officer corps ranked in the first position, who is trained in exclusively military skills at the Royal Air Force College, identifies himself almost completely with occupational ideologies. He believes that the asserted goals of the organization are the only occupational goals of importance, and to ensure that they are achieved he rejects the validity of any occupational activity which does not demonstrate military 'purity'. His involvement is directly related to the exercise of command functions, and he tries to avoid participation in activities in an advisory or research capacity, which, although they are characteristics of group professionalization, tend to be contrary to his evaluation of military purity.

The command function is accepted not only because its implementation necessitates the development of a high level of military purity, but also because officers can be ranked according to the degree of success which they achieve in this field. Advancement prospects are directly related to the degree of 'purity' attached to a specific military assignment, and the scale is so clearly defined that every officer knows fairly well what to expect. The need to be imitative and to adhere to this concept of 'purity' encourages group membership and the sense of belonging to the military organization. This sense, moreover, is reinforced through the exercise of the command function, for implementation of the latter cannot be attained if the officer participates in the military process as an individual. The characteristics of the command function are such — the need to plan, to organize, to motivate and to control — that success can only be achieved through group cooperation. The high degree of cooperation which is necessary for success, also ensures that involvement is a means of satisfying various psychological needs. Participation in 'pure' military activities as a member of the formal group, becomes, for the individual, a 'means of developing, enhancing, or confirming a sense of identity and maintaining self-esteem'.[1] This participation is most easily achieved when the officer accepts without question the value of two of the discriminating characteristics of ascriptive professionalism — service and leadership — for, then, his implementation of group activities emphasizes his adherence to traditional *mores* and conventions. 'Service' suggests a willingness to subordinate personal interests to the demands of the officer corps. It is a recognition

---

1 Edgar H. Schein, *Organizational Psychology* (Englewood Cliffs, 1965), p. 70.

of the need to accept restrictions on individual freedom of action, and to accept the obligations of uncritical loyalty. 'Leadership', too, imposes obligations on the individual, for it necessitates the acceptance of responsibility. It denotes qualities of chivalrous and honourable conduct, and its reciprocal nature, since the rights of leadership are balanced by the obligations of obedience, confirms the loyalty of the individual to the group.

In accepting these concepts, the officer who is trained in exclusively military skills at the Royal Air Force College, is obliged to respect the dictates of the group. He follows both the written rules and the unwritten conventions of the officer corps, and, ultimately, the officer, because of the demands imposed on him by these concepts, becomes completely submerged in military life, to the exclusion of his outside interests. His individual personality is merged with the corporate personality of the group, but, in return for this commitment, group membership enables him to satisfy more of his psychological needs. In particular, it enables him to test reality, that is, to verify the real nature of the relationship between the officer and the men for whom he is responsible, and group membership becomes a means of meeting his affiliation needs.[1]

In complete contrast, the ideological commitment to the occupational group by the achievement professional who has undergone only a limited amount of socialization, is characterized by the emphasis which he places on his external skills, his extra-occupational experience, and his civilian training. He often demonstrates little loyalty to the organization, for he is *in but not of* the officer corps, and the low level of his integration in either the formal or informal organizational structure is associated with his orientation to the outer reference group. His pronounced commitment to external occupational skills is accompanied by a tendency to association with external peers, and this, in turn, reduces the degree of commitment to the military organization. Because these external skills and the association with external group members create a sense of economic dependence, this type of officer is less dependent on the functional group with its sense of security and concomitant sense of power.

Paradoxically, however, an analysis of military professionalization suggests that these achievement professionals often exhibit evidence of a higher level of group professionalization, than the ascriptive professionals who have been entirely trained within the organization. For the latter, the need to ensure the continuing existence of the occupational group as a closed community, means that the group is perpetually resisting external threats. Additionally, ascriptive professionals are continually concerned with the power which is wielded over the

1   One of the characteristics of the Prerogative Association, which differentiates it from the more usual form of Qualifying Association, is that it is based on a highly developed corporate personality to which individual personality is subordinated. This suggests that the affiliation needs of the ascriptive professional can only be met through his membership of the functional group, and that the latter replaces, rather than supplements, the more usual form of professional Association.

organization by the external civil power. To meet these threats, and to offset this civil power, the ascriptive professional tends to accentuate the importance of the bureaucratic structure as a means of protecting the organization. Bureaucratic career commitment replaces professional involvement. The ascriptive professional is deeply committed to the group because it embodies values which he regards as important, and there is a tendency for him to seek effective goal realization though insisting upon the importance of the bureaucratic rules of the organization. Its practices become sacrosanct. The rules are regarded as the embodiment of rational practice, and the individual who refuses to demonstrate uncritical loyalty to the organization, is rejected as a deviant. Lines of communication become formalized. A structured hierarchy exercises bureaucratic and not professional authority, and the ideological commitment of the individual is oriented towards the bureaucratic organization and not the professional occupation.

A limitation on this tendency, which if unchecked, leads to a total rejection of the professionalism of the officer corps, is derived from the presence within the group of the remaining two categories of the ascriptive professional who has undergone a limited process of socialization, and the achievement professional who has been trained within the organization. Ideological commitment in these two categories is clearly distinguishable, for each is derived from a different base. A high level of commitment is associated with the ascriptive military professional who has undergone a limited amount of group socialization, but since it is primarily based on a wish to be imitative, it does not reach an extreme level. The sense of 'service' is less well-developed, and there is a reaction against a concept which demands the subordination of personal interests to the needs of the group. Commitment is often pragmatically based, for it is derived from a realization of the advantages which are associated with membership of the officer corps, and, when these advantages are no longer readily apparent, the level of ideological commitment is rapidly reduced. Concomitantly, the level of bureaucratic career commitment, in the absence of readily transferable civilian skills, always continues at a high level, and this ensures the loyalty of the individual to the organization.

The achievement professional who is trained within the military organization occupies a position of transition. He has accepted the demands of 'service' and 'leadership' which are indicative of the ascriptive professional, but his training in an external transferable skill leads him to reject the concept of a bureaucratic career commitment. He knows that if he becomes dissatisfied with the nature of his occupational activities, he can withdraw from the organization and exercise an influence in association with his external peers. He is not committed to the demands of the 'pure' military attitude, and, since the achievement professional wishes to establish a self-image which can be distinguished from that of the ascriptive professional, he will emphasize discriminating characteristics which are indicative of his external associations. His ideological commitment to the officer corps resembles that of the externally trained achievement professional, for neither category of officers can participate fully in command functions. A difference between these two types, however, is that the former lacks the professional self-esteem of the latter, because he is forced to participate to a greater extent in group activities, so that the officer corps can become for him a formal psychological group which meets a variety of psychological needs.

Although we can note these intra-organizational differences, an analysis of the ideological commitment of the officer corps as a whole, suggests that there is, in comparison with many external occupations, a high level of commitment. A problem which remains unsolved is the extent to which this level of commitment, normally subsumed as a criterion of professionalization, can be used as an indicator of a level of ascriptive professionalization. It is evident that the fusion of organization and profession which is a characteristic of these special organizations, is accompanied by a fusion of ideological and bureaucratic commitment. In many instances, it is clear that commitment is associated with the wish of the group to secure the legitimacy of the structure by ensuring group solidarity. A cohesive group culture, which is deliberately developed in the assimilating institutions through which all officers pass, is indicative of a high level of professionalization, particularly since the group believes that the service it renders to the remainder of society is for the good of the whole, and that withdrawal of the service would cause immeasurable harm. There is, however, always a suggestion that this culture, and the associated group identity, are derived from the bureaucratic base of the organization, and that they are exploited as a means of furthering the maintenance of the hierarchical authority pyramid. This suggestion appears to be confirmed by the manner in which the officer corps excludes from membership the deviants who might query the *rationale* of the structure, and by the way in which the military, by insisting on group conformity, seeks to ensure universal internal support for a self-image which can not be evaluated by outsiders.

A conclusion that a high level of ideological commitment is not necessarily indicative of a high level of group professionalization, can be deduced from the attitude of the ascriptive professional towards his *status*. The specific status determinant which is adopted is usually that of bureaucratic rank, and it is only the achievement professionals who have been trained outside the organization, who support an interpretation of status which is based on work satisfaction and its value to society. The status of the ascriptive professional has, both in his own eyes and in the evaluation of society, declined since 1939 and there is ample evidence of an over-preoccupation with this concept. Both factors suggest that, in this context the military is characterized by a low level of professionalization, and this conclusion is supported by the almost complete absence of *transferred prestige* between the achievement and ascriptive professionals within the officer corps. Indeed, it is also clear that many achievement professionals suffer from a diminution of status because of their membership of the officer corps, since they are subject to overriding bureaucratic decisions as to the type of work they will perform and are unable to obtain the requisite experience for post-graduate qualifications as easily as they would in other work situations.[1] This, in turn, leads to a potential role conflict which weakens the development of a group consensus and the concomitant growth of a high level of group professionalization.

In the same way that an examination of the military organization through a use of the *ideological* sub-elements of the variable of professionalization, indicates the problems which arise from the fusion of profession and organization, the use of the *behavioural* sub-elements in analysis suggests that the existence of a highly structured code of conduct may not be indicative of a high level of group professionalization. The written military code is to a very large extent 'imposed' upon the individual officer and many of its articles reinforce the prescriptions of the employing authority. In common with external 'professional' codes, it is a code of ethics, albeit in general rather than specific terms, and indeed, it is a distinct recognized code, so that a degree of professionalization can be related to the quantitative evaluation by group members of the existence of a code which can be effectively enforced by a central body of control. Nevertheless, it can be distinguished from a true professional code on several counts. Of these, the most important, is the extent to which the military code of behaviour is a *negative* code. The true professional code confers on occupational group members both positive rights and positive obligations, and it is on the basis of both of these that the member behaves as part of the group. In contrast, the military code is primarily a code of punishment in which individual rights are recognized only in so far as actions taken to limit these unexpressed rights, may be punishable as a breach of the disciplinary code. Essentially, the code is designed to protect hierarchy of rank and not the fraternal equality which is a discrimating characteristic of the free professional. Moreover, since the code, in the shape of Military law, is imposed on the officer corps from outside the collectivity, it reflects the wish of the client-government, as a monopolist, to subject group members to a set of rules and regulations.

In the Military, the external code of occupational ethics is more clearly seen in the unwritten set of conventions which reflect an inherited neo-feudal code of honour. In the past, these conventions were primarily relevant to the position of the officer as a member of a privileged social group, and not to his position as a member of an occupational group. In this situation, group reaction to external and internal stimuli took the form of a complex mix in which behavioural atti-

---

1 For doctors, these professional disadvantages were recognized in the Report of the National Board for Prices and Incomes, 1969 on the Pay of the Armed Forces. See *Report, op. cit.,* para 135, p. 36. The Board also acknowledged that other 'specialist Service officers' suffered a limitation which they did not see as being different in kind or any less in extent than that of Service doctors.

tudes were derived from social group membership rather than occupational group membership. In the contemporary military organization, changes which have occurred in the socio-economic basis of recruitment to the officer corps, have produced a concomitant amendment to the relevancy of these codes. To justify their retention, particularly in the Royal Air Force which has been most affected among the British military forces by such factors as technological developments, the established officer corps argues that they reflect the professional ethos of the military establishment. In many respects, the arguments which are advanced to support this thesis are similar to those put forward by groups which, in striving for external recognition of their claim to professional status, formulate written codes to cover both the formal and informal norms of the ideal-type professionalized occupation. In the Royal Air Force, moreover, it is apparent that the achievement professional who has experienced the constraints of an external professional code, rejects the validity of these arguments, claiming that these conventions are outdated and that they inhibit the growth of professionalization. Conversely, the ascriptive professional accepts the validity of these conventions, since their provisions, by differentiating the military and the remainder of society, contribute to the maintenance of military 'purity'. Both instances suggest that the presence of these unwritten conventions cannot be used as a viable index of professionalization, since the factor common to both rejection and acceptance, is the acknowledgement that these conventions are anachronistic and ascriptive.

One of the reasons for the rejection of the validity of these conventions by the achievement professional, is his contention that their provisions affect the development of the *objective peer evaluation of merit,* which is one of the discriminating characteristics of a high degree of group professionalization. Concepts, such as the importance of ensuring uncritical group loyalty, encourage, particularly in their breach, the lay evaluation of occupational performance. They also conflict with the achievement professional's interpretation of the informal norms which govern group behaviour. In many cases, where he is employed in an advisory or research role within the organization, the achievement professional concludes that these conventions are irrelevant criteria in the assessment of his professional ability. He feels that in these conventions 'merit' is interpreted to mean character rather than intellect, and that this is a further limitation on the establishment of a peer evaluation of merit.

If this peer evaluation of merit is accepted as a discriminating characteristic of professionalization, then it must be concluded that the system of merit evaluation in a military organization is indicative of a low level of group professionalization. In the contemporary Royal Air Force, a formalized pattern of merit evaluation has been established, in which, to allow for the employment of specialists within the organization, a sharp distinction is made between the ascriptive and the achievement professional. For the latter, the extent to which lay evaluation is allowed, is related to the degree to which it is permissible in the comparable external occupational group. Nevertheless, although this precludes lay evaluation of specialist skills, such as those of the doctor, the lawyer or the nurse, this does not prevent the lay evaluation of character, and, as we have seen, this is often equated in the Military organization with the evaluation of ability.

For ascriptive professionals, and for those achievement professionals who are less well identified with that mystique of professionalism which makes lay evaluation of skills difficult, if not impossible, the system of merit evaluation is a complex one. In general terms, the system reflects the existence of two distinct lines of authority in the Royal Air Force, so that the individual is evaluated, firstly, by the immediate superior to whom he is responsible, and, secondly, by the collegial superior in his area of specialization. The initial evaluation is indicative, both in its form and in the adopted criteria of assessment, of a low level of group professionalization. There is a specific requirement for the lay evaluation of individual ability in the performance of specialist skills, and, additionally, assessment is oriented towards the evaluation of character. In contrast, the second evaluation is more reminiscent of a true professional peer evaluation, for it is primarily concerned with the assessment by a collegial superior of the manner in which the individual performs his specialist occupational activities. A factor which limits the extent to which this type of evaluation can be taken as an indicator of a high level of group professionalization, is however, the rank element associated with the assessment. In all cases of merit evaluation in the Military organization, the assessment is carried out by a hierarchical superior, and however much the evaluator may try to model his assessment on the principles of peer evaluation, he must consider both bureaucratic and professional ability. As a result, some part of his assessment must be oriented towards the evaluation of bureaucratic skills which may be the antithesis of professional skills. Moreover, where the performance of both types of skills engenders role conflict, the position of the evaluator in the pyramidical rank structure forces him to recognize the superordinate position of ability in bureaucratic task performance. Consequently, he minimizes the importance to the organization of individual ability in the performance of professional skills, and, to this extent, the form and nature of merit evaluation is again indicative of a low level of group professionalization.

From this brief analysis of the Royal Air Force, as an exemplar of a special organization, we reach the not unexpected conclusion that different aspects of organizational activity reflect variations in the level of attained professionalization. Initially, these variations endorse the importance of a multivariate form of analysis, for it is apparent that an appraisal which is based on a single indicator of professionalization, such as 'expertise', 'monopoly of skill', 'autonomy', 'commitment' or 'responsibility', may lead to distorted conclusions. It is also clear that encountered analytical problems are not unique to the military organization. for, in essence, they result from the dysfunctional consequences which are

associated with the fusion of profession and organization. In the absence of a
neoteric organizational system which could provide a realistic and practical alternative to the authoritarian bias of traditional organization theory, 'special' organizations remain characterized by the ubiquity of their hierarchical patterns. As
we have seen, these impose specific limitations on the development of group
professionalization, particularly in the context of professional training, ideological commitment, and the evaluation of merit, all of which are affected by the
ruled-ruler relationship inherent in legal-rational authority systems. Although the
organization and the individual may attempt to escape from these limitations,
or, indeed, may claim that the basis of authority in the military or other special
organizations has been amended, analysis suggests that the model of organizational behaviour continues to be an amalgam of characteristics derived from the
autocratic, custodial or supportive models. The ascriptive professional, who
carries out his work activities within these parameters, consequently continues
to be denied decisional autonomy, and he is perpetually constrained by the
bureaucratic demands of the employing environment.

Concomitantly, differentiated organizational needs encourage the development of those characteristics of professionalization which support the legitimation of group activities. Specialization, centralization and standardization,
for example, are favoured, because, in establishing a high level of group professionalization, they not only maintain the effectiveness of the military profession, but also ensure that organizational decision making is carried out within
a formal matrix characterized by its expertise, its exclusiveness and its monopoly
of skill. Here, the aims of the structural elements of professionalization endorse
the bureaucratic aims of the central sanctions authority mechanism, for the
fusion of profession and organization is so complete, that the ascriptive professional, in formulating his own activity goals, participates with fellow professionals in the establishment of organizational goals. A derived problem, however, is
the extent to which hyper-professionalization, in this context, produces resistance to new techniques and ideas, so that by rejecting innovation, the legitimation of group activities encourages dysfunctional trends.

The officer corps is more prone to suffer from these dysfunctional consequences which limit the development of group professionalization, than are the
members of other special organizations. A considerable part of military professionalism is based on a long historical tradition. The Military pioneered the development of a comprehensive process of assimiliation. Staff colleges preceded
the business schools. The foundations of many professional characteristics, in
thought, technique and structure, were laid down by the officer corps of the
past, so that the Victorian creation of the professions absorbed, either consciously or unconsciously, concepts originally formulated in the Military environment. Yet, while external occupational groups moved from this nineteenth-
century base to a position indicative of a growth in the level of group profession-

alization, internal factors restricted a similar development in the officer corps. As a result, the legal rationalization of traditional military characteristics, noticeably concepts of honour, loyalty and conformity, has encouraged role strain and status incongruency. Additionally, although members of a highly professionalized occupational group should feel no inihibiting sense of moral obligation to the employing organization for the support it gives them, the officer is often socialized into a position of organizational dependency. The excessive institutional commitment, subsumed as a characteristic of the custodial model of organizational behaviour, induces a pattern of conservatism which, in rejecting changes in professional norms and standards, is indicative of a low level of group professionalization.

The continuing problem which is encountered by the Royal Air Force and other special organizations, is derived from the conflict between the demands of a bureaucratic career commitment and the requirements of professional personality involvement. The Military is not alone in attempting to overcome the dysfunctional consequences of this conflict, but, for the officer corps, the need to find a viable solution to the problem is most acute. If the organization is to continue as an effective means of controlling the management of violence, recruitment and task performance must be oriented towards the development of a high level of group professionalization. The Royal Air Force has been at some pains to encourage this development, and many of its proposals will, if they are allowed to come to fruition, greatly enhance the established level of ascriptive professionalization. A major difficulty, however, is that too often in the past, reliance on a single causal variable of professionalization drawn from concepts applicable to the performance of the 'free' professional, has overemphasized the importance of some aspects of professionalism, to the total exclusion of other considerations. This difficulty can be overcome, if multivariate analysis is employed in a critical examination of the form and nature of ascriptive professionalization. This enables us to identify the criteria of the dynamic process as it is applicable in the context of the special organization. The problem areas can be isolated, and further empirical testing which employs the conceptualized subelements of professionalization, can determine the extent to which the conclusions reached in this study of a military organization are of a wider applicability. It is suggested that the conclusions which have been reached are so applicable, and that we can infer from them that the method of multivariate analysis which we have employed, is the most effective means of analysing those special organizations in which work practitioners can be identified as ascriptive, rather than 'free', professionals.

4 Professions or Self-Perpetuating Systems? Changes in the French University - Hospital System

H. JAMOUS and B. PELOILLE

4

CHANGES IN THE FRENCH
UNIVERSITY - HOSPITAL SYSTEM

H. JAMOUS and B. PELOILLE

The greater part of this contribution is an analysis of the transformations undergone and instituted by the French university-hospital *corps* since the beginning
of the nineteenth century. It stems from a body of research the aim of which
was to understand the social and historical conditions of a governmental decision
— the 1958 Debré reform — aimed at reorganizing medical studies and changing
the conditions of practice of hospital doctors and faculty professors who in
France form a sort of medical elite and aristocracy.[1] A reform or a governmental
decision is, most often, destined to remedy a situation which is usually described
as a state of crisis. The 'decision -making' orientation we have adopted, which
consists in seeking the origins of this crisis, and in explaining the reasons which
have led to the choice of such and such a train of argument rather than another,
has proved fruitful in understanding the role of the social and professional
categories which are at the centre of this crisis. But, with regard to the concepts
suggested by the idea of profession or the theme of professionalization, these
have turned out to be inadequate to account for the transformations in these
professional groups. Thus, in the elaboration of this paper we have tried to state
explicitly the ideas which have guided our own analysis, asking ourselves if they
could not provide general insights for a better understanding of the activities and
the groups which are usually approached through the notions of profession or
of professionalization. Therefore, we shall first discuss these ideas, and then we
shall proceed with the analysis of the changes which have occurred within the
university-hospital *corps*. This analysis, in turn will enable us to finally take up
again the first theoretical considerations in order to suggest and comment on
some general hypotheses.

THEORETICAL PROLEGOMENA

There is an inherent problem of definition in any work of research. Our analytical procedure is best characterized by a refusal to define initially both the
specificity of the product provided by the so-called 'professionals' and the
nature of these social categories; likewise, this procedure precludes any prelimi-

1 H. Jamous, *Sociologie de la décision : la réforme des études médicales et des structures
hospitalières* (Paris, 1969).

nary definition of the social functions thought to be fulfilled by these professions. Indeed, the sociological interest of our research lies in demonstrating that we are dealing with products whose definition and social function are *end results* of: (1) an Indetermination/Technicality (I/T) ratio which characterizes the production process making it possible to arrive at the results expected of any given occupation or activity; (2) the way in which the general balance of social forces, and the system of legitimacy which corresponds to it, uses and expresses this ratio in each historical situation.

This unusual, indeed reverse approach to our subject,[1] generates other problems of definition and difficulties of exposition which in turn require precision. The I/T ratio expresses the possibility of transmitting, by means of apprenticeship, the mastery of intellectual or material instruments used to achieve a given result. This makes it possible to appreciate the limits of this transmissibility; i.e. the part played in the production process by 'means' that can be mastered and communicated in the form of rules (T), in proportion to the 'means' that escape rules and, at a given historical moment are attributed to virtualities of producers (I). It can in theory characterize any given process of production. Made operational, the I/T index would provide a dimension along which it would be possible to order any given set of activities.

We shall delineate our field of thought and research by saying that the occupations and activities which concern us are the ones which lie on that sector of the dimension where the I/Ts are usually high. This sector does not include all occupations nor only the occupations usually called 'professions'. One might remark that the many definitions of this notion proposed in sociological literature are far from being in agreement or without ambiguity. Without embarking upon a debate of the kind which would involve a discussion of the whole of the argument which we oppose, we shall be content to outline an example in the light of Parsons' recent comments,[2] to show how the dimension which we are introducing allows a certain clarification of the object of our research.

If one considers, for instance, the realm of pharmacy, and the way in which Parsons defines the limits of the field of study: 'profession of learning' which embraces those who take part in the creation of knowledge, its transmission and in its application, and the 'sector of the cultural system where the primacy of the values of cognitive rationality is presumed' — one realizes that our dimension will have the advantage of discriminating researchers and professors from those modern pharmacists who have become commercial distributors. This immediately draws one's attention to the significance and exact function of what the

1 It is, however, necessary to indicate that, for the present systematization, we owe some of our ideas to Freidson whose most recent approach coincided with the first conclusion of our research. H. Jamous. *Contribution à une sociologie de la décision : la réforme des études médicales et des structures hospitalières* (Paris, 1967).

2 T. Parsons, 'Professions', *International Encyclopedia of the Social Sciences* (New York, 1968), pp. 536-46.

authors have called the criteria of a profession: length of the apprenticeship and its level of specialization, judgement by equals, taking over of a social value, etc. These no longer appear as elements of a definition to be admitted as such, but as survivals of times past which require explanation.

But, as the operationalization of such a dimension demands a complete reformulation of the processes of production which are intrinsically connected to the different occupations, we have to be content with a theoretical delimitation; if we happen in this article to speak of 'profession' or of 'professionals' we shall not be referring to categories defined by specialized literature, but to those which might be pin-pointed by means of an operative definition of I/T. These terms, like those of 'activities' or of 'occupation', which we shall use, will mean in effect: 'occupations or activities whose I/T ratio, intrinsic to the systems of production, is generally high.' These theoretical prolegomena, which we ask the reader to grant us, will be made clearer in the course of the essay.

This type of production is seen to be peculiar in that is is difficult to evaluate in terms of unanimously accepted measurable and objective criteria. Even when some indicators exist, they do not apply directly to the result itself, but to a number of general consequences which one supposes to be linked to it by a long and complex chain of intermediate stages. We can even say that, in certain extreme cases, it is difficult to characterize even this production or its result.

It follows that the system of evaluation of production and the system of sanction and control which can be applied to the producers can be established only with some difficulty on the basis of a comparison and a direct estimate of performances. They will be constructed; above all, either on the basis of the virtualities attributed to the producing agents or on the basis of the institutions and organizations which produce the latter. But obstacles may arise in the form of a vicious circle when it is a question of knowing how to estimate the value of these agents, or of the institutions and organizations themselves. For these, in their turn, run the risk of being assessed on the basis of the results obtained by the agents which they produce, a result whose value was itself guaranteed by these organizations. Recourse to a transcendental value or to a principle of external legitimacy is therefore necessary. This value which is the expression of a balance of social forces will: (1) either guarantee at the same time the value of the institutions, of the producers which it creates, and the results of the latter; (2) or else, attribute to the producers, as to the institutions, exceptional virtualities which serve as a guarantee of results.

The modern universities, schools or professional associations which provide training and knowledge and which hand out diplomas recognized by the public authorities, guaranteeing in some way the output of their possessors, form examples of the first case. Illustrative of the second case is what happens in the

so-called primitive societies, where the role of our 'professionals' is generally
filled either by the senior members — the closest to the ancestors who are the
guardians of the values and principles of legitimacy of the society — or else by
the members of certain noble families or by individuals provided with exceptional magical powers. In these cases which are, moreover, not exclusive, the
way in which these virtualities are 'acquired' is through experience, ascription or
initiation. In the same way it was the charisma of the priests rather than their
skills which justified in the past their monopolization of the principal roles in the
field of knowledge and which guaranteed the 'effectiveness' or adequacy of their
actions.

It is known that the specificity of sociologists of the professions, the
majority of whom do not stray far from the ideas of Parsons, consists in charac-
terizing western societies and the contemporary period by 'the primacy of the
values of cognitive rationality' which nowadays is a marked feature of the training and role of professionals. More objective means of evaluation having been
provided by science, it is by means of its criteria that technical apprenticeship,
as supplied by the universities, takes the place of initiation, ascription or
charisma. In fact, the two systems which have just been mentioned always contain the seeds of a dilemma and potential crisis which may erupt as soon as it
comes up against results obtained by new means: i.e. every result liable to be
judged equivalent to, or better than, that reached by recognized procedures, but
having been obtained by a person who does not possess the recognized virtualities, who has not acquired them by the customary methods or who does not belong to a social group whose 'qualities' serve as a guarantee. The dilemma then
appears thus: either the equivalence or the superiority of this 'new result' is
recognized, but in this case doubt may be cast not only on the value of the institutions which up till then handed out or sanctioned these virtuality-guaran-
tees, but also by the same token the principles of legitimacy on which they are
based; or else these institutions and these principles are maintained, but then
they must be strengthened and given a value in such a way as to show that only
the results which may be obtained by means of them have any value, that only
the definition which they assume is adequate. In systems with a religious or
charismatic basis, it is generally the second solution which is adopted, using
various forms and procedures of anathema; this produces the perpetuation and
self-support of the system and of its values. In systems where 'the values of
cognitive rationality' are predominant, it is the first solution which ought in
principle to be the rule since this scientific rationality has provided an outlet
from closed and religious systems by supplying 'universalist' methods of evaluation and control.

The choice which guides our analysis leads us to deny this clear-cut distinction. The reason for this firstly is that the production processes partic-
lar to 'professional' activities always contain an important margin of indeter-

mination which rationalized and transferable rules do not take into account, and because, secondly, the institutions and the organizations which turn out these 'professionals' are the product of an overall relationship of social forces; it is difficult then to claim that the system of evaluation of production, training, sanction and control of the producing agents is governed only by the 'values of cognitive rationality'.

It is known in fact that the 'natural' selection of technical or intellectual aptitudes carried out by the school or the university is also and above all a social selection.[1] Thus, the value of production expected from professionals is always guaranteed by this mixture of competence and social qualities confirmed by a diploma.[2] This apparently simple and 'natural' fact is the result of the combination of several phenomena:

(a) The internalization of the surrounding ideology which makes us assume that those who are best-placed on the social scale are the most competent.

(b) The impossibility of making comparisons since the others generally have no chance to show their skills, a fact which moreover is the basis of the ideology and upholds it.

(c) The fact that generally when criteria of appreciation are lacking, there is a tendency to take into account the most striking characteristics and those which are socially most highly valued.

It follows that, here as well, any debate around the value of the results obtained outside of the authorized channels reproduces the dilemma mentioned above, while giving it a social content. It is not a question of opposition between religious principles and 'cognitive rationality' where the very conditions of existence of the latter were at the centre of the debate. Given that 'cognitive rationality' has achieved a position of privilege, it is the part that it plays in the methods of arriving at the results in relation to what is indeterminate which is the object of conflict. This new solution which makes it more possible to rationalize, to codify and therefore to transmit the processes of production intrinsic to the activity, becomes a 'polemical solution' as much from the scientific and technical point of view as from the social one. It leads in fact to the appearance of a technical dysfunction, since it reveals that the approved means which are linked to training (institutions, rules, norms, etc.) are no longer adapted to the expected goal. But, at the same time, it denounces a social injustice, since it shows that the qualities considered until then as virtual and as a guarantee of effectiveness can no longer play this role.

Results of this kind, which contain within them a new definition of a given activity or discipline, become a threat for those who, by controlling the system

---

1 P. Bourdieu and J. C. Passeron, *Les Héritiers* (Paris, 1964).
2 'This domestic detail did much harm to the doctor; people did not want to recognize in him talent, while seeing him so poor.' This remark, taken from a novel by Balzac, *Le Cousin Pons,* remains true today, if one considers the psycho-sociological mechanisms which it implies.

of evaluation and of sanctions óf this activity, control in this way its definition. This group, if they are not anxious to allow any discussion concerning the basis of their privileges and their prerogatives, as well as their own identity, have the choice of two means of defence: (a) to deny that these results can be compared with those established hitherto; it is this type of reaction which is usually the source of false distinctions, of exclusions and of 'schools', each having its own definition, rules and code; (b) to refuse to recognize the potentialities of innovation and rationalization of the new result, to attribute it to chance, or to intuition, to reduce it to a technical detail with no general significance, etc. In both these cases, indetermination linked up with the production processes is emphasized, so that the social qualities which filled it out, which served as a guarantee of production and justified its mastery by a group, could continue to play their part. In both cases, there is a deviation of the rules and forms of apprenticeship governing entrance to the activity. To be sure, these rules and forms still provide the skills, but they also serve, in particular, to select and to socialize the members who will not risk questioning the definition which is to be perpetuated. That is to say, those who possess the qualities so far associated with the results which are given value by this definition, and who will have an interest in perpetuating it.[1] Thus, for a long period, until a new definition gets the upper hand — in a way which we shall see further on — the length and the form of apprenticeship, the obstacles which it assumes, its esoteric and specialized nature which distinguishes the competent person from the layman, the institutions and the organizations composed of equals, masters of the system of evaluation, sanction, control and what is called the code of ethics, etc., all these elements which the sociology of the professions presents as the criteria which define and delineate a profession, become — sometimes without the agents concerned being aware — a means of defence, of exclusiveness and of self-perpetuation. They become the support of a whole system of belief which could be called a *professional ideology*. And in this ideology, the most strategic and most profitable dividing line to detect is not so much that which separates the specialist from the laymen — although it too plays its part in the professional ideology on account of the esoteric element, exclusiveness and subordination — but rather that which is

1   There is no point in emphasizing the fact that our line of argument implies that we do not make the usual distinctions between two sectors, on the one hand, that of knowledge (W. Goode, 'The librarian : from occupation to profession?', *The Library Quarterly,* 31 (1961), 306-18), of theory (E. Greenwood, 'Attributes of a Profession', *Social Work,* 2 (1957), 44-55) or of cognitive rationality (T. Parsons, *op. cit.*) in which only 'rational' arguments, motivations and social relationships intervene, setting up innovation and openness, and on the other hand that of 'social values and norms' (E. Greenwood, *op. cit.*) in which tradition, perpetuation and exclusiveness dominate. This purely formal distinction gets rid of a fundamental relation for all sociology of knowledge or of the professions, which ought, on the contrary, to centre its thoughts on the complex relationship which all theoretical argument maintains not only with cultural norms and values but with the social and material advantages which it procures.

intended to distinguish between those who claim their authority from an expertise and a definition which are recognized but threatened and those who hold the potentialities of innovation and rationalization.

As long as the preponderance of the first coincides with an overall balance of social forces, as long as the dominant principles of legitimacy are able to reinforce and maintain this professional ideology, this duality will be hidden or attenuated, the dominant definition of the activity will be presented as the only definition, the rules and the institutions which correspond to it as the only ones adequate. Those who are the bearers of new definitions and new potentialities are liable to what may be called a sort of 'secular anathema', or else they are put in a position of subordination where the fact that they are equipped with a greater degree of rationality enables their role to be reduced to that of 'technicians' or operatives.

Authors have, therefore, had some difficulty, understandably, in delineating the frontiers of a profession and in fixing exactly who belongs or does not belong to a profession on the basis of what they call its 'criteria' or its 'elements'. This is because the latter are no more than elements of the professional ideology and constitute the weapons and the most favoured tools of a struggle in which the frontiers of a profession, the definition of the activities which correspond to it, are the object of a never-ending conflict, and in which the concept of profession itself, expresses only the preponderance of one term of a duality which it is necessary always to put at the centre of the analysis.

This does not mean that it is necessary always to seek the *origin* of this duality in the different social groups or professional categories. Although splits and fusions may subsequently occur and crystalize, this duality, this contradiction, is inherent in all processes of production which contain an important margin of indetermination. Alternatively, and sometimes even at the same time, the attempt at rationality and the emphasizing of indetermination are in opposition to each other, the desire to codify and to make more technical a process of production while at the same time attempting not to give up exclusive control. Two contradictory endeavours in which within the act of codification, there exist the beginnings of withdrawal and the possibility of a takeover by others.

In fact, it is as if the agents of an activity — the individual himself — have constantly to face the following dilemma: either to act with a view to greater and greater control of their practice by making it more technical, by codifying it, but in doing this, to give the possibilities of intervention and access to all those whose social qualities set them outside it. Or on the other hand to make use of their qualities in order to continue to monopolize their field by ideological rationalizations about its nature, its functions, and so to avoid all possibility of intervention and reappraisal from outside.

No longer considered in relation to others who might exercise sanctions and control, but in relation to others excluded from the advantage provided by a given activity, the simplified dilemma can be expressed in the following way: either I seek to have better control over the process of production underlying my activity, and in consequence I rationalize it and it gives me the possibility of making better forecasts, but I give to others, other than my son or a member of my group, the chance of replacing me, or of pursuing the same activity and enjoying its advantages. Or alternatively if I insist that it be my son, or another member of the group possessing the same qualities as myself who replaces me and enjoys these advantages, it is then better to codify less, but I deny myself the possibility of better control of my field and of being in a position to make predictions.

It is this inherent duality and contradiction in the process of production which enable us to understand that the legitimacy of monopoly, the definition and the function of an activity are, by reason of technical changes, social struggles and divisions, perpetually objects of confrontation and conflict. But they also allow us to understand that the evolution and the changes in a profession do not usually take place continuously and according to any self-regulated process, but by the successive formation of systems which seek to close themselves off and to maintain and perpetuate themselves; they achieve this in the course of a certain period, then they are themselves called in question by the very elements which they themselves have helped to make. These elements, bearers of a new definition extolling openness and leaning on forces external to the profession, will try, when victorious, to perpetuate and keep for themselves, in their turn, the privileges, rules and codes which are the basis of this triumphant definition. This mechanism of which we here evoke only the most general aspects will be described more precisely and more completely in the third part of this article and in the analysis of our empirical example. But before embarking upon this, it is necessary to make two comments of a general nature:

(1) This duality makes it possible to explain the contradictory interpretations and the polemics raised by the problem of the role and functions of professions in modern societies. In fact, each orientation which favours only one term of this duality, could show either that the professions constituted closed and esoteric groups whose monopolistic practices were economically dysfunctional and presented a menace to 'democratic' equilibrium[1] or that, on the contrary, thanks to the scientific rationality which governed the rules of entry, they formed relief-groups allowing a greater social mobility whose values, founded on collective control and regulation, in the long term would lead towards social harmony and peace.[2] It could be said that these two orientations are unilateral,

1   Reuben A. Kessel, 'Price discrimination in medicine', *The Journal of Law and Economics*, 1 (1958), 20-53; O. Garceau, *Political life of the American Medical Association* (Cambridge, Mass., 1941); M. Friedman and S. Kuznets, *Income from Independent Medical Practice* (New York, 1945).
2   A. M. Carr-Saunders and P. A. Wilson, *The Professions* (Oxford, 1933); T. H. Marshall,

because each one is founded on one aspect of the duality. It would be more appropriate to add that this type of proposition becomes senseless from the moment the unity of the notion of profession is questioned and when, in order to understand the roles and the functions which it presupposes, it is necessary to take into account the contrary effects which arise from its two terms.

An analogous argument can be made in order to take account of the existence of two contradictory themes in sociological literature: one of professionalization and the other of de-professionalization.[1] It would be seen that there too, each of the two themes can be developed only because it takes account of one single aspect of this double dynamic. It is this unilateral orientation which finally permits the explanation of a number of contradictions and ambiguities in sociological literature and which authors reject by moral wishes or evaluative propositions.[2] It would be possible to provide many quotations but we shall content ourselves with drawing attention to the following typical and significant words of Carr-Saunders. Speaking of associations which train their own members, he writes: 'It is no means true that the interest of the organization is confined to technical education. A charge of exclusiveness has been brought against them because they demand evidence of good general education before specialization. *But it is not their fault* that only a small percentage of the population can fulfill these requirements.'[3] A simple evaluative formula (which we have underlined) allows the author easily to get rid of the problem, which we consider to be the central one from the sociological point of view. It is, in a word through not knowing how to place the contradiction right at the centre of the analysis that the study of the professions often seems to result in contradictions in the analysis.

(2) The second remark concerns the changes which the I/T ratio undergoes in any given activity. In fact, under the action of increasing rationality, and of the 'counter-action' which consists in emphasizing indetermination, the definition of the activity and its social function change. But so too does this I/T ratio change. That is to say that the 'attempt at rationality' and 'the valorization of indetermination' are only descriptive of general patterns about which one ought to be able to be specific and to particularize, not only in each con-

'The Recent History of Professionalism in relation to Social Structure', *Canadian Journal of Economics and Political Science*, 5 (1939) reprinted in *Citizenship and Social Class* (Cambridge, 1950); J. Ben-David, 'Professions in the Class Sytem of Present-day Societies', *Current Sociology*, 12, 3 (1963-4), 247-98.

1 H. L. Wilensky, 'The Professionalization of Everyone?', *American Journal of Sociology*, 70 (1964), 137-58.

2 The text of Greenwood (*op. cit.*) which presents the general attributes of a profession is the most curious in this respect. We find original and lucid remarks which deserve to be enlarged upon but are continually cut short or thinned out by observations inspired by the well-known 'pattern variables' of Parsons which either contradict them or deprive them of all heuristic possibility.

3 Carr-Saunders and Wilson, *op. cit.*

crete example, but also in each phase of the history of an activity. Here it would be possible to see an outline of Weber's pattern of increased rationalization or the theme of the end of struggles and ideologies which certain authors have substituted for Weber's idea of 'disenchantment of the world'. But in fact with the increasing rationality of an activity the conflicts and the ideologies which are bound to it do not disappear but change their point of application. It may be suggested that three phases generally correspond to the history of an occupation and these partially overlap. In the first, both the professional ideology put out by the dominant members and the struggles develop around the conditions governing the existence, in the activity in question, of scientific rationality or transferable techniques. In the second, it is the role played by the latter, in the means of attaining the results, which is saturated with ideology and which is at the centre of each confrontation. Finally in the third, it is the social function of the activity and of production which becomes primarily the object of conflict and of ideological rationalizations. The problem of the social function is in fact continually present, but it becomes central only when 'cognitive rationality' saturates an activity in an overwhelming fashion and when a precise definition of functions is realized.

The empirical case which will make this abstract essay more explicit and on the analysis of which we shall now embark, bridges the second and third phases.

THE DOUBLE DYNAMIC WHICH DETERMINES AND IS DIRECTED BY THE FRENCH UNIVERSITY-HOSPITAL CORPS

It is not an exaggeration to say that the Debré reform is the most important attempt at change which has been made since the *Consultat* which, by numerous laws, ratified the beginning of the end of the *Ancien Régime* and of the French Revolution. In the following paragraph we shall describe neither the content of this reform nor all of the conditions which made its promulgation possible, nor the reasons which permit an explanation of its very relative practical success. We shall concentrate our attention on the main people involved in this attempted transformation, namely the university-hospital *corps,* and we shall analyse it in accordance with the theoretical points of view suggested above. We shall examine this social and professional category which at the beginning of the nineteenth century monopolized three types of production: (*a*) the production of medical knowledge; (*b*) the transmission of this knowledge, that is to say the production of practitioners; (*c*) the application of this knowledge, that is to say the production of medical care in the hospitals. We shall show how this category came to be considered as the driving force in medical knowledge and the principal builder of modern medicine. We shall then be in a position to explain the subsequent establishment of a system of defence, extolling a fixed definition of medical knowledge and its social function, and intended to perpetuate and to preserve this monopoly, the rules, norms and values on which it is based, in the face of a double threat: (1) The threat born of socio-economic struggles and changes which sought to redefine the social aim of medical and hospital activity by calling in question the conditions of production of hospital care and the quality of such care. (2) The other threat produced by scientific and technical changes — issuing partly, therefore, from the 'professional' group itself — which set itself the task of redefining the nature of medical knowledge by disputing the quality of what was produced and transmitted.

THE EXTERNAL DYNAMIC OR THE SOCIO-ECONOMIC FRONT

The beginning of the nineteenth century in France confirmed the rise of the bourgeoisie, and the triumph of liberalism. The doctors who belonged to this great bourgeoisie came into hospitals which had been freed from the ascendancy of the religious orders shaken by the Revolution, and freed from the whims and desires of the former founders. The hospitals were now placed under the formal authority of the *communes* which were made up of these new triumphant notables, of whom the doctors themselves formed a part.

These hospitals owed their existence, above all, to the legacies and gifts of the well-off classes. The doctor who was a product of these classes, and who belonged to a liberal profession came there for some hours each day 'as a visitor'.[1] His purpose was to perform a charitable act and he drew no material profit from the care he gave to the needy who were the only patients in the hospitals during all of the nineteenth century and at the beginning of the twentieth. He could, on the other hand, profit from an inexhaustible source of objects of observation made possible by the accumulation of a large amount of 'human material'; hospital service constituted in effect — as we shall show later — the ideal place for observation and research and a kind of 'natural laboratory' of the period where clinical knowledge was progressing and the training and initiation of future doctors was being achieved.

What Foucault calls 'the terms of the contract drawn up by wealth and poverty in the organization of clinical experience', and which were given concrete form by the post-revolutionary laws of the *Directoire* and the *Consulat,* governed, and still essentially govern, in the middle of this present century, the organization and the activity of hospitals.

'And on account of its reciprocal structure the rich man clearly sees the usefulness of coming to the aid of the poor man in hospital: by paying to have him looked after, he will thereby be paying so that the illnesses by which he himself might be attacked will be better known; that which is benevolence with regard to the poor is transformed into knowledge which is applicable to the rich.'

1 R. Savatier, 'Les métamorphoses de la médecine hospitalière dans leurs modernes expressions juridiques', *Droit Social,* nos. 9-10 (1962), 479.

Following this, there is a quotation from an author writing at the end of the *Ancien Régime*:

'The charitable gifts are going to lessen the ills of the poor, from which comes new knowledge for the conservation of the rich. Yes, rich benefactors, noble gentlemen, this sick man who is laid down on the bed which you have provided, is experiencing at this moment the illness with which you yourself will soon be stricken; he will recover or he will die; but whatever the outcome, his fate may enlighten your doctor and save your life.'

Following which Foucault concludes : 'These then are the terms of the contract drawn up by wealth and poverty in the organization of clinical experience.'[1]

It would be quite inadequate to think that one could analyse this doctor's situation or his role or function which have changed little in a century and a half, on the basis of the theme of a profession inserted into a bureaucratic organization or of that of professionalization. If doctors ruled themselves in the very heart of the hospitals and possessed rules and norms which made them masters and over-lords in their departments, and if the administrators fell in with their wishes and the sick agreed with their prescriptions and with their observations, this was not only because they alone possessed knowledge and skill. It was because the anxiety and the mystery which are linked with illness aroused on the part of every potential sick person an emotional investment, an attitude of subordination and of dependence, which was translated in the attribution to the doctor of potentialities and almost charismatic power. It was also because the doctor possessed a political and social power due to his class origin and to the web of influence which he wove by taking care of the powerful and important figures in his region, these *notables* to whom he himself belonged and who by their legacies and their gifts subsidized the hospitals. Hospital administrators and sick people were certainly 'laymen' but they were also members of the lower social categories, being more often in a situation of subordination or dependence, and, having provisionally internalized the liberal ideological system, which justified the organization of society as a whole and also the organization of the hospitals, which, as we have just seen, was a particular expression of it.

Likewise, to try to describe the autonomy and the power of self-government which this group acquired in terms of an occupation which was to become 'professionalized' would seem completely inappropriate. The importance of the hospital *corps*, in the hospital as well as in society, and the new clinical medicine which it fashioned and defined, were the product of the social conflicts which reached their culmination in the French Revolution. At the end of an extraordinary period of creative effervescence in this sphere, when, while still believing in the myth of the end of illness, of misery, and of hospitals, innumerable new

1 M. Foucault, *Naissance de la Clinique* (Paris, 1963).

ventures were embarked upon, the 'medicine at liberty'[1] of the Revolution found itself framed by liberal laws which authorized the triumph of the ideas of a social class, of a medical and hospital organization, and thereby, of a particular conception of medicine. The hospital doctors were, in this process, those who gathered the fruits of victory over the Faculties, the medical guilds and the religious orders of the hospitals, all of which were so many closed and esoteric organizations of the *Ancien Régime*, themselves possessing their own definitions of medioine and sickness which saw their social privileges totter and then vanish along with the medico-philosophical systems connected to them.

There was not therefore, within the hospital, a confrontation between a profession and a bureaucracy; nor was there a process of professionalization. What there was consisted firstly of the victory of one class and of one socio-economic system which produced an adequate hospital organization and, secondly, of the development of clinical medicine which — as we shall see later — was linked with it. Throughout a century and a half the hospital doctors could enjoy this double victory; during all this time a certain number of implicit principles were the basis of, and the guide for, their activities: (1) They alone were masters and overlords in the hospital services created for the needy, where they practised for two to three hours per day. (2) They belonged to a liberal profession and were ruled by their own system of self-government. (3) Thanks to their origin and their political power, and in view of the way in which hospitals were financed, they orientated and determined what might today be called 'Health policy' and the ideology which justified it.

The scientific and technical changes, the breaks made with socio-economic liberalism were, little by little, to call these principles into question. We lack space to describe these changes in detail; we can only concentrate here on one strategic point wherein the essential can be best understood. And this is the creation and then the spread of Social Security.

Social Security was the result of by no means recent struggles on the part of the workers' organizations to attempt to substitute for the ideas of charity and assistance those of the right to good health and security for everyone. Born in 1930, it became general in 1947, just after the Liberation, at a time when the balance of social forces was to the advantage of the Trade Unions and those political parties which represented the working class.

The consequences of the creation of Social Security — which Imbert[2] calls the 'revolution of the twentieth century in this field' — are fundamental ones. Its organizations, on which sat representatives of the salaried class, constituted a 'third party' which intervened between the sick man and the doctor. The latter could no longer claim to be doing an act of charity since the patient paid him fees through the intermediary of Social Security. Moreover, this latter played a

1 *Ibid.*
2 J. Imbert, *Les hôpitaux en France* (Paris, 1958).

greater and greater part in the investments and the expenses of the hospital. It financed costly equipment which the growing technicality of medicine demanded and which only the public hospitals could hope to pay for. This participation was thus substituted more and more for the traditional methods of financing which were of communal or private origin (legacies and donations). At the same time a greater number of patients from a much more varied social background, were thus brought to frequent the hospital. Members of the bourgeoisie were often obliged to choose this institution rather than a private clinic, which lacked the basic and costly technical apparatus, and so they came face to face with an arrangement reserved until then only for the underprivileged classes of society. The material conditions and a whole style of human relationships which had prevailed for the latter for more than a century became 'visible' and a source of intolerable scandal once the upper social classes, representing 'public opinion' had to experience them themselves. Numerous books and newspaper articles were published on the 'scandal of the public hospitals'. They denounced the delapidation of the buildings, the lack of staff, the condescending attitude of the · doctors, but also very often their absence or negligence. They stigmatized the differences in the relationships which were set up between the doctor and the patient according to whether the patient went for a consultation at the hospital or at the private clinic of the practitioner. The Audit Office (*Cour des Comptes*) spoke of 'abuse' and quoted figures of doctors' fees considered excessive in relation to the time spent with the patient, etc. In such a context the organization of the Social Security could legitimately consider themselves representatives of the patients, and what is more, of each potential patient, which is to say of every worker. They demanded the right to inspect the use of what they called the 'public funds' or the 'investment of the workers' whose trustees they were. Thus they brought together certain trends existing at the centre of the State organizations such as the Plan, the Ministry of Health and Ministry of Finance whose aim was the better coordination and the rationalization of the organization of hospitals throughout the country.

And what was primarily involved and contested in all these criticisms was the conditions of practice of the hospital doctor, whose liberal nature was considered to be the greatest obstacle to changes facilitating the realization of a rational hospital policy which would be just and humane. The hospital doctors were no longer confronted with a docile and conciliatory administration; they saw appearing in opposition to them a bureaucratic authority with a financial basis, and yet which put in concrete form social demands, considered as a symbol of the worker's victory. And these demands called into question the juridical framework which until then sanctioned the doctors' power and autonomy.

The terms of the conflict crystallized in the year 1953 concerning the theme of full-time work. The idea that the hospitals could no longer function as in the past and that the presence of the doctors was necessary for more than two to three hours per day was apparently accepted by both protagonists. Both declared that, in essence, an increasing rationality was imperative, that full-time work could lead to an improvement in diagnostics, to a better supervision of patients, and to less expenditure and to shorter periods of hospitalization – in short to an increased efficiency, profitability and humanity. But the practical realization of this idea sets the Social Security in opposition to the medical associations. The latter defended the formula of 'full-time service' which provided an option whereby the doctors guaranteed the continued functioning of the service by organizing *themselves* the work-shifts and replacements wherever technical considerations, of which they claimed to be the only judges, demanded presence over a long period. They declared that such a solution enabled the desired goals to be reached while necessitating the minimum expense and upheaval. But the strongest point of their argument consisted in linking indissolubly their technical autonomy with the liberal principles which governed their activity and which made them alone guarantors of the quality and the humanity of their medical care.

'Full-time, freely chosen, according to a pliable formula, and of high quality: wholehearted agreement. Widespread and obligatory full-time, according to one formula only, totalitarian and at a cheap rate: never. And no *ukase* will rule the day.'[1]

It was this unjustified association between two quite distinct types of freedoms which the Social Security denounced and which, moreover, was well-placed to show how the quality and the humanity of the medical care were not necessarily bound to liberalism, and how, in any case, the different prerogatives which the doctors enjoyed until then were used only to their own advantage and profit. So, without questioning their technical independence or their professional code of ethics, the Social Security expected to impose the solution of the 'full-time doctor' which made of the practitioner a sort of civil servant attached to his service and to nothing else. This would remove from the most prestigious elements of the medical group the possibility of 'having their cake and eating it', of using the autonomy left to them by the liberal system, in order to devote themselves essentially to their private patients and clinics, and so take advantage of the unbalanced competition between the public sector and the private one. Were they not to a great extent answerable, implicitly or explicitly, for the low standard of the public hospitals since their interests were certainly not focused there? And did they not accentuate this 'unbalanced' competitive struggle *by taking the cream* of the 'good risks' to the profit of the private clinics, leaving the difficult and costly cases to the hospitals? Only such a freedom made it possible for example,

1 P. Mollaret, 'La médecine à temps plein dans les hôpitaux de Paris', *La Presse Médicale*, supplément 58 (1957).

'to build or to arrange to have built a clinic which will work at 100 per cent capacity, by the side of a modern hospital, obliged to have the most highly perfected equipment, but which only works at 30-40 per cent capacity. The same doctors practise in both establishments, and organise themselves to draw profit from the burdensome equipment of the hospital, and also from the comfort offered to the patients by the clinic.'[1]

Here is a quick outline of the confrontation of ideas and convictions which shook the hospital scene and the administrative organizations concerned around the year 1953, and at the outcome of which all the medical associations took up positions. At the same time liberal medicine was also challenged in terms of the simple practitioner by the same Social Security which wanted to impose fixed rates of fees. From this battle which has been called the battle of the medical charter,[2] the Social Security emerged victorious in spite of some strikes and a large minority of refusals to 'adhere to the charter'. As regards full-time, the Social Security did not have the same success. However it succeeded in negotiating an agreement with the most highly reputed doctors' organization, the Joint-Syndicate of the doctors of the Paris hospitals which made allowances for two parallel experimental attempts of a duration of two years, in ten services in the Paris region.[3] Five of them worked according to the 'full-time service' formula, five others according to the 'full-time doctor' alternative proposed by the Social Security. The results of such an experiment were intended to guide subsequent decisions.

Therefore, on this 'front', where the group which occupies our attention had to confront, at hospital level, the repercussions of economic and social changes, it still seemed to be all-powerful. To be sure, a fundamental doctrinal debate shook it, and revealed some unsuspected flaws; certainly, one of its organizations, the most prestigious one, agreed to negotiate with an adversary, which radically called into question the value-system to which the doctors subscribed. Moreover, much blame was cast upon it by the majority of medical syndicates adhering to the *status quo*, who saw in these experiments a breach, the consequences of which might well raise doubts about the foundations of liberal medicine. Nevertheless, the principles which by and large governed the activity of hospital doctors were the very principles which dated from the beginning of the nineteenth century and it was difficult to foresee what use would finally be made of experiments from which each party expected results which would confirm its own thesis.

It is in fact important to underline the fact that in this argument where there were no unanimously accepted intrinsic criteria for evaluating medical production and where the parties concerned referred to an external criterion of evaluation,

---

1 Actual cases frequently quoted by higher staff of the Social Security.
2 H. Hatzfeld, *Le grand tournant de la médecine libérale* (Paris, 1963).
3 P. Mollaret, 'Naissance d'une médecine hospitalière à temps plein', *La Presse Médicale*, supplément 53 (1954); 'La médecine à temps plein dans les hôpitaux de Paris', *La Presse Médicale*, suppléments 50, 51, 52, 53 (1955).

liberalism or not, the debate turned in fact on the problem of the social function of hospital medicine and, more generally, of medicine pure and simple. It was this social objective which was implicitly at the centre of the polemics which became the object of the conflict, and it is therefore only from the consequences of this conflict that it will be possible to redefine it. And in the same way it will not be possible to redefine the medical activity itself, except on the basis of the outcome of another conflict which divided 'the profession' itself, and whose history we shall now rapidly outline.

THE INTERNAL DYNAMIC OR THE SCIENTIFIC FRONT

In the preceding analysis we have considered the activity of hospital doctors only from the point of view of the medical care provided by them. We must emphasize that is was on this group too that responsibility fell for the teaching and the furthering of medical knowledge. The state of medical science in the nineteenth century which was essentially clinical, demanded the combination in one and the same person of these three 'functions'. With medical knowledge consisting above all in widening and making more precise anatomical-pathological knowledge, these could be acquired only as a result of long practice and of precise and laborious observation. It was, therefore, the *clinicians* who having seen and observed a great deal amongst their own patients but most of all in the hospitals, were in a position to classify and order their observations, and could transmit an experiment or a piece of medical knowledge, and so bring about an advancement of the latter.

The System in its Heuristic Phase

The conditions in which appeared the experiment and the whole clinical terminology — 'the first scientifically structured terminology devoted to the individual' — have been brilliantly described by Foucault in *La naissance de la clinique.*[1] A great part of this work is devoted to the debates, experiments and innovations of the revolutionary period, which favoured the expansion of this field of study and created in the hospitals an unlimited range of possibilities where it could fully come into its own. We have already quoted a significant extract which suggested how the class structure of the period and the ideological system which corresponded to it could amply justify the 'scientific' use which could be made of ready patients in hospital. This point is of great importance if we wish to understand the great rise of the French clinical school at the beginning of the nineteenth century. But to it we must add three other structural and organizational conditions.

(a) The existence in Paris of a concentration of hospitals, exceptional in

[1] Foucault, *op. cit.*

E X

Europe, thus providing incomparable opportunities for observation and investigation.

(b) The founding in the hospital system of a process of apprenticeship and of selection which was completely appropriate, designed to create a sort of 'medical elite'.

(c) The fact that the faculties of medicine chose their instructors from among these carefully selected and highly qualified clinical experts from hospitals.

(a) On the first point we shall simply refer the reader to Shryock[1] and to Imbert[2] who quote relevant figures; it is the two other points which deserve our further attention.

(b) Parallel to and conjointly with the official instruction of the faculties and schools of medicine which awarded the doctorate and trained the general practitioners, there existed — still exists — a series of 'hospital competitive examinations' which the students of the 'elite' sat and which alone allowed entry to hospital appointments. We also find here the ratification of new ideas and of suggestions resulting from the Revolution and even from the end of the *Ancien Régime*, whose purpose was to counterbalance and even to make a breach in the petrified teaching of the Faculties who were more preoccupied with 'systems' and 'rhetoric' than with observations and facts. It was in this way that the *Externat* and the *Internat*, both founded in 1802, but prepared for by numerous earlier debates, appeared as 'progressive' institutions, in the social sense as much as in the scientific sense of the term. Based upon liberal and egalitarian ideas, they claimed to give an equal chance to all students whatever their origin, and leave to 'competition' the demonstration of ability. They sanctioned, moreover, the victory of those who defended the practical and positive tendency in medicine: for the first time the titles given to doctors and surgeons were considered to have equivalent value. This fact is in itself highly significant in relation to our discussion, when it is known that more than centenarian conflicts opposed the two guilds and that the first had the upper hand and despised the second for their 'lack of general culture', and for the essentially manual work which they provided. Moreover, the surgeons, most often compared to barbers, had usually the subordinate role of handiwork men for the 'erudite' who was the doctor.[3]

It is difficult to claim that the anonymity of the competitive examination and the principle of equality of opportunity were more respected in the past than at

1 R. H. Shryock, *Histoire de la médecine moderne* (Paris, 1956).
2 Imbert, *op. cit.*
3 These are the terms in which they are described by a doctor who is trying to write a history of medicine. 'Less restrained by general culture, nearer to the people, and dissatisfied, the surgeon will go more willingly and by instinct, to the subversive groups.' P. Delaunay, 'L'évolution médicale du XVIème au XXème siècle', *Bulletin de la Société Française d'Histoire de la Médecine*, 22 (1928), 17-56.

present. There are on this subject criticism and grievances which date from the beginning of the nineteenth century. The important thing is to know that at this time, and for more than fifty years, 'social selection' did not clash with scientific selection. There is no doubt that these competitive examinations were intended to choose the members of a social elite who would be responsible for taking care of those who were part of this same elite, but contrary to what was to happen later, these privileged students became at the same time the scientific elite. The work necessary for the preparation of the competitive examinations, and the practical work which was demanded of them at the hospital, gained for them a knowledge and breadth of experience quite adequate for the medicine of the time.

What then was the *Internat*, this so highly valued institution founded in 1802, and which, up to the present time has been described as the 'keystone or foundation of French medicine'? It was a difficult examination which made possible the selection during their fourth or fifth year of study in the Faculty of students who were already *externes* and as such had already been selected by prior examination. Its preparation necessitated an apprenticeship of two, three or even four years, in anatomy, pathology, and semiology, fields of study which, at the time, made up the essential foundations of medical knowledge. Once nominated, the *interne* became for four or five years, working full-time, the 'mainspring' of a hospital department, in a system consisting of an eminent *patron* and his assistants (all former *internes*). The intense work which he had to carry out, the variety and the number of cases presented to him at the hospital, the responsibilities entrusted to him, the nature of the system in which he was placed and the opportunities for discussion which it offered, the lessons and the guidance which he in his turn gave to the external students and to the undergraduates formed a busy and ideal school and an incomparable clinical experience. It was, moreover, from among these internes, who had already gone twice through a selection-board and who had been broken in to the hospital work that, again by examination, the 'assistants' and the 'doctors and surgeons of the hospitals' were recruited who were to become the future heads of the departments. But what made this series of tests worthwhile was not so much the successive selection which it made possible *as the adequacy of the criteria of selection for the medical and scientific necessities of the time.* The knowledge acquired during the preparation for these examinations, as much as the experience which they provided, was in some way adapted to the needs of medical sciences of the period. Moreover, one can even say that this sytem formed a privileged driving force in medical progress: because the practitioners distributed throughout the departments possessed a thorough knowledge of the sciences which were useful to them; because the hospital ward provided ideal opportunities for practice and observation where a whole team, could exchange and discuss its experiences; because this group could at the same time fulfil a function of nursing and one of research. Thus it was in the hospital wards, these 'natural laboratories', that medical science was born and fashioned.

Shryock even tells us that the French school, renowned in the nineteenth century to the point where 'it is not an exaggeration to say that modern medicine was born in Paris between 1800 and 1850', paid for this reputation by being accused of 'therapeutic nihilism'. He declares that the thorough exploration of the principal branches of anatomical-pathology was sometimes made to the detriment of healing and the interest of the patients and that in the polemics which opposed Laennec and Broussais, the latter loved to accuse Laennec of 'being more interested in autopsies than in ways of preventing them'.[1]

(c) It is therefore understandable that this hospital framework where doctors, chosen and trained by this succession of examinations, worked, became for the faculties of medicine a sort of 'pool' from which they recruited the majority of their teachers and researchers. The well-known *agrégation* of medicine, a 'university' examination which opened up the way to a Faculty chair, was the last barrier which the hospital doctors had to overcome before being considered for a chair. But it is important to stress that this progression did not follow any formal rules; it constituted a custom, considered, deservedly at that time, to be the most practical.

There was, to be sure, in the faculties, a purely academic path, which the socially less well-placed students chose, or those who were not attracted by practical clinical work or by the hospital, and who devoted themselves entirely to activities of research and teaching, but this was little followed. Some went to the dissecting room and the laboratories of the faculty, after having passed through the *internat*; others followed their apprenticeship there right from the beginning under the direction of *chefs de travaux* and professors. Some of these 'fundamentalists' as they gradually came to be called, succeeded in presenting their *agrégation* and in becoming professors. But they formed a small minority in comparison with those hospital surgeons and doctors, called in France *Chirurgiens et Médecins de Hôpitaux*, who, after a career consisting mainly of hospital and clinical practice, passed the *agrégation* much more easily and canvassed for a faculty chair.

The teaching body of the medical faculties was then made up, on the one hand, of a great majority of practitioners belonging to the most privileged classes having had the chance to sit the hospital exams, then the *agrégation*, and thus practising a teaching role while still being a member of a liberal profession; on the other hand it was composed of a purely academic minority, of more modest social origin, having the status of civil servants. This unequal and socially differentiated division depended on no official regulations. It was the expression of a social structure, and the result of custom; it expressed a fact which, as will be understood after what has just been said, corresponded very adequately to

1 Shryock, *op. cit.*

the state of medical knowledge of the time.

So for more than fifty years, social selection and scientific selection coincided; those who by their social background attained the highest status and were in the majority within the system, acquired at the same time the skills and the clinical experience which shaped in a determining way progress and medical knowledge at the time. The new scientific discoveries were gradually to break this coincidence asunder.

The System Seeks to Perpetuate and Maintain Itself

It is, oddly enough, in France too, but in the second half of the nineteenth century that the specialists place the emergence of new fields of study which were to enable medical science to progress in a new way. These were: physiology with Magendie and Claude Bernard and bacteriology with Pasteur.[1] It is important to know that already Claude Bernard had failed the *agrégation* and could not have a chair in the Faculty of Medicine in Paris, that Pasteur was not a doctor but a chemist and worked neither in a hospital nor in a Faculty. These details are significant and seem *a posteriori* 'predictive' in so far as they suggest that as soon as these new basic fields of study were launched and had proved to be fertile there were men, a system built up of acquired positions, traditions, customs, formal and informal norms and a relationship of social forces, already established. The valorization of the clinical orientation in medicine and the attachment to the norms and balances of forces underlying it which were to be responsible for the fame of the French school were gradually to become ideological rationalizations and the instruments of defence of a sort of 'social caste' when faced with changes imposed by these expanding fields of study. The aim of this 'caste' was more to preserve its acquired positions and privileges and perpetuate its own identity than to open up and to share in the new stock of scientific knowledge which was to be progressively built up outside itself.

This will be made more precise. What it is essential to note in what is to follow and which could relate just as much to the sociology of the professions as to the sociology of knowledge, is not only that there is a possibility of understanding how medical progress and the development of biology have escaped from a previously fertile system. It is above all the fact that an organization and a relationship of social forces have fixed a specific definition of medical knowledge, to which a system of valorization and sanctions corresponded, and of which for nearly a century it has been difficult to say that it was better or less good than any other.

It was in fact by the creation of new Faculty chairs and around them that the

1 It would be interesting to study the exact conditions which favoured the birth of these new fields of study, and it would lead to a somewhat different interpretation to declare, on the one hand, that it was not a question of 'birth' but of systematization of ideas and of former discoveries, and on the other, to investigate how these fields of study (especially physiology) were the extension of certain anatomical-pathologists' investigations. See Shryock *ibid* on this subject.

new fields of study were able to develop. In fact, with these no longer dealing exclusively with man, and acquiring an experimental character, the strategic bond of research was expected to move from the hospital services towards the laboratories which were liable to be created around the teaching chairs. But all through the nineteenth century and right up to the last few years the greatest number of chairs, and the most prestigious, remained those associated with the clinics. The 'functional' proportion, originally an expression of a given state in the medical sciences, became gradually in the Faculty Councils a semi-formal law governing the balance of forces to which one can even give a numerical value: two clincial chairs to one fundamentalist'. If then the creation of new chairs and of new teaching depended on the public authorities and on generous donations it was the maintenance and the perpetuation of this 'equilibrium' which above all determined the title of the chair, even the choice of its holder. Even when, later than in other countries, chairs in the basic fields of study were created (in 1907 the Paris Faculty of Medicine had no chair for Pasteur's science of bacteriology), they often formed what could be called 'temporary chairs' where a clinician trained in a hospital would wait for a few years before obtaining a clinical chair, the final and most highly valued accolade. The interpretation of the contents of the teaching itself was only another expression of the balance of forces in the Faculty Councils. Thus, for example, the chair of 'experimental medicine' − also created late − was not considered to be a chair in a 'basic' field of study but, like a chair of medicine, it was assigned to the clinicians.

In fact, one could have expected these professors, even those elected for a temporary period, to develop around these chairs and in connection with their hospital services an activity of busy and creative research (some rare and exceptional personalities did this), but two principal reasons made this difficult, if not impossible.

(1) Only clinical medicine could be content with a dividing of time between the private patients and the hospital. Hospital practice was a necessary condition for research and discovery and even extended the private activitiy of hospital doctors. The expansion of the experimental sciences which transported the place of research from the hospital service to the laboratories, obliged doctors who wanted to devote themselves to research to give up an appreciable part of their incomes. It was, on the whole, the opposite that happened. The hospital doctor had a far bigger private practice than his predecessors, and neither the hospital services nor the Faculty chairs were busy with important research.

(2) A still more important reason was that the obstacle course marked by examinations, which it was still necessary to follow in order to arrive at the supreme accolades − including the chair − no longer prepared him to assume this kind of responsibility. The different barriers to selection which it was necessary to cross, among them the well-known *Internat*, still made necessary the training in subject-matter, essay forms and their presentation, which had

little connection with the practice of the new medicine. Up till the middle of the twentieth century questions in the *Internat,* on which candidates concentrated all their effort for three to four years, were exclusively based on anatomy and pathology.

The answers to these 'questions' which together were considered the 'mass of the knowledge required by the best qualified juries'[1] were learned by heart, in stereotyped forms, by entire generations. The real apprenticeship of the *interne* began only after this harassing trial. Here are the terms used by an eminent hospital doctor to describe it:

'These exercises of the mind had the culminating point in competitive examinations such as that of the *Internat.* In order to achieve the title of *interne* in the hospitals of Paris it was necessary, I assure you, to spend as many hours training oneself in the art of seducing hostile or distrustful juries, as in learning the real fundamentals of the job of doctor. The great "lecturers" and the masters of the "cross examination" on whom our success depended, had to be masters of eloquence as much as of biology. I remember even today the revelation that Jean Gosset's exposition on the sensitivity of a sworn surgeon to certain forms of verbal imprudence on the subject of therapeutic surgery was for me. It is to this prowess of style that I owe my becoming an *interne* and I am ashamed to state that, at that time, even if I had, thanks to Jean Gossett, Jean Bernard and some others, learned the art of seducing a jury, even if I knew how to discourse with charm on the electrocardiogram, or the treatment of a diabetic with insulin, I was in fact incapable of reading a real cardiogram or of treating a diabetic in flesh and blood. Of this superficial, verbose, and unreal approach to medicine, there were some of us in my generation who were to feel the deepest disgust.'[2]

This extract dates from 1963 but criticisms in this vein had often been expressed since the beginning of the century.[3] In fact, the function of these different stages of 'training' and of selection, supervised by the hospital doctors themselves, changed. They became in each region, and in each Faculty seat, barriers and *social trials* which a local group possessing a monopoly forced those who tried to become a member of it to undergo. The 'art of seducing a jury' by adequate rhetoric and the 'prowess of style', which indicated social rank, geographic or religious origin, became the predominant criteria of selection and choice. The different exams where the juries decided beforehand by trading with 'votes' who would be selected thus resembled more and more *rites de passage* ratifying adherence to an elite strata, and the progression of these examinations consisted of a process of socialization and selection making it possible to choose those who were considered worthy to belong to this strata and capable of perpetuating its rules and values.

1   G. Herand, *Histoire d'une institution : l'internat des hôpitaux de Paris,* Thèse de doctorat, Faculté de Médecine de Paris (1952).
2   J. Hamburger, *Conseil aux étudiants en médecine de mon service* (Paris, 1963).
3   F. Jayle, 'Du recrutement de chirurgiens des hospitaux', *La Presse Médicale,* 20 (1904), 153-5.

Progress along this ascending pathway depended also on the service rendered by the junior to his superior. At each stage the 'pupil' would receive in exchange for his services and his loyalty to a master the benefit of the experience which he had acquired under his master's protection and the fruit of his past devotion. With each master trying thus to secure the career of his pupils it was up to the juniors to 'back the best one', which meant the professor who, by virtue of the field of study which he represented (the more traditional it was, the more prestigious) and by the same token his influence, his credit and his power, gave them the best chance of getting as high as possible in the hierarchy. For, to progress in the ranks there corresponded a possible increase in income. The clinician working in the hospital in the mornings only, adjusted the rate of his professional fee each time he moved on a stage. This economic asepct tended to maintain those different systems which have been called 'feudal', since the 'exchange of services' which implicitly bound together master and candidates included the patients whom the latter would be sending to the man who would 'judge' them in the future.

This enables us to understand that every scientific deviation, every geographical displacement and every non-conformist initiative were penalized by the very rules of the system. This affords a glimpse of the reasons which allowed the latter to be called 'self-perpetuating' since nothing could be developed or increased, which had not already been traditionally approved. It is this single essentially clinical *voie royale* which gave access to the highest incomes, the power and the prestige bound to the university-hospital appointments. And no one could follow this path with any chance of success except those who, by their origins, were well-placed in the social pyramid, and who were most capable of perpetuating it.

The Anti-System

In fact the system still produced practitioners and professors considered to be great clinical men, some 'fundamentalists', who all very skillfully integrated the new therapeutic medicine and discoveries. But the creation of the latter took place outside the system. Nevertheless, at the end of the nineteenth century, criticisms and violent arguments were raised within this very *milieu.*[1] This explains how, at this period, several *internes,* among them Roux, a pupil of Pasteur, or much later Nicolle (the last French Nobel prize-winner in 1928, before Lwoff, Monod and Jacob in 1965, all four from the *Institut Pasteur,* and none of whom had passed the hospital exams) left this circuit, for a longer or a shorter period, in order to be initiated into the new sciences and techniques. This could happen only in the few research institutes which existed outside of the hospitals or the medical faculties: there were the Laboratories of the Faculties of Science, the Institut Curie, the Museum of Natural History, the Collège de France and the Institut Pasteur. But, up to the end of

1   *Ibid.*

the Second World War the number of these 'non conformists' were few since
no reward was forthcoming to ratify or to acknowledge their skill. They had
to improvise their scientific education at their own risk and peril, while well
knowing that they were placing themselves on the outer fringe of a system and
scientific orientation which was socially as well as materially the most
'rewarding' and the most highly valued.

The upheavals and splits brought about by the Occupation and Resistance,
even if they did not affect the system as such, favoured the creation of a medical
resistance group with leftist political tendencies. Along with some *grands patrons*
of this university-hospital aristocracy were grouped practitioners and researchers
of more modest origin. In the atmosphere of solidarity and of hope of rebirth
created by the Occupation, this group worked out, already under the direction
of Robert Debré,[1] plans for a complete transformation of the organization of
Health, within the framework of a complete remodelling of French society.
These novel and courageous ideas did not come to fruition, however, and the
system continues to function, broadly speaking, as in the past. In contrast, as
we have indicated, Social Security became widespread, and more and more
organs of basic research were created which did not demand of the candidates
these 'socio-scientific' titles deriving from success in these examinations. Young
people could enter who not only did not wish to, but what is more, had no
possibility of following the only worthwhile career opened up by the *voie
royale*.

So, in the years which followed the Liberation there was formed gradually,
on the outer fringes of the system described above, a whole category of
doctors and scientists of whom it is difficult to say that they formed a profession, or a univocally definable group but whose importance was to increase.
Some belonged to the 'fundamentalists' already mentioned, some were biologists
in the service of chiefs of hospital staff, others even worked in the institutes of
research. The characteristics which were common to them all, and which were
to enable them to constitute a potential force, are the following:

(*a*) The fact that they had taken the risk of not following the traditional
clinical path or had no choice but not to follow it made them more flexible, as
much in the geographical sense as the scientific. Several of them, moreover,
encouraged by certain 'patrons' who, though members of the system were
mindful of its limitations, travelled abroad, went into the study of biology and
discovered the importance of this field in medical scholarship and practice.

(*b*) The very form of the activity involved in this new type of medicine
convinced them that the liberal character of the profession was in no way bound
to the quality of medical production or to their own personal selfrealization. On
the contrary, they were tempted to believe that these would be better favoured
in those large organizations which alone possessed the burdensome equipment

1 R. Debré, *Médecine, santé publique, population* (Paris, 1945).

which modern medical or scientific work demands, and that the existence and the smooth running of these organizations were in no way linked with the safeguarding of socio-economic liberalism.

(c) They became aware that, even while possessing and mastering the technology and knowledge essential to the smooth running of modern medicine, they were not receiving from the university-hospital system, society or the public authorities either the reward or the opportunities of work to which they considered they had a right. So there would be no point in increasing their skills and their knowledge since they would remain in a position of inferiority and of dependence in relation to a group which monopolized the means of work and the positions associated with high incomes, power and prestige.

Consequently it was not only the allocation of certain status that they were all led to call into question, but a closed system of organization which emphasized a particular definition of medicine and, more generally, the socio-economic ideology which favoured it. Their aims then coincided with the radical, political and scientific leanings of underprivileged medical practitioners, of groups of students and even certain personalities within the system who were seeking or vainly waiting for change. In the end, and significantly, it was not within professional organizations that the most active among them militated with a view to bringing about this change but in the political parties. By refusing to see the hospital and medical problems merely as touching upon the professional body these 'fringe groups' distinguished themselves from the best-placed members of the profession who might have wished to resolve these problems within the esoteric framework formed by the only 'competent people' as defined by them.

So on this front were contested both the clinical valorization of medical activity and the organizational system which perpetuated it, and also the liberal framework which was linked to it for a century and a half. In this respect, this movement, and the menaces contained within it, linked up with the aims of Social Security mentioned above. But whereas on the hospital 'front' we concluded by revealing some attempts at negotiation and experiment from which one might have expected some possibility of change, we find ourselves here faced with the self-perpetuating aspect of the system, which blocked it at every level. Although criticizing and challenging it verbally most students inwardly realized very quickly that 'outside of the hospital examinations and the clinic, there was no salvation'. Most of them disregarded the teaching of the Faculty and put all their energies into embarking upon that *voie royale* which alone could lead to high incomes and social approval.[1] We have seen, moreover, how the norms of the Faculty Councils, and the processes leading to the creation of the Chairs and to the choosing of their holders, did nothing but reinforce the balance of existing forces. As for the numerous commissions of reform nominated by the

---

1 We must add that the *Externat* and the *Internat* also formed the only means the students had of practical apprenticeship.

public authorities, they were for the most part, made up of these professors, clinicians and hospital-trained people of liberal calling, who had arrived at this position of power and who were able to stay there only by virtue of their control over the means of access to the system. And it was demanded of them that they change the very system which was the source of their own authority and privilege and which had given them the power to bring about reform. It is therefore understandable that around the year 1955 all the groups concerned were in agreement in speaking of the 'crisis' in medicine, in medical research and in the university medical system of France and that innumerable propositions and suggestions were made and published, that numerous governmental commissions of reform were nominated and assembled one after the other – but that not one of these combined attempts could get beyond the stage of pious wishes and declarations of intent.

The 'coup de force'

Yet in 1958, a decision was taken, probably the most important in this field since the French Revolution. It created the University and Hospital Centres, where the full-time medical groups were bound to develop medical care, teaching and research.

The detailed contents of this reform, the procedure adopted to draw it up and put it out have been described in a publication already quoted.[1] It is sufficient here to draw attention to some characteristics which will be useful in approaching the theoretical conclusions of this analysis.

(*a*) This decision was taken shortly after a serious political crisis, caused by events in Algeria, which provoked a change of régime and the coming to power of General de Gaulle. It could be said that the reform was imposed in a context of charismatic power.

(*b*) It was worked out by an *ad hoc* committee in which, for the first time, the hospital and university medical associations who were the most 'representative' were not in the majority. The influence of the representatives of the Social Security, of the Central Administration, of the biologists and of the young doctors who did not possess all of the cherished titles, was predominant there.

(*c*) The president of the committee was Professor Robert Debré who had been in favour of change for a considerable time. An eminent personality in the university-hospital group, possessing great authority, and knowing how to make use of it, he was radical and intransigent and could impose his ideas all the more easily by virtue of the fact that his son was at this time the Prime Minister.

(*d*) Finally, thanks to the new Constitution, the law was not referred to the National Assembly but was passed in the form of an Ordinance.

In short, this decision was considered by its opponents as much as by its

1   H. Jamous, *Contribution à une sociologie de la décision* (1967) and *Sociologie de la décision* (1969).

adherents to be a *coup de force*, with the latter adding that this was the only way of introducing, or at least of beginning to set in motion, a change.

SOME HYPOTHETICAL SUGGESTIONS

It is in this third part that we shall be able to establish links of a more subtle kind between the theoretical prolegomena laid out at the beginning of this article, and the detailed analysis which followed. Four groups of propositions will be presented in the form of hypotheses which may have a general bearing on the understanding of the activities and of the groups which are usually approached with the help of the concept of 'profession' or the changes studied under the theme of 'professionalization'. Set forth at first in a very foreshortened form, commentaries will be made about these propositions by means of a selection and a synthesis of facts already mentioned as well as by new facts to back them up. Thus, as far as the ideological aspect of the definition of an activity is concerned, we shall examine in greater detail the significance of the valorization of clinical medicine, and, on the subject of changes in a profession, we shall refer to some significant facts about the 'crisis of May and June 1968'. It is perhaps superfluous to emphasize again that these propositions have no claim to being definitive conclusions. They form the basis of hypotheses necessitating several supplementary empirical analyses which might, moreover, help to make them more precise.

PROBLEMS OF DEFINITION AND PROFESSIONAL IDEOLOGY

The object of study which in sociological literature takes the name of 'profession' is not a stable or univocal entity which can be strictly delineated. It is the historic product of a struggle which, at the heart of a system, divides amongst themselves those who try to control the process or processes of production underlying the system, and who strive to put forward a particular definition of these activities.

Those who, at a given moment in history, thanks to their skill and their social qualities, control the system of evaluation, of sanction and control, impose their definition of the production(s), have a tendency to exclude or to place in a position of subordination those who could be brought by technical and scientific changes to redefine these productions. It is possible to say that the system includes dominant members and dominated members.

The former can perpetuate their definition only by emphasizing the margin of indetermination inherent in the production process and, by the same token, the rules, the norms and the institutions which are their supports.

These criteria, which specialized sociology considers to be the characteristics of a 'profession' are in fact an expression of the professional ideology of the dominant members.

This professional ideology is strengthened by, and strengthens in its turn, the general ideology which is an expression of a balance of social forces.

Commentaries

These first propositions condense a part of the analysis of the empirical case, by taking up again some theoretical prolegomena from the first part. In the commentaries which follow, we shall develop these by showing precisely how the professional ideology has been translated into the valorization of clinical medicine and the functions which it has been able to carry out.

We saw that the French Revolution and the laws which followed upon it made it possible for a social and professional group to remove from the esoteric *corps* of the *Ancien Régime*, the monopoly over the production of medical knowledge and its transmission. Since that time and throughout the first half of the nineteenth century their clinical medical practice contained creative potentialities. From the moment when profitable discoveries could also be made by people who were not treating the sick, or who had not followed the apprenticeship and training considered until then as the necessary way of obtaining such results, this monopoly was endangered. There appeared the need for a differentiation of functions, where the clinical doctors risked losing the monopoly over the production of medical knowledge. What is more, they were in danger of being gradually reduced over a longer period to the role of simple practitioners of this knowledge, and by the same token, of no longer being considered as those best-placed to transmit it. The professional ideology, by emphasizing clinical medicine, anticipated these dangers and made it possible, moreover, for medicine to be set on the supports of the general ideological system of society.

In accentuating the indetermination inherent in the production process of medical care, the clinicans emphasized individual and social potentialities, experience, talent, intuition, etc., all of which they alone controlled and defined and which, moreover, enabled the result to be evaluated on the basis of qualities which they themselves possessed, or according to criteria of selection and of choice which only reproduce these qualities. Moreover, to create or to allow indetermination in the process of the application of knowledge to be perpetuated is to continue to believe that this practice is not so highly technical and differentiated, and that possibilities of discovery are still inherent in it. In consequence, those who treat the sick, that is, those who apply their knowledge, are still those who have the greatest chance of producing knowledge, and are the best placed to transmit it.

Thus, the affirmation of an essentially clinical definition of medicine and the constant repetition that it 'is learned only at the patient's bedside', has the function of delaying as long as possible this differentiation which tends to turn the clinical doctor into one who simply applies medical knowledge. Only this ideology makes it possible to consider that hospital and therapeutic practice, on account of its large indetermination, remains a privileged driving force of medical progress and that in this practice the lengthy contact between master and pupil confronted by the patient is the privileged means of instruction and of the transmission of medical knowledge.

This defence system whose organizational and institutional foundations have been described at length is, paradoxically, not intended for 'laymen' only. It serves too, and perhaps more importantly, to counter other 'skilled men' and 'professionals', potential rivals supporting a more rationalized definition of medical activity and knowledge, and who are to be excluded or kept in a subordinate position. This self-maintained structure, and the ideology produced by it are therefore neither the whole system nor the whole profession, but express the dominant term of a duality. Thus, they are not, either, the expression of a sort of 'pathological' or dysfunctional state explicable by cultural[1] or organizational[2] determinants. They are the 'natural' exasperation of a term of the dialectic peculiar to every activity and every system of production containing a wide margin of indetermination, and of which its possessors wish to perpetuate their control. The other term is represented by that constant threat — sometimes coming from these very possessors — which is composed of the ineluctable attempt at rationalization of those seeking to reduce this indetermination. We shall see that between these two terms — about which it is useful to be specific in each activity or 'profession' in order to understand their dynamic — there is seldom any chance of integration. From a given moment, all opposition springs from a disagreement of definition and all conflict, at its limits, is a conflict about legitimacy claimed for themselves by the dominant members in order to impose their own definition, and to control the system of evaluation, sanctions and control.

But professional ideology cannot perpetuate itself, govern itself and resist for long the threat it faces without settling down and being legitimized by the dominant ideology. The valorization of indetermination, that is to say in our case, of the clinical orientation, also makes possible this kind of reinforcement which ends up moreover in becoming reciprocal. In effect, to valorize clinical medicine is to valorize the potentialities and the talent of the producer in obtaining the result; it is to make the quality of this result depend less on techniques and transmissible rules than on an always particular and hazardous relationship, 'the coming together of conscience and confidence', as the majority of doctors love to repeat. It is easy to conclude from this that only a liberal system made up of individuals 'free to choose' favours this type of meeting or relationship, and that it is indispensable not to make rules for or predetermine

1 M. Crozier, *Le phénomène bureaucratique* (Paris, 1963).
2 Ben-David, *op. cit.*

these if one wants to have the best chance of obtaining results of quality. Clinical medicine and liberalism emerge reinforced the one by the other, the idea of 'free choice' sustaining the illusion that their union is the best guarantee of quality, that is to say of a country's good health.

From this point of view, it is the 'layman' who finds himself paradoxically excluded, because he is not competent, but at the same time he is supposed to be free. It is here, in fact, that the valorization of indetermination accomplishes two masterly strokes. (1) It makes possible the creation and maintenance of a 'code of ethics' founded on liberalism with the purpose of legitimizing the relationships which completely evade the criteria of liberalism. This is apparent in their individual characteristics such as the subordination of the patient to the doctor, as well as in their collective characteristics of a supply which continually provokes an increase in demand. (2) It apparently unites antinomic ideas; esotericism and 'freedom of choice'. And since it is only possible to get beyond this twofold contradiction by calling on transcendental values, one sees why there is recourse to moral and evaluative notions such as confidence, conscience, etc., which take us far from 'the primacy of the values of cognitive rationality'. Moreover, it is with situations and relationships containing the seeds of the *production of charisma* that we are dealing, charisma which can just as well concern a particular individual as a social category as a whole. The specificity of the medical relationship, 'concerned with both life and death', has often been stressed in order to account for the charisma of doctors, but not enough mention has been made of the way in which this relationship can be exploited by the accentuation of the indetermination which is connected with it, and the stressing of a distance which the layman as well as patient or student, ends up by expecting and valuing. This would make it possible, as Freidson[1] suggests to detect behind this process the production of a specific definition of sickness itself, which can be understood only with regard to the definition of the activity imposed by the preponderant professional ideology.

Finally, if one looks at the medical activity from the point of view of the production of medical care and the monetary advantages which it procures, it will be noticed that the process of 'over-indetermination' helps to emphasize the rarity of the 'good' product, and hence its price. It is in this way that charisma and profit can support each other. Thus are facilitated the imposition and finally the interiorization of the commonplaces which affirm alternatively that a professor, because he is 'good' can demand high payments and that, if he has a high income, it must be the case that he is good. Wealth becomes the guarantee of talent, this in its turn justifies wealth, which makes one believe in talent — the wheel turns full circle. Professional ideology makes us forget that deprived people who are able to reach this status are few; it joins up here with

1   E. Freidson, 'Medical personnel : Physicians', *International Encyclopedia of the Social Sciences* (1968), pp. 105-13.

what Bourdieu[1] calls the ideology of the gift, both referring back to a liberalism which in medicine more than elsewhere has always been a seductive illusion.

But it is all this structure which was beginning to totter when we reached the end of our analysis. It brings us to the problems of change.

THE TRANSFORMATION OF A PROFESSION

Given what precedes, transformations of a 'profession' can be explained only by taking a twofold dynamic into account. One dynamic, internal to the system and determined chiefly by scientific or technical discoveries which make it possible better to rationalize the means of arriving at the expected results of the activity in question, awakens in those who take part in this growing rationalization demands which bring them to redefine the nature of this activity. The other, which is external and expresses an overall balance of forces, provokes new demands as far as the social use of the production underlying this activity is concerned.[2]

The major transformations have the greatest chance of occurring when these two demands meet and come together in order to fight against the resistance of those who control the definition and the social function of the production.

The confrontations thus created are conflicts of legitimacy; they crystallize around the legitimacy claimed by the dominant members in order to dominate and perpetuate the system of evaluation, of sanction and control.

Transformations of a profession are not made by a self-regulating system but by sudden jolts, when the principles of the dominant legitimacy are shaken.

Commentaries

The general conclusion does not more than resume, while synthesizing to an extreme, the twofold analysis of the empirical case. We shall therefore stress the particular propositions which follow and which go beyond the facts presented by putting forward some further remarks and clarifications.

The coming together of the two demands which favour change ought not to be considered as an instantaneous and unique phenomenon. The path is prepared for it by an alteration of partial changes which affects either the increasing technicality of an activity or the general balance of forces and which are not integrated within the system.

There are two essential ideas here: (1) A new definition of the activity which is opposed to the dominant one, even if it does provide some 'objective' criteria

1 Bourdieu and Passeron, *op. cit.*
2 The notions 'internal' and 'external' are themselves polemical terms which must be used with caution. They should be made explicit in every concrete example, while keeping in mind that the frontiers of a 'profession' or of a system become the major element of conflicts in moments of crisis. This point will be elucidated in the comments which follow.

enabling its greatest riches to be evaluated, is not enough to provoke the change; it needs a suitable combination of social forces which could make use of it. (2) The mobilization which inequality or social injustice may cause, cannot, either, on its own, lead to change; it must be able to make use of technical dysfunctions. In sum the notion of technical dysfunction is not a key force and at its limits cannot be said to exist unless it becomes a social instrument.

When, as early as 1904, Jayle, an eminent professor, denounced the fruitlessness of the competitive examinations which do not allow doctors to embark upon the field of bacteriology and Pasteur's sciences, there was another eminent professor to protest 'against the tendency of certain modern authors who think they may find in laboratory research the solution to the problems which are raised by the study of illness . . . I cannot admit', he adds, 'the abdication of clinical medicine before the rising tide of bacteriology.'[1] If these peremptory declarations make us smile today — and must have done so at the time — this does not prevent another eminent professor writing in 1968:

'I find it irritating, however, that the biological sciences carry, in our faculties, the label of fundamental sciences. Does not calling them 'fundamental' signify that clinical medicine has been relegated to the back room? Now, what is fundamental to us, is clinical medicine. The other branches of medicine, however indispensable they may be, remain subsidiary to it.'[2]

If, at the time of Roger and Jayle the system which we know now, was maintained and continued to be perpetuated, it was not because the fruitfulness and the superiority of clinical medicine had been proved. If, sixty years later, a decision was taken which ought in principle to sanction a new definition of medical activity, it was not only because it had finally been proved that clinical medicine was no longer the privileged driving force of medical knowledge. This fact could have been proved, or what is more, challenged for a very long time. For a very long time too there have been in France fruitless arguments about the 'so-called advance of foreign countries': was Germany, at the beginning of the century, really ahead in bacteriology and physiology and the United States, more recently, in biology? But if, on the one hand, scientific and technical discoveries did not succeed in changing a system which perpetuated itself in this way, in spite of 'dysfunctions', for more than sixty years, the demands caused by the spread of Social Security could hardly be expected to succeed in shaking the system earlier. The most that they could do, which is in fact the least, was to promote some local experiments the utilization of which could be predicted. A moment of crisis of legitimacy, which had created a situation of charismatic power, was needed for this twofold demand to be able to converge and act as one, following a process which was considered to be a *coup de force*. To be sure, a legal text does not constitute change, but by its contents and its results, it

1 H. Roger, *Introduction à l'étude de la médecine* (Paris, 1904).
2 Gilbert-Dreyfus, *Origine et devenir de la médecine* (Paris, 1968).

can be said to have been the major step in this process of change.[1] Moreover, it was on the occasion of another crisis of legitimacy — May and June 1968 — that the system was again summoned to change by a unification of this twofold demand. And in connection with the problem which preoccupies us, two elements in this recent crisis ought to be mentioned.

(1) The phenomena which, in our view, deserve the greatest attention in the multiple events of May and June 1968, were not the workers' strikes, nor the student agitation as such. They were the splits and violent contestations which divided what could be called the professional groups and associations (professors, executive staff, doctors, lawyers, etc.). It is not a question of claiming that these phenomena are new and characterize what is specific about the May crisis, but of emphasizing that the internal duality of these systems can only be expressed in open conflict and only, perhaps, create changes when the chance arises to call into question the principles of legitimacy. In fact, to find other examples of such violent divisions in these groups, we must go back to the different revolutionary periods or to the time of the Occupation and the Liberation. Such is not the case as far as the students and the workers are concerned.

(2) But in this regular occurrence the new fact was that this twofold demand was able to be fused into a whole and be taken in hand by a single social group — the students. Not yet belonging to a system, they took as their cause the demands, the claims and the resentments of all those whom the different self-perpetuating systems excluded, relegated to the sidelines or placed in a position of subordination. But from the very fact that they could not yet, like the latter, claim a skill, they could, and at the same time had to, lean on external social demands. They demanded a new definition of activities while at the same time trying to attribute a different social function to them. This phenomenon is, in fact, at the same time both new and old. It is old in so far as the essential pattern seems to be preserved, the meeting and coming together of a twofold demand at a time when the dominant principles of legitimacy are tottering. It is new in so far as a single and important group exists which is able to take charge of this twofold demand.

In referring to the Debré reform, it can be said that it was the committee presided over by Robert Debré, which through charismatic power was able to take charge of these two demands to bring about a sort of 'micro-revolution from above', while in May 1968 it was the students who, fulfilling this function, were able to create a sort of 'micro-revolution from below'.

It is, moreover, important to point out the similarity of the mechanisms which take over in this sort of confrontation, where the dominant members of the system demand and try to justify the esoteric and closed nature of their activity whereas those dominated and excluded demand openness and

1 When the present article is published, a paper on the effective implementation of this decision, written by B. Peloille will be put into circulation.

'popularization'.

The Debré committee which worked out the reform, the well-known 'general assemblies' of May 1968, which debated the changes to be brought in, the committee which worked out the reform of Higher Education following the May crisis have all suffered the same great reproach from those well-placed members of the profession: it is of not being 'democratic' or representative. The first was reproached with having been composed above all of 'non-professionals' and of attributing too much importance to members of the Administration – notably those of the Social Security – to young doctors, to biologists and to researchers, all of whom were considered not competent, or not yet competent, or not quite competent. The presence of members 'outside of' or 'strangers to' the profession was constantly stigmatized in the 'general assemblies' of May: this meant students of other fields of study, workers, nurses, ward orderlies, etc. The obsession with 'representativity' was the *leitmotiv* of all these assemblies. Those in favour of change did not contest these facts, rather the contrary, they assumed them by claiming for themselves a representativity which overflowed the limits of what their opponents called the 'profession' and which touched upon the whole of society, serving as a basis for a new legitimacy. This gave rise to propositions of generous scope recalling the revolutionary period and the Liberation: medicine, research, hospitals each in the service of the people, or in the service of the workers.

These facts are significant and essential to the understanding of the reasons why the transformation of a system can be made only through a sort of violation of the dominant legitimacy. Given that there do not exist objective indicators, unanimously accepted, which make possible an evaluation of the production(s) underlying an activity and that the definition of the activity, the system of evaluation, of sanction and control, are in the hands of its dominant members, the recognition of dysfunctions, the stigmatization of a situation and its exasperation in the form of a 'crisis' generally comes only from the outside; from those who bring a new definition or from those who demand a different social function. If the dominant members of a profession can be brought gradually to recognize the defects and the dysfunctions of the system, and themselves to speak of crises, each of the protagonists will propose a different definition and different solutions for the crises. The fundamental question: 'Who is legitimately most highly qualified or best placed to define this crises and propose fresh solutions?' cannot be resolved by the traditional and hallowed options, or by negotiation between 'representative elements'. For on the one hand, the most powerful will try to perpetuate their previous state and on the other hand, and above all, because the problem posed consists precisely either in calling into question the definition and frontiers of the said profession or else in affirming that laymen and 'outsiders' may demand to be involved in it. This renders senseless the very notion of 'representativity' or, more exactly, places it at the very centre of the debate.

It may, therefore, be understood that a major change can take place only after *coups de force* coming from those who, officially or not, have control over the sources of legitimacy and of authority in a society, or on the occasion of a general shake-up of the principles of ratified legitimacy. But it can also be understood that these events, where the notion of representativity is always the subject of strife and of redefinition, react upon these principles, and that the notion of 'democracy' itself is continually being redefined.

ARE WE DEALING WITH A PHENOMENON OF PROFESSIONALIZATION?

The phenomenon which has been described and analysed cannot be called a phenomenon of 'professionalization'.

It cannot be considered as an illustration of general hypotheses, which attribute to the 'professionals' an increasingly important role and position in present day society.

Commentaries

We shall comment very briefly on these propositions which may be deduced from what has just been set out, only to forestall a certain number of objections. The epithet 'professional' could, in fact, be applied to those new types of doctor, men of research or of laboratories, who thanks to successive upheavals – the Occupation and the Liberation, Gaullism and the Debré Reform, the Crisis of May 1968 – have gradually come to occupy the forefront of the scene. This would enable our case to be considered as an illustration of the general hypotheses about growing professionalization as made by Carr-Saunders,[1] Parsons[2] or Ben-David.[3] This sort of overall objection contains within it several others which must be broken down.

It is useless to show how the application of the principal criteria of a profession, usually used to detect an occurrence of professionalization, would not have enabled us to understand the emergence and the action of these new physicians. The whole analysis which precedes shows rather how this kind of criterion formed the polemical and ideological arguments of the dominant group who sought to defend and perpetuate themselves, and that it was possible to catch their significance only by placing them within the twofold conflict analysed.

More serious would be an objection of a Personian type which would integrate this analysis and make of it a case typical of the past, when 'cognitive rationality' was not predominant and when 'non-technical concerns' could interfere to a

1 Carr-Saunders and Wilson, *op. cit.*
2 Parsons, *op. cit.*
3 Ben-David, *op. cit.*

considerable extent with the 'professional functions'. The conflicts, the ideologies, the particularism or charisma, whose action we have stressed, would be 'neutralized' by the appearance and victory of these new physicians who constitute a kind of 'professional expert', more 'rational' and with functions more specific. In fact such an 'integration' could take place only through the looseness of the notion of 'cognitive rationality' denounced above.

After all, not only was the clinical approach in medicine not stripped of 'cognitive rationality' but it could be considered as one of the conditions of the development of modern medicine. When we recall that 'specificity', 'universalism' and 'achievement', etc., have also been presented by Parsons as the functional prerequisites of scientific medical practice, and when we see the way in which clinical medicine has been able to set off a professional ideology giving rise to particularism, 'quality', valorization and charisma, we wonder why such mechanisms should not be renewed. We cannot in fact see why these researchers, these new 'professionals' whose system of production will always contain a large margin of indetermination, should not produce in their turn a professional ideology with the purpose of preserving and perpetuating rules and protective norms. As we do not see why new excluded groups of the future, having a different definition of research and a new balance of forces attributing to it a different social function should not give rise to conflicts and ideological rationalizations homologous to those we have just described. We must point out, in passing, that this stage has not yet been reached. The work carried out by Peloille[1] on the implementation of the reform sheds light rather on facts which suggest what might be called 'a revenge of the clinician', a revenge in which 'cognitive rationality' remains closely bound to 'non-technical concerns' as much as, if not more than, before.

As far as these hypotheses about the growing importance of the 'professionals' are concerned, everything depends on the meaning which we give to the notion of importance. If this is expressed by the conclusion of Ben-David[2] who sees the 'professionals' as taking in modern society 'the place of the self-made *entrepreneur*, which in its turn has replaced the nobleman-landlord and the knight', or by the following phrase of Parsons: 'The massive emergence of the professional complex, not the special states of capitalistic or socialistic modes or organization, is the crucial structural development in twentieth-century society', such general terms are being used that it is difficult to embark upon a fruitful debate.[3] It is

1 Research in progress on the implementation of the Debré reform to be published in mid 1970.
2 Ben-David, *op. cit.*
3 There too it can be said that such hypotheses can be made only with the help of an abusive extension of the notion of 'professionalization'. With many works trying to show that we are in a society of growing professionalization, it is legitimate to wonder whether it is society which is being professionalized or if it is the looseness of the conceptional tool serving the analysis which is on the increase (cf. : Wilensky, *op. cit.*; G. Benguigui, 'La professionalisation des cadres dans l'industrie', *Sociologie du Travail,* 9 (1967), 134-43;

tempting to reply: and why not 'the massive emergence of the organizational complex', or else that of the 'marginal men', of the 'technostructures', of the 'managers', etc.[1]

This kind of hypothesis is so difficult to verify that, every so many years, a talented sociologist can write a book telling us that present-day society is characterized by the emergence of a new type of man, of a new 'complex' or of a new class without it being possible to invalidate or to confirm these seductive speculations.

In truth, these general hypotheses give a more interesting significance to the notion of importance, that of historical and sociological determination, i.e. the elements which serve as driving forces and explain modern societies would have to be sought in the activities, the production, the rules and the norms of these social categories called 'professional'. With this interpretation in mind, the analysis which has just been made, in so far as it can be considered a good example, tries to show how this type of hypothesis is at one and the same time true and false.

But, as this case is both unique and special we shall change our fourth proposition into a question.

ARE THE DESCRIBED MECHANISMS PECULIAR TO FRANCE?

The question here posed is in fact that of the degree of generality of the hypotheses previously formulated. In so far as we consider them as indicative hypotheses, an answer to this question can be given only subsequent to a certain amount of comparative research. It is however possible to answer some objections raised by existing research and theories, to gather together results and arguments enabling us to give some kind of backing to these hypotheses.

There is a culturalist interpretation of the phenomenon which we have analysed. It explains the different components of the phenomenon on the basis of national characteristics. It is the theory of change *à la française* put forward by Michel Crozier[2] who integrates some conclusions made by Pitts[3] and Willie.[4] We cannot here take up again the facts and arguments developed in our work in order to show the difficulty which this theory has in accounting for our phenomenon. We shall content ourselves with referring the reader to them.

D. Monjardet, C. Raguin and J. Saliba, 'Pour une sociologie des travailleurs intellectuels', Laboratoire de Sociologie Industrielle (Paris, 1968).

1   These remarks are more than mere gibes : we lack space for a discussion of the important and erudite work of Ben-David whose conclusions concerning 'The professional class' are derived from an over-bold leap from empirical indicators to its interpretations.

2   Crozier, *op. cit.*

3   J. R. Pitts, 'Change in bourgeois France', *In Search of France* (Cambridge, Mass., 1963).

4   L. Wylie, *Village in the Vaucluse* (Cambridge, 1958).

A work of Ben-David[1] 'Scientific productivity and academic organization in nineteenth-century medicine' puts forward the notions of 'decentralization' and of 'competition' to explain the differences in scientific productivity between France, the United States, Great Britain and Germany. The author's mode of analysis and interpretation is fundamentally different from ours since he considers the academic organization of each country as univocal entity, while we see in it a duality made by a system which creates around itself its own 'anti-system'. The marginal situation of Magendie, of Claude Bernard or of Pasteur and the ostracism which they and their successors experienced at the hands of the members of the university-hospital system, thus constitute strategic phenomena whose significance was bound to escape the author. These important facts were not the result of centralization or of non-competition – the system, moreover, was rather decentralized and still is – they were the conditions for it. And when Ben-David concludes in these terms :

'It is not argued, however, that competition is the only possible outcome of any state of decentralisation, or that competition, once established, is self-maintaining. Decentralisation may lead to collusion or mutual isolation as well as to competition; and competition may be replaced by either of these alternatives. Determination of the general conditions that ensure competition, therefore, is another problem which needs further study';[2]

he thus seems to call into question that which he has just tried to demonstrate and conclude with those points with which we would rather have begun.

Another way of searching for a specifically French definition is to give special consideration to the dualism which governed the system – neither completely liberal nor wholly state-controlled – thus enabling a professional group, placed in a strategic position, to take advantage of two systems, and to block the means of self-regulation.

Such a suggestion would have deserved more extensive development, had not 'non-French' results and facts existed, which show that the productions and occupations which concern us involve relationships which rule out self-regulation. It is sufficient to refer to the works of Perrow,[3] Freidson,[4] Kessel[5] and Garceau.[6] The first shows the determining influence of the state of technical knowledge and of the nature of the work on the goal and the power-structure of hospital organization. Freidson insists on the idea of emphasizing indetermination in medical

1 J. Ben-David, 'Scientific productivity and academic organization in nineteenth century medicine', *American Sociological Review*, 25 (1960), 828-43.
2 *Ibid.*
3 C. Perrow, 'Goals and Power Structures : a Historical Case Study' in B. Freidson (ed.), *The Hospital in Modern Society* (New York, 1963) and 'Hospitals : Technology, Structure and Goals', in J. C. March (ed.), *Handbook of Organizations* (Chicago, 1965).
4 Freidson, *op. cit.*
5 R. A. Kessel, 'Price Discriminations in Medicine', *The Journal of Law and Economics*, 1 (1958), 20-53.
6 Garceau, *op. cit.*

practice and shows that, in consequence, the informal organization of the profession is not made up of exchanges, of reciprocal apprenticeship and control, but of boycott and mutual ignorance, which gives rise to processes of segregation and to self-maintaining collectivities of like people, heterogeneous as much from the point of view of professional norms as of techniques. As for Kessel and Garceau, they describe the omnipotence of the medical organization of the United States whose monopolistic practices affect prices as much as the exclusion of those accused of 'unethical practices'. Apart from the works of Kessel and Garceau who suggest how the potentialities of self-maintenance exist even in the case of practical practitioners, the idea common to these different results which, at first sight, may seem heteroclite, is the manner in which they invert the usual way of posing the problem of the professionals. And it is in this sense that we are in agreement with their approach. The social function of activities and their very definition are not, in any one case, set down at the outset, but are deduced on the basis of precise analyses of the technicality and the nature of the work, of the system of real control which this can set up, of the existing balance of forces, whether in the organizations or in society. This conclusion of Freidson is explicit:

'it follows that physicians are responsible for the *social creation* of disease in the course of "discovery" and diagnosis. It would follow, further, that in medical practice the social organization of work biases the way in which diseases are created, and shapes the way in which patients are managed and even created by diagnosis. Thus a major task of the sociology of medicine is to study the causes and consequences of physicians' conceptions of disease, showing how disease as a social object is created or formed by medical institutions.'[1]

It would suffice to add 'and socio-economic institutions' to make such a conception which results from the analysis of Anglo-Saxon research only, come quite close to that which we have distinguished in the French case.

Finally, there is one innovation which, in the year 1910, transformed the medical profession and medical studies in the United States and of which certain characteristics seem to consolidate to some extent our hypotheses about change: this is the famous Flexner reform. The study of this reform, being carried out by Dorin at the present time at the *Centre de Sociologie de l'Innovation,* fits into the framework of that comparative research which it is necessary to undertake in order to verify and refine the hypotheses proposed above. The few aspects which we shall very briefly quote seem to indicate that a certain number of mechanisms which have presided over the change are independent of national characteristics:

(1) This reform ratified the failure of the liberal system in the realm of medicine. It was in favour of intervention and invalidated the laws of competition and of supply and demand in the field of medical training, which were considered as not being able to guarantee the quality of what was produced :

1 Freidson, *op. cit.*

medical care or practitioners.

(2) Professional associations were divided and could not play a self-regulating role. For a short space of time, the American Association of Medical Colleges (A.A.M.C.) attempted to establish criteria and prerequisites capable of raising the standard of medical instruction. The formal adherence of the schools to the resolutions worked out during the annual congresses and their participation in these did not cause any raising of standards. This attempt at 'internal' change, which could be linked with a phenomenon of increasing professionalization failed.

(3) For the resolution of this crisis, the intervention of an external and voluntarist action was needed, which made this reform a result of a twofold initiative; the one stemming from a section of the profession and represented by the person of Colwell, secretary of the Council of Medical Education; the other from the major Foundations (Carnegie, Rockefeller) concerned at this time with the reorganization of the whole of the American system of education. In this enterprise Abraham Flexner was the central personality around whom these two demands crystalized.

(4) The reform too could be branded as a kind of centralizing *coup de force* violating the principles of legitimacy of American society, since it called into question the orthodox criteria of liberalism and the local independence of the states.

(5) In fact this reform already expressed the triumph of the new principles of legitimacy which were neither those of the majority of professionals nor those of Congress or of the Federal Government, but those which were borne by the emerging and powerful Foundations into the socio-economic system of America and which ratified the end of liberalism as a fact but not yet as a myth.

Conclusion

The comparison just made between the Debré reform of 1958 in France, and the Flexner reform of 1910 in the United States, allows us to conclude with the mention of some problems which our analysis leaves temporarily in abeyance. Briefly, the most important will be to locate in a meaningful way the points of similarity and of dissimilarity in every comparison made, for the purpose of supporting the general hypotheses. To show that medicine in 1910 and medicine in 1958 both imply specific types of change linked with the national institutions peculiar to the time, constitutes in some way a commonplace continuation of research in progress. On the other hand, the most complex problem, but for that very reason the most fruitful, consists in going beyond the formal similarities of the mechanisms that have been detected and to reveal the exact content which is implied by the passage from one type of dominant legitimacy to another. This brings us back to the general socio-economic changes concerning which we have only made special mention of their manifestations. In fact, the Social Security and the State organizations in France and the Foundations in the United States

F

constitute in this first stage of our comparison the points on which are hinged what we have called the 'external prerequisites'. The problem of knowing the exact nature of these in any one situation has not been touched upon. In fact it presents us with the question of the role and the function in the general structure of power in these two countries of the Social Security and the State organizations in France, and of the Foundations in the United States.

In this respect the analysis which we offer may be considered as incomplete. But it has the advantage of being based on an approach which indicates the ways in which it could be completed. By detecting the appropriate intermediate steps this approach attempts not to cut off the analysis of activities and groups called 'professional' from the general social dynamic and yet not thereby to lose itself in the confusion of an overall historical approach of a too general nature.

5 Teaching as a Profession

T. LEGGATT

5

TEACHING AS A PROFESSION

T. LEGGATT

Much of the sociological writing of recent years on professions and profession-alization has been concerned with three major themes: the characteristics of the 'true' profession, the process whereby an occupation develops into and achieves the status of a profession, and the conflict between two principal trends of all industrial societies — bureaucratization and professionalization. In the handling of these first two themes there has been a lack of substantial agreement between writers upon much beyond somewhat tentative conclusions at a high level of generality. In relation to the third theme there have been a number of insightful analyses but, although persuasive formulations, they tend to lack sufficient precision to be usefully applied to the detailed examination of a particular professional field.

The aim of this paper is to offer a critique of some of the principal contributions on these themes, to carry out a systematic analysis of the characteristic features of teaching as a profession from an alternative perspective, and to look forward to new modes of enquiry into professional work suggested by this critique and analysis.

The first theme, that of identifying the characteristics of professional work, has been of recurrent interest to sociologists from Flexner's discussion in 1915 to the publication of Goode's latest statement in 1969.[1] These writers' interests have been of two kinds: to assess the credentials of a particular occupation aspiring to professional status, or to define in the wider context of occupational sociology as a whole the category of professional employment. Each writer gives his own evaluative analysis and then proposes a unique list of defining characteristics. These lists contain from five to fourteen characteristics and although they are indeed different they are necessarily overlapping. The characteristics that appear with greatest regularity are these:

(*a*) Practice is founded upon a base of theoretical, esoteric knowledge.

(*b*) The acquisition of knowledge requires a long period of education and

[1] Abraham Flexner, 'Is Social Work a Profession?' in *Proceedings, National Conferences of Charities and Corrections* (New York, 1915), pp. 576-90, and William J. Goode, 'The Theoretical Limits of Professionalization', in Amitai Etzioni (ed.), *The Semi-Professions and Their Organization : Teachers, Nurses, Social Workers* (New York, 1969), pp. 216-313. See also Howard S. Becker, 'The Nature of a Profession', in *Education for the Professions*, National Society for the Study of Education Yearbook, (Chicago, 1962), 61, pt. II, pp. 27-46, Ernest Greenwood, 'Attributes of a Profession', *Social Work*, 2 (July 1957), 45-55, and Everett C. Hughes, *Men and Their Work*, (Glencoe, 1958).

socialization.

(*c*) Practitioners are motivated by an ideal of altruistic service rather than the pursuit of material and economic gain.

(*d*) Careful control is exercised over recruitment, training, certification and standards of practice.

(*e*) The colleague group is well organized and has disciplinary powers to enforce a code of ethical practice.

What these conclusions reveal is the wide agreement of the various observers about the characteristic features of the long-established professions, namely medicine, the law and the church, against which the claims of those that aspire to similar status, such as schoolteaching and social work, should be judged. This process identifies ideal typical criteria, to which no actual occupation does or can conform but which may serve to order occupations along a number of dimensions. These lists, then, give no definition, but a series of non-quantifiable indicators of the closeness of a given occupational group to achieving fully recognizable professional status.

The second major theme, of identifying the processes whereby an occupation moves toward full professionalization, has been developed by Bucher and Strauss, who emphasize its indeterminacy, and by Wilensky, who seeks to establish that there is a 'natural history of professionalisation'.[1] Wilensky identifies these stages as those followed on the route to professional status by the established professions: (1) the occupation is followed full-time, (2) formal training is established, (3) this training is provided within universities, (4) local and then national professional associations are formed as the core tasks are defined in competition with neighbouring occupations, (5) political activity leads to legally controlled licensing and certification, and (6) a formal code of ethical practice is developed. However, Wilensky also finds a difference in progress between the older professions, for example architecture and dentistry, and those whose status has been improved more recently and is still marginal, for example social work and librarianship. He deals with the discrepancy in two ways. He explains the variations in terms of particular power struggles that occurred in the histories of the out-of-line occupations. He also argues that there may be two modes of progression, one typical of the older professions and the other of the newer. But this amounts to *ex post facto* special pleading to save a weak hypothesis that does not fit the empirical evidence. As Goode comments, the scheme is 'neither empirically correct nor theoretically convincing'. He names several occupations whose histories do not fit the scheme and points out that it is unlikely that 'a list of the specific historical *events* in the structuring of a profession will yield the organic sequences in its development'. Goode's principal

1 Rue Bucher and Anselm Strauss, 'Professions in Process', *American Journal of Sociology,* 66 (January 1961), 325-34, and Harold L. Wilensky, 'The Professionalization of Everyone?', *American Journal of Sociology,* 70 (September 1964), 137-58.

objection is that the approach that identifies formal steps toward professionalization misses what is important, for it does not 'separate the core, *generating*
traits from the derivative ones'.[1]

The third major theme in the literature, of the opposition of the trends
towards professionalization and bureaucratization, has attracted massive
attention, but the greater part of it lies outside the concerns of this paper. However, one recent approach is of direct relevance. Etzioni and his associates argue
that there is a continuum of professionalism upon which two important types,
the fully-fledged professions and the semi-professions, can be identified. Semi-
professions are distinguished from fully-fledged professions in that they have a
high proportion of female members and they are employed largely in bureaucratic organizations. Their associated characteristics are a shorter period of
training than the fully-fledged professions, a less legitimated status, a less
specialized body of knowledge and less established rights to privileged communication. The prime examples of semi-professions are schoolteaching, nursing and
social work.[2] The distinction is genuine and useful, but it will be argued below
that it is still too crude to advance understanding of these professions to more
than a limited degree.

To return to the first major theme, two directions have been taken in its
more recent development: first, through analysis of the lists of professional
attributes the identification of increasingly more truly professional credentials
and the establishment of a hierarchy of occupations to separate those that make
just claim to professionalism from those that do not; and secondly, the reduction
of the list of ideal typical characteristics in order to disclose what Goode calls the
core or generating traits of professionalism.

The first of these directions is taken by Hickson and Thomas. They seek to
establish a hierarchy of professions by fitting different occupational qualifying
associations into a Guttman cumulative scale using the professional attributes
identified by a variety of observers.[3] This exercise is successful, yet it is of
dubious value. The authors find themselves unable to take account of the most
important features of professionalism: the extent of autonomy in professional
practice, the degree of observation of the ideal of service and the relationship of
practice to a theoretical knowledge base. Further, they are concerned with
qualifying associations and not with occupations as such. This obliges them to
leave out of consideration clergymen, teachers, nurses and social workers, or 53
per cent of the professional labour force in this country.[4] The scope of their
findings is therefore limited narrowly.

The second direction of analysis is pursued by both Wilensky and Goode.

1 Goode, *op. cit.* pp. 274-6.
2 Etzioni, *op. cit.* Preface.
3 D. J. Hickson and M. W. Thomas, 'Professionalization in Britain: A Preliminary Measurement', *Sociology*, 3 (January 1969), 1966, 37-53.
4 Sample Census Tables, Part I, Table 2, p. 50, Great Britain, Economic Activity.

These writers are agreed that the core characteristics of professions are their foundation upon systematic, technical knowledge and their devotion to the service ideal, and they derive from these generative traits all other characteristic attributes. Wilensky argues that high status professions have a knowledge base founded both in theory and the long practice that gives 'tacit knowledge', that residual element identified by Polanyi that remains when all knowledge that can be has been communicated.[1] The acquisition of both open and tacit knowledge necessitates long training and impresses the public with the feelings of awe and inferiority that secure a mandate for the wide exercise of professional discretion.[2] Goode maintains that what he calls the 'person professions' (of the law, the church, medicine and university teaching) owe their status to their salience and to the potential harmfulness of their indiscriminate practice which could follow from practitioners' access to private knowledge and involvement in matters with a high emotional charge and against which open devotion to the service ideal is the most effective defence.[3]

This line of argument is surely sound, yet once the process of distillation of common usage is embarked on it is idle to shrink from the final reduction, especially as this coincides with the authoritative view of the Oxford English Dictionary which defines profession thus: 'a vocation in which a professed knowledge of some department of learning or science is used in its application to the affairs of others or in the practice of an art founded upon it.'[4] To follow this definition is first of all to clarify the fact that scientists such as physicists, chemists and biologists should not be considered professionals.[5] They become so when they apply their knowledge, as, for example, engineers, meteorologists, pharmacists or veterinary surgeons. But secondly it suggests that the service ideal is an added rather than an essential feature of professionalism, readily employed as a defensive shield against threats to the high status of the professions. Indeed the power that the older professions derived from their exclusive knowledge was such that it was only acceptable if wielded by men whose morality was beyond dispute. What is now referred to as a long period of training was developed not only that the technical knowledge could be mastered but also to permit on the one hand the process of initiation into the morality and responsibility to be associated with the proper exercise of professional power and on the other the reduction of bonds, especially familial bonds, based in ascriptive relationships.

The professions that Goode names are the very professions for which in the middle ages of European history universities were developed, for the teaching of

1 Michael Polanyi, 'Tacit Knowing: Its Bearing on Some Problems of Philosophy', *Reviews of Modern Physics*, 34 (October 1962), 601.
2 Wilensky, *op. cit.* pp. 149-50.
3 Goode, *op. cit.* pp. 297-304.
4 *Shorter Oxford English Dictionary* (London, 1933).
5 Unless they are employed as university teachers, in which case they are professional *teachers.*

theology, medicine and law. In an age when power was predominantly based upon ascription, when education in abstract knowledge was necessary only for the few, these fields of learning were encouraged to develop. What they had in common was a central concern with the powers of life and death. (Goode's fourth person profession, university teaching, is of different status since it is an occupation for the dissemination of powerful knowledge, not for the application of that knowledge to the affairs of everyday life.) This kind of knowledge is indeed mysterious and esoteric and the practitioners of arts based upon it were inevitably regarded as having remarkable and awesome powers and in need of the sanction of God himself for their practice. In those ages of faith it is no surprise that the majority of such men of knowledge were employed in the service of the church or were as closely as possible under its surveillance. The men of knowledge had to be seen to be good or working in the service of the good.[1] The expansion of secular learning, the natural sciences, at the time of the European Renaissance and their divergence from the domain of natural theology led to new sources of powerful knowledge. Yet these sciences were both lacking, through this very process, an association with the sacred and the mysterious, and seldom applied in everyday affairs; they did not, therefore, in the very first meaning of the word, need to be 'professed'.[2]

In short, professionals as we know them today are the non-ascriptive achievement-based elite, whose power has grown as the processes of industrialization and rationalization have eroded the ascriptive order; and they are the elect, in a true sense of the most knowledgeable and morally superior of men whose dealings are with other men in the conduct of practical affairs. This surely provides an explanation for why Goode's professions have held such privileged status, but it also provides a means of assessing the future prestige of occupations. It emphasizes that there is necessarily a limit to the number of occupational groups that can attain elite status. It suggests that the study of the process of professionalization is of more interest to the historian than to the sociologist, for it is related to one time period of Western European development. It accounts for the fact that the status of the priesthood is declining and will continue to do so in societies where the churches are no longer seen to have relevant knowledge of life and death. The doctors and lawyers continue to hold their ground, though the lawyer's power in countries where physical, including capital punishment is of declining importance is founded more upon his expertise in relation to the handling of property matters.

The significant challenge to this group of occupational elites evidently comes now from secular rivals, the natural scientists, and battle for the highest prestige

1 The ideal typical professional is perhaps most fully depicted in Plato's philosopher ruler whose superior knowledge and goodness are attained only after continuous education to the age of fifty and whose participation in practical affairs and government is indeed out of dedicated service, 'an unavoidable necessity'. See Plato, *The Republic* (London, 1955).

2 'To have made one's profession of religion', *Oxford English Dictionary, op. cit.*

is already joined between the traditional professionals and these modern masters of esoteric and powerful knowledge. For the future it can be predicted with fair certainty that the continuing increase in specialized knowledge based upon the advance of science will lead to four consequences in the field of professionalism: the splitting of the medical profession into a number of narrow speciality-based professions; the relative decline in prestige of the legal profession, unable to take advantage of this advance in knowledge; the development of rivalries between an increasing number of new specialized sciences, including even the social sciences; and lastly, the more frequent application by scientists themselves of their knowledge as they are increasingly often called upon to take important decisions in the management of practical affairs — whether or not this earns them the title of professionals.

THE PROFESSIONAL STATUS OF TEACHING

This long introduction now provides a vantage point from which to judge the status of the teaching profession. Without question, the profession cannot lay claim to elite status. With the spread of literacy it has lost any esoteric knowledge base. With the growth of white-collar employment teachers have also lost in relative income and become, in Mills's phrase, 'the economic proletarians of the professions'.[1] Employed in bureaucratic institutions teachers lack professional authority and independence: they do not control recruitment to the profession, training or certification nor do they determine their own practice (they cannot turn away clients or fix fees) or conditions of service. They need no code of ethics for the protection of the public and if such a code existed the teachers' loosely organized colleague group lacks the necessary disciplinary powers for its enforcement. It may well be that while an elite profession can maintain status in the context of bureaucratic employment, as do lawyers in the field of industry, no profession can win this standing for itself for the first time in this environment.

Yet it would be foolish to deny teachers the title of professionals which is enshrined in popular usage and census classification. Etzioni's preference for semi-professional, though advancing analytic precision, seems unlikely to become a stable category. The group of occupations most easily and usefully distinguished are those with the highest prestige, and these are readily identifiable under the title of the elite or the esteemed professions. A more descriptive title for Etzioni's semi-professions might be the bureaucratic professions.

CHARACTERISTICS OF TEACHERS AS AN OCCUPATIONAL GROUP

The comparative approach to the study of professions cannot be developed

1 C. Wright Mills, *White Collar : The American Middle Classes* (New York, 1951), p. 129.

substantially without more systematic and detailed data about each individual profession than exists at present. The questions of greatest sociological interest in relation to each professional field are the following. What are the characteristics of (a) the practitioner group, (b) the group's clientele, (c) practitioner-client relations, (d) the organizational context, and (e) the environmental setting? What are the characteristic acts of professional practice? And what are the effects of these upon the quality of professional experience and the status of the occupational group? Answers to these questions will give a fuller understanding of the *peculiar* character of an occupation (from which comparative study can then proceed) and will allow well-informed speculation about the occupation's future.

The outstanding characteristics of teachers as an occupational group[1] are the large size of the group, its high proportion of female members, its lowly social class composition, its small measure of autonomy as a group[2] and its segmentation. These features, although bearing on each other, have independent effects upon the nature of the occupation and its status. Others, such as the high rate of turnover of teachers, their low degree of commitment to their work, and the low prestige and disadvantageous stereotype of the group and its members are more consequences and reinforcements of these primary characteristics than of primary significance in themselves.

The size of the group is readily demonstrated. Sample census figures for Great Britain show there to have been approximately 549,680 teachers in 1966, 27.9 per cent of the professional labour force. This compares with approximately 394,850 nurses, the next largest professional group, and with 35,490 lawyers, 59,360 doctors and 125,290 accountants from the older professions. These groups constituted respectively 20 per cent, 1.8 per cent, 3 per cent and 6.3 per cent of the professional labour force. Percentage figures relating to the United States in 1960 are very similar.[3] These percentage figures are fully set out in Table 1 overleaf.

Group size in itself has many consequences. First, through the ordinary processes of wastage the number of recruits needed annually remains high. Any shift of policy that requires a change in the size of the client population, for example, in the case of teaching, raising the secondary school leaving age, or in the ratio of practitioners to clients, for example through reductions in class size, immediately increases the necessary annual scale of recruitment. Continual pressure to increase recruitment renders impossible the introduction of any new restrictions upon entry in the interest of raising the qualifications of teachers or their standards of practice. From the professional group's viewpoint there is a con-

1 This paper is wholly based on data referring to primary and secondary schoolteachers in Great Britain and the United States.
2 The autonomy of the group is to be sharply contrasted with the autonomy of the individual teacher in the classroom which is discussed below.
3 Sample Census, *op. cit.*, and *Statistical Abstract of the United States* (1967).

tinual danger of standards declining or, in order to maintain — or perhaps even increase — standards, a possibility of having to employ sub-professionals (auxiliaries or aides) to do work previously carried out by professionals. A further consequence of this constant pressure on recruitment is the necessity of employing people with only a limited commitment to the job.

Table 1. *Selected Professional Groups as a Proportion of All Professional Workers* in Great Britain (1966) and the United States (1960)*

	Percentage	
Professional group	Great Britain	United States
Medical practitioners†	3.0	3.1
Lawyers	1.8	2.9
Accountants, etc. +	6.3	6.5
Social welfare workers	2.6	1.8
Nurses	20.0	?**
Schoolteachers	27.9	20.8

Sources: Sample Census 1966, Statistical Abstract of the United States, 1967. (Washington, D.C., 1967), Table No. 330, pp. 232 and 234.

Notes: *All professional workers in Great Britain are those classified as professionals, technical workers and artists less draughtsmen, laboratory assistants, technicians, technical and engineering assistants, and technical and related workers not elsewhere classified.

　†For Great Britain, medical practitioners: for the United States, physicians and surgeons.

　+For Great Britain, professional accountants, company secretaries and registrars: for the United States, accountants and auditors.

　**No reliable figure for male nurses was obtainable.

A second direct consequence of large group size is the near impossibility of susbstantial salary raises, especially in a centralized national system, since even a small increment granted to such a large number makes far greater demands on the budget than the claims of any other professional group. In the United States there is plentiful evidence of teachers' need to take additional employment to supplement their earnings.[1] There is also evidence that the public recognizes the level of pay to be low,[2] as do students who consider, but thereupon reject, teaching as a career.[3] A third major consequence of all these effects of group size is the most obvious of all, as compared with other professions the low prestige of teaching. Size is directly related to modest prestige, since high prestige is in normal times[4] reserved for elites; and this is emphasized by low entry

1 See, for example, National Education Association of the United States, *The Status of the American Public-School Teacher,* Research Bulletin of the Research Division, 35 (Washington, D.C.: N.E.A., February 1957).

2 F. W. Terrien, 'Who Thinks What About Educators?', *American Journal of Sociology,* 59 (September 1953), 150-8.

3 S. C. T. Clark and W. Pilkington, 'Why Teaching is Chosen as a Career', *Alberta Journal of Educational Research,* 1 (March 1955).

4 In times of crisis groups even as large as armies can attain the highest prestige.

qualifications and low salary.

The second distinguishing feature of the occupational group, that characterizes all Etzioni's semi-professions, is its high proportion of women members.[1] In Great Britain in 1966 58 per cent of teachers were women and in the United States in 1960 the equivalent figure was 72.5 per cent (47 per cent of secondary school and 80 per cent of elementary teachers). Figures that demonstrate the contrast between teaching and other professions are given in Table 2 below.

Table 2. *Percentage of Female Practitioners in Selected Professional Occupations in Great Britain (1966) and the United States (1960)*

Profession	Great Britain	United States
Medicine	18	7
Law	5	4
Accountancy	14	17
Social welfare work	52	57
Nursing	94	?*
Schoolteaching	58	73

Sources: Sample Census 1966; Statistical Abstract of the United States, 1967.
Note: *No reliable figure for male nurses was obtainable.

Teaching is an occupation of high prestige for women, despite its general low ranking,[2] and, although men experience dissatisfaction, it is one with which women are well satisfied. In the United States, Collins and Nelson found women teachers' morale to be higher than mens' and a study by the National Education Association also found women more satisfied than men.[3] In this country Rudd and Wiseman found women quite content but men substantially dissatisfied.[4] Male dissatisfaction may in part be directly due to the occupation, and certainly primary school teaching, being stereotyped as a women's profession,[5] although the other low prestige features mentioned are no doubt important in their own right.

Several observers have suggested that the teaching occupation peculiarly well fits the life style and work orientation of women. The occupation can be undertaken by those with the low career commitment[6] characteristic of women who

1 For a full discussion of this feature see Richard L. Simpson and Ida Harper Simpson, 'Women and Bureaucracy in the Semi-Professions', in Etzioni, *op. cit.* pp. 196-265.
2 See National Opinion Research Center, 'Jobs and Occupations: A Popular Evaluation', in R. Bendix and S. M. Lipset (eds.), *Class, Status and Power* (New York, 1953), pp. 411-26.
3 Harold W. Collins and Norbert J. Nelson, 'A Study of Teacher Morale – Union (AFT) Teachers versus Non-Union (NEA) Teachers', *Journal of Educational Research*, 62 (1968), 3-10, and N.E.A., *op. cit.*
4 W. G. A. Rudd and S. Wiseman, 'Sources of Dissatisfaction among a Group of Teachers', *British Journal of Educational Psychology*, 32 (1962), 275-91.
5 See Myron Lieberman, *Education as a Profession* (New Jersey, 1956), pp. 241-56. Lieberman's work is relevant to many of the themes touched on in this paper.
6 See Blanche Geer, 'Occupational Commitment and the Teaching Profession', *School Review*, 74 (1966), 31-47, for many perceptive observations relevant to this issue.

wish to raise a family at some point in their lives. Today almost all women work but only a minority have long-range occupational commitments.[1] Its lack of a specialized and rapidly changing knowledge base makes a period of absence from practice – even of sufficient length to allow the raising of a family – quite manageable for a teacher, without the need of a period of re-training. It also requires a shorter period of initial training than do the elite professions, and this is less delaying of marriage than would be other forms of professional training. Further, lack of accumulated experience on the job, so important in many other occupations, from industrial management to police work, is no bar to resumption of work in teaching after a prolonged absence.

The bureaucratic nature of the work context, compatible only with a weak concern for autonomy, is more acceptable to women than to men who have traditionally played more submissive roles than men and have therefore been more accepting of authority. They have, in general, less ambition than men for advancement, a stance that is well suited to teaching in which promotion leads to administrative posts and away from the classroom work that characterizes the occupation and provides its greatest rewards.[2] The fact that employers do not require schoolteachers to be geographically mobile is also convenient to married women, who constitute 53.6 per cent of women teachers in this country.[3] Yet if their husbands' jobs necessitate a move, there are always ready openings for schoolteaching in any new community. One of the barriers to a higher level of professionalization in teaching is the rudimentary development of colleague groups, but while in this respect disadvantageous this is of small concern to women employees whose family activities and commitments are less compatible than men's with extra-familial group loyalties.[4] Finally, at least in primary schoolteaching, the role itself is closer to the maternal than to the paternal familial role: it calls upon nurturant skills, and an holistic approach towards other people that is more culturally developed among women. The client of the primary schoolteacher is the child, struggling to learn, with low levels of mastery of language and emotions, and in all societies women are more socialized than men to give them care and guidance.

The stereotype of teaching as a women's occupation is, then, founded in empirical fact in two respects: it is an occupation with a predominance of women members and it involves work, at least in primary schools, for which women are

1 Mason reports that in a United States national sample of beginning teachers in 1956 80 per cent of the men expected to remain continuously employed as teachers or school administrators until retirement, but only 25 per cent of the women had this expectation. See Ward S. Mason, *The Beginning Teacher : Status and Career Orientations,* Circular no. 644 (Washington, D.C., 1961). p. 103.
2 See Lortie's thorough discussion of teachers' rewards in his paper that has been drawn upon at many points in this chapter: Dan C. Lortie, 'The Balance of Control and Autonomy in Elementary School Teaching', in Etzioni, *op. cit.* pp. 1-53.
3 Sample Census, *op. cit.*
4 A suggestive, wide-ranging discussion of biologically-based sex differences in joining and maintaining group bonds is Lionel Tiger, *Men in Groups* (London, 1969).

especially fitted. Yet the differences between primary and secondary schools in
these respects are more apparent than real, for all teachers are parent-surrogates.
The experience of supervising and taking some responsibility for growing
children and adolescents, common to all parents, is shared of all professional
people only with schoolteachers, at whatever level. The habit of ex-pupils
returning to their secondary schools to visit their old teachers is not matched
in any other professional context and is most akin to periodic visits to somewhat
distant relatives. Teachers, like parents, though to lesser degree, have to cope
with the experience of children with whom they are familiar and to some of ᵥ
whom they are genuinely attached passing out of their realm of jurisdiction into
adulthood. They too experience with parents the strain of value-clashes between
the generations. Teachers, then, have in their working lives to share experiences
closer to those of parents' than do other professionals.

What is of importance in the context of this paper is not only the fact that
teaching is an occupation suited and attractive to women but also the consequences of this. These are profound. The high proportion of women members
combining teaching with family life or returning to teaching after leaving it for
family reasons involves high rates of turnover and this in association with the
large number of teachers results in a loosely organized professional group. Both
Caplow and Lieberman assert baldly that the preponderance of women leads
directly to what they term 'the unorganisability of the profession'.[1] There is
certainly a direct relationship between group size, membership turnover and
growth on the one hand and loose structure and loose controls on the other.
Coser has argued that the larger a group becomes the looser will be the common
element shared by members and the less cohesive will be the group.[2] Caplow has
applied this proposition to occupational groups and pointed out that it leads to
a low degree of control. He also suggests that growth of an occupational group
is far more threatening than is decline of group solidarity.[3] Indeed it seems self-
evident that the casualness of entry into and exit from teaching associated with
high rates of turnover of personnel precludes any but a loosely organized
membership group.

This structural cause of loose organization is reinforced by the tenuous
loyalty of women members. The presence of so large a female element requires
that family values be compatible with those of the occupation. As Roe has
argued, much needs to be done for benefit of society ' . . . in terms of reorgan-
ising work patterns and opportunities, whether part-time or not, whereby
those who are not adequately satisfied with their traditional housewife role may
find other outlets, and still not give up this socially necessary role.'[4] From this it·

1 Theodore Caplow, *The Sociology of Work* (Minneapolis, 1954), p. 246, and Lieberman,
   op. cit. pp. 247-56.
2 Lewis Coser, *The Functions of Social Conflict* (Glencoe, 1956), pp. 144-5.
3 Caplow, *op. cit.* p. 138.
4 Anne Roe, *The Psychology of Occupations* (New York, 1956).

would follow that teaching cannot be organized, as are the elite professions on the ready assumption that its practitioners equally value and draw equal satisfaction from their work. Thus the predominance of women contributes heavily to a loose organization of the teaching profession beyond the power of exhortation for rational planning and cooperation to dispel.[1]

As a reinforcement of how different is the situation in respect of these two group characteristics, size and the predominance of women, of teachers as compared with all other professional groups save nursing, the two quantifiable variables are combined in the matrix shown in Table 3.

Table 3. *Proportion of Female Members and Proportion of All Professional Workers of Selected Professional Occupations in Great Britain (1966)*

	Occupational group as % of all professionals		
% female members	Less than 5%	5-15%	Over 15%
0-5%	Law Architecture	Engineering	–
6-25%	Medicine	Accountancy	–
26-50%	–	–	–
Over 50%	Social work	–	Nursing Schoolteaching

Source: Sample Census 1966.

This emphasizes clearly how these two structural features distinguish schoolteaching and nursing from other professional groups, with consequences that have been discussed. The occupational similarities of teaching and nursing are explored further below.

The third principal feature of teachers as a group is their social class origin. As compared with the elite professions, Marshall's occupations for gentlemen,[2] teaching draws recruits of modest social class origin. The best data on teachers in England and Wales is still that gathered for 1955 by Floud and Scott. These show that among primary teachers 52 per cent of men and 47.5 per cent of women were of lower class and 26 per cent of both sex groups were of lower middle class origin. Among secondary school teachers proportions of men of lower class origin varied from 52.5 per cent in modern schools to 25 per cent in direct-grant grammar schools and for those of lower middle class origin from

1 Yet Lieberman and other critics continue to believe that exhortation to teachers to cooperate more effectively will change the situation.
2 T. H. Marshall, 'The Recent History of Professionalism in Relation to Social Structure and Social Policy', *Canadian Journal of Economics and Political Science*, 5 (August 1939), 325-40.

31 per cent in maintained grammar schools to 23 per cent in modern schools; comparable data for women ranged from 39 per cent of lower class origin in modern schools to 15 per cent in direct-grant grammar schools, and from 30 per cent of lower middle class origin in modern schools to 25 per cent in maintained grammar schools.[1] The full data are given in Table 4 below.

Table 4. *Proportions of Men and Women Teachers of Lower Class and Lower Middle Class Origin in Grant-Earning Schools in England and Wales (1955)*

Type of School

Social class %	Primary %	Modern %	Technical %	Maintained Grammar %	Direct Grant Grammar %
			(A) Men		
Lower middle	25.6	23.1	28.8	31.1	26.7
Lower	51.9	52.5	47.0	36.7	24.7
			(B) Women		
Lower middle	25.9	29.8	28.5	24.6	26.6
Lower	47.5	39.8	30.5	25.2	15.0

Source: J. Floud and W. Scott, 'Recruitment to Teaching in England and Wales', Table II, adapted.

Note: Lower middle: small enterprise and own account, and clerical; excludes teaching, and lesser professions, administrative and business.

Lower: all manual, farming, and personal service.

Floud and Scott also established that this class composition has changed very little over the years in primary schools, although there has been a decline in the social class of grammar school teachers. Data from the United States are very similar. Mason reports that of those starting to teach in the 1956/57 school year 62 per cent of the men and 49 per cent of the women were from blue-collar or farm backgrounds.[2] In both countries therefore teaching seems to be an important avenue of upward social mobility, especially for men. Simpson and Simpson comment on Mason's data that if teachers who are children of clerks, salesmen, blue-collar workers or farmers are considered upwardly mobile, 61 per cent of Mason's sample had moved up.[3] The superior class background of women teachers confirms earlier statements of the comparatively high prestige

1 Jean Floud and W. Scott, 'Recruitment to Teaching in England and Wales', in A. H. Halsey, Jean Floud and C. Arnold Anderson (eds.), *Education, Economy and Society: A Reader in the Sociology of Education* (New York, 1961). pp. 527-44.
2 Mason, *op. cit.* p. 13. See also Lindley J. Stiles (ed.), *The Teacher's Role in American Society* (New York, 1957), pp. 13-41.
3 Simpson and Simpson, *op. cit.* p. 200.

of teaching as a career for women. Clearly an occupational group that recruits
so heavily from the lower social classes and that provides an important avenue
for social mobility can have no more than intermediate standing itself.

The fourth main characteristic of the occupational group is its relatively low
degree of autonomy as compared with other professions. The high degree of
autonomy of the elite professions is their most significant organizational characteristic, but this can in no way be matched by a semi-profession employed in a
bureaucratic structure. Teachers, as already noted, lack this autonomy. They are
effectively government servants conforming in the practices of their institutions
to government regulation. In the United States teachers are the employees of
local school boards elected by the community who vote upon and control
directly tax monies for the schools.

This lack of autonomy has causes rooted in the histories of the two countries.
In this country education in the state sector was developed by a ruling elite
that expanded the provision as it thought necessary for the well-being of the
economy and polity, while sending its own children to separate, private schools.
In the United States the early settlers established and maintained their local
schools under community control, a tradition that has always been stoutly
defended.[1] Goode has put forward the proposition that autonomy is only won
when it is necessary and that this necessity only arises when an occupational
group has the power to do harm to its clients.[2] However, this seems to be a
somewhat contrary view since the necessity for control need not at all lead to
autonomous control: the control by civil governments of professional armies is
a case in point.

A final feature of the teaching profession that requires comment is its segmented state. Cleavage in this country derives from several sources: the existence
of public and private sectors, the different levels of schooling, the competing
interests of administrators, school principals and teachers, the separate disciplines
at the secondary level, and the various teacher associations that match these
differences. In the United States these sources of differences are overlaid by a
major division between the American Federation of Teachers on the one hand
with unionized workers as its reference group and the National Education Association on the other which admits administrators as members and looks instead
to the 'free' professions.[3] These cleavages preclude any but a fragile unity, leaving
effective power in both countries with administrators. They prevent the cohesion
so vital for the generation of informal work norms common to all teachers, upon
which a more developed autonomy might be founded. Bucher and Strauss in
their discussion of segments in professional occupations have maintained that

1 For a full account see Bernard Bailyn, *Education in the Forming of American Society*
   (Chapel Hill, 1960).
2 Goode, *op. cit.* pp. 297-303.
3 For full discussion of the United States teacher organizations see Lieberman, *op. cit.*

they may be a source of strength, a focus for an effective pressure group that can transform an occupation. They exemplify their thesis by reference to various sub-branches of medicine.[1] However, the profession of medicine has long been established and the jockeying for position of established specialities cannot be taken to imply that the segmentation of the teaching profession will be advantageous to their struggle for status also. In contrast, a more promising development would seem to be a move towards common objectives on a united front, as may in the future be achieved in this country.[2] This move is itself further evidence of the felt need of an occupational group to unite in order to act as a significant political force. Nonetheless, though unity is seen to be necessary for political purposes, it remains to be seen how well it can be maintained in view of the very real, differing interests that the various segments of the profession legitimately represent, the structural features already noted that preclude any but a loose form of organization and the disparate values that reduce the possibility of agreement on any but diffuse and vague goals.

Consideration of these five principal features of the occupational group, relating to the ascribed characteristics of members, characteristics of membership structure and the structure of employment, forces the conclusion that relative to the elite professions teachers have no likelihood of markedly improving their public prestige, their internal cohesiveness and their status according to any proposed scale of professionalism. However, if one looks closely at the clientele of teachers and their relations with them, and at the teachers' work itself, the real uniqueness of the profession and its activities and the small value at the present time of comparing teaching with other occupations before its distinguishing characteristics are fully examined and understood will become further apparent. This examination now follows.

TEACHERS' CLIENTS AND CLIENT-RELATIONS

Numerous characteristics of schoolchildren and of teachers' relations with them are quite unlike the clients and client relations that other professionals are accustomed to. Yet little attention has been drawn to this. First and foremost the clients are of low status. Westwood describes teachers as mediating between the world of children and the world of adults,[3] and this surely gives teachers themselves a marginal role and status. Geer states firmly that children are clients of inferior status, presumably because they are immature people in need of control and guidance, and it no doubt follows that their dealing solely with low

1 Bucher and Strauss, *op. cit.*
2 A report of a Bill to be tabled in Parliament for the establishment of a Teachers' General Council to give teachers in England and Wales 'a genuine professional status' appeared in *The Times*, 12 August 1969.
3 L. J. Westwood, 'The Role of the Teacher – II', *Educational Research*, 10 (November 1967), 21-37.

status clients depresses the status of teachers. Geer also makes the point that serving clients who are compelled to attend likewise is damaging to status.[1] The requirement of compulsory attendance changes ordinary parental concern for their children into *rights* to know and therefore appraise what is going on in schools. Given that this is so, the question arises whether indeed children are the teacher's clients. Are not parents the real clients, since teachers are providing their children with instruction which they lack the skills to give themselves and in which process they are likely to see more importance than do the children? Or, since the children's attendance is not only compulsory but also free and teachers are hired employees, is the state or the community the one big client suggested by Lortie?[2] Certainly the matter is not as clear here as in most other professional work where the multiple client is rare.[3] The only satisfactory answer is that all three parties are clients with a legitimate interest in teachers' work and all standing to gain benefit from their proper performance.

Of the three clients those with most immediate interest are children and their parents, and their interests are neither of them satisfactorily represented, for parents are adults too distant from the classroom, even when fully interested, to be well-informed about what is going on in school and children are well-informed non-adults open to the suspicion of immaturity in the proper judgement of adult behaviour and of espousing values positively hostile to the adult world. This measure of ambiguity is in part functional for teachers, who are thus enabled to control both varieties of client and their challenges to teacher authority.[4] Yet it is clearly also dysfunctional with respect to high professional status since it distorts a proper professional-client relationship by forcing teachers to use discipline and bureaucratic authority to control their compulsorily-attending immature students and by allowing them to define parents as ill-informed, meddlesome, intrusive and the like.[5]

Lortie notes that would-be teachers have had about 10,000 hours of exposure to practising teachers prior to starting their own training, and he points out that no other initiate has this kind of experience of his occupation and its practitioners.[6] But so too have all parents who have completed secondary schooling which likewise gives them an acquaintanceship with practising teachers and therefore an empirical basis for appraising them that is without comparison in their relations with other professional workers. Parents with secondary schooling cannot be persuaded of the arcane nature of the teacher's art. Further, teachers

1 Geer, *op. cit.*
2 Lortie, *op. cit.* p. 23.
3 Although with the development of the welfare state the combination of the individual client and the state as massive client is becoming more common.
4 See Howard S. Becker, 'The Teacher in the Authority System of the Public School', *Journal of Educational Sociology*, 27 (November 1953).
5 *Ibid.* The definition varies according to the social class of the parents.
6 Lortie, *op. cit.* p. 10.

are in several respects acting *in loco parentis*, serving as role-models and as instruments of socialization, integration and social control.[1] They have traditionally been allowed powers of discipline and punishment, even of corporal punishment, as have no other adults outside the family and they are in some measure the guardians of morals and arbiters of conduct of their charges as well as the academic instructors. Further, as Naegele has noted, by grace of modern psychological theory, teachers have access to information about parents and their ways through inference from the behaviour of their children.[2] These are very exceptional privileges for which parents may truly claim the reciprocal right if not of close scrutiny at least of free criticism. And they suffice to give the parent-teacher relationship an emotional charge that no professional with aspirations to universalistic objectivity could tolerate.[3]

The teacher's relationship with pupils is equally unusual. As noted above, the clients are all minors, they meet the professional teacher not by virtue of the attraction of high reputation but through compulsion, and they often see little or no purpose in classroom activity. These circumstances in themselves would not allow an ideal typical professional relationship, but this is further complicated by two other features. First, the pupil-clients meet the teacher in a group seldom of less than twenty-five[4] and secondly, the relationship is intensive, regular and protracted over a long period of time. Each pupil receives the teacher's undivided attention only on very rare occasions. He has a fragment of the teacher's concentrated effort while being continually exposed to generalized attention and having great opportunity to observe the teacher dealing with other pupils. The difference from other professional situations is striking. While a patient in a hospital ward has occasion to observe the nurse tending to others this is not at a loss of personal attention and the nurse's conversational exchanges are not overheard by all patients in the ward. Only in teaching is a professional's unique personal service to clients so attenuated and public. The regularity of school classes and the long time span of pupils' contact with teachers[5] deny to teachers the opportunity to act as impersonal and impartial professionals.[6] However much he may attempt to hold his distance, his exposure is too constant and in time he is sure to be seen as a human of the usual, or more than usual, frailty whose foibles and idiosyncracies are noted, exploited and passed on through the oral tradition of schoolchildren. Ultimately, no mystery, no semblance of secret art, no impervious professional front can be convincingly sustained.

1 See Kaspar D. Naegele, 'Clergymen, Teachers and Psychiatrists: A Study in Roles and Socialization', *Canadian Journal of Economics and Political Science,* 22 (February 1956), 46-62.
2 *Ibid.* p. 55.
3 See Talcott Parsons, 'The Professions and Social Structure', in *Essays in Sociological Theory* (New York, 1957), pp. 34-49.
4 This generalization holds good only of the public sector.
5 Up to 12 years.
6 This is of course not even attempted in primary schools.

CHARACTERISTICS OF THE TEACHER'S WORK

Discussions of the teacher's classroom role usually focus upon such issues as the diffuseness of the role, the teacher's difficulty in reconciling the bureaucratic need for discipline and social distance with a personal need for what Bidwell has called 'affectively laden interaction', or the conflict of role-expectations and personality disposition.[1] In the present context other less discussed aspects of the nature of teaching are more central. These are the teacher's knowledge and the evaluation of his work; the language of the primary school teacher; the teacher's 'holistic orientation';[2] the autonomy of the classroom.

The knowledge base of Etzioni's semi-professions is admittedly weak. As noted above, every educated adult has a basis for critical evaluation. Education is not in itself a recognized intellectual discipline but a composite subject which draws upon other disciplines that have not yet themselves earned great respect, such as psychology and sociology. Wilensky argues that respect for these subjects is low because they deal with behaviour that we all have many years familiarity with.[3] Courses in the methodology of teaching therefore tend to be judged as somewhat fraudulent attempts to establish an illusory expertise. The disciplines taught in secondary school, and especially the natural sciences, are indeed intellectually respectable. But still the high status given by esoteric knowledge is evasive, because the schoolteacher's function is only to transmit knowledge and not to create it. Only at the university level is the teacher's specialized knowledge clearly out of reach of the secondary school-educated citizen and only at that level is it prestigiously associated with the creative processes of research. Whitehead's prescription that ' . . . foresight based upon theory, and theory based upon understanding of the nature of things, are essential to a profession' is far from being fulfilled.[4] All schoolteachers employ a very simple technology, and what technology they do use – audiovisual aids and the like – has been developed by workers in other fields. Further, teaching does not allow the accumulation of experience over generations. Teachers are isolated in their class-room work, they do not work together, so that the arts of an outstanding teacher die with him.[5]

Despite this, or perhaps because of it, evaluation of teaching is an uncertain process. There is little agreement about what are the objectives of education, about what constitutes success in teaching, and therefore about the criteria by which 'success' may properly be judged. Hughes has commented as follows: 'In

1 Charles E. Bidwell, 'The School as a Formal Organization', in James G. March (ed.), *Handbook of Organizations* (Chicago, 1965), pp. 972-1022. See also Willard Waller, *The Sociology of Teaching,* (New York, 1932).
2 Simpson and Simpson, *op. cit.* pp. 234-40.
3 Wilensky, *op. cit.* p. 149.
4 A. N. Whitehead, 'Aspects of Freedom, in *Adventures of Ideas* (Cambridge, 1932).
5 Lortie, *op. cit.* p. 29.

teaching, where ends are very ill-defined — and consequently mistakes are equally so — where the lay world is quick to criticize and blame, correct handling becomes ritual as much as or even more than an art.'[1]

Thus, argues Hughes, responsibility for failure is put upon the student. But so too may be the credit for success. When a pupil performs well in an examination, is it his success or the teacher's? There are no criteria for discrimination, so that honours can seldom be more than shared. And those with most relevant experience for passing judgement, a teacher's own peers, are prevented from so doing by their exclusion from the classroom. As a consequence a remarkable situation arises in which parents and pupils feel that they can readily evaluate teachers, and do so — and for this additional reason have less respect for teachers than for other professionals, while the only people well placed to make judgements on an informed basis and according to consistently applied criteria are the teachers themselves. Jackson's research among outstanding teachers in Chicago illustrates this conclusion. The teachers whom he interviewed expressed great hostility to outsiders' evaluations of their classroom performance, sharply mistrusted tests because they served to assess the child's natural ability rather than the teacher's effectiveness, yet were fully confident that they could directly and immediately assess their own performance: as one teacher replied on being asked how this was done, 'oh, look at their faces'.[2] Lortie, too, stresses the importance of what he calls intrinsic and transitive rewards: 'transitive rewards arise when effective communication with students produces student responses which the teacher defines as learning.'[3] The difficulty that teachers have in eliciting respect for their learning and expertise when combined with this lack of clarity about the nature of success in teaching inevitably exposes them to criticism, and to the insecurity that can follow this, and undermines their claims to respect. The further inevitable result, much commented upon, is that the teacher is forced toward a reliance upon a bureaucratic style of authority.[4]

The features of a weak knowledge base and of problematic evaluation give teaching at the primary level an anti-intellectual flavour, and this is reinforced by a characteristic of their language to which both Jackson and Lortie have drawn attention, its conceptual simplicity. Jackson associates this trait with a simplified view of causality and intuitive rather than rational decision-making in the classroom ('playing by ear'), and attributes all three traits to the primary teacher's very specific concerns and highly intensive contact with children — he calculates a normal rate of two hundred to three hundred interpersonal interchanges per hour — and to her need to tolerate ambiguity, unpredictability and

1 Everett C. Hughes, 'Mistakes at Work', *Canadian Journal of Economics and Political Science,* 17 (August 1951), 322-5.
2 P. W. Jackson, *Life in Classrooms* (New York, 1968), chapter 4.
3 Lortie, *op. cit.* p. 33.
4 See Bidwell, *op. cit.* and Lortie, *op. cit.*

occasional chaos.[1] Lortie quo es from research by Haller who found that 90 per cent of the vocabulary used by elementary teachers in ordinary conversation (with an adult) were the 2,200 most commonly used words in the English language. As Lortie himself concludes, this suggests that teachers do not 'possess and employ an extensive technical rhetoric'.[2] These findings draw attention to a much under-researched area. They also illustrate the primary schoolteacher's distance from the technical and learned professions with their specialized and in part private languages.

Again in contrast to the traditional professional's highly specific[3] concern with his clients the teacher's approach to his pupils is characterized by his 'holistic orientation'. To the teacher the response of the pupil as a total person is frequently as important for his satisfaction as his own exercise of skills; indeed such a response may be seen as the only good evidence of a proper exercise of skills. This concern accounts for the teacher's interest and pleasure in ex-pupils who return to school: the fortunes of the whole person are of importance, for the teacher's full responsibilities embrace the overall socialization of the child into the values of the adult society.

THE BUREAUCRATIC CONTEXT

Much has been written about the bureaucratic features of school organization and of the effects this has upon teachers and the nature of their role. A summary comment is relevant here. The organizational setting of the school is bureaucratic in the classic Weberian sense, at least in a rudimentary form: there is a functional division of labour; the authority structure is hierarchical, disputes being settled by reference to superiors, and each employee derives his or her authority in the first instance from the office rather than from any personal qualities; great importance is attached to rules and to formal records; each client or pupil is treated impartially according to universalistic criteria; there are clear qualifications for recruitment and promotion is according to seniority.[4] However, while many students of bureaucracy have been concerned with the dilemma of the professional working as a staff member in a bureaucratic setting, a common situation in industry, the position of the teacher is quite distinct in that all members of the school hierarchy are professional educators who have shared the same training. So that, although some degree of conflict may be inevitable for the professional working in a bureaucratic organization[5] owing to the clash of criteria in relation to proper work practice and to the authority

1 Jackson, *op. cit.*
2 Lortie, *op. cit.* p. 52.
3 Parsons, *op. cit.*
4 See Bidwell, *op. cit.* for a full discussion of the school as a bureaucracy.
5 For evidence for this see Ronald G. Corwin, 'Militant Professionalism, Initiative and Compliance in Public Education', *Sociology of Education*, 38 (1965), 310-31.

system, and especially to the enfeeblement of the service ideal at the hands of the client orientation of the teacher, the bureaucracy is one of low constraint. As Lortie points out, there is in schools what he calls 'zoned decision-making'. Although the professional teacher has to accept his superiors' authority in many areas, he nonetheless has his own free and independent zone of decision-making in the privacy of the classroom.[1] It is precisely this very real autonomy that makes bearable for the teacher employment in a bureaucracy. The content of his teaching is his to determine, however defined the curriculum. Yet this too is in part dysfunctional from the perspective of professionalism. The very autonomy that is such an important characteristic of teaching and one of the sources of its rewards for the teacher, also divides teachers from each other and prevents the development of those significant colleague relations that would allow the emergence of a cohesive community of professionals.

THE DISTINCTIVENESS OF TEACHING

The object of this paper has been twofold. First, an attempt has been made to establish more clearly the nature of the professional status of teaching, so as to lead discussion away from disputes about whether it is a profession at all and how the occupation is progressing towards further professionalization. Teaching is a profession but not a highly esteemed one, and this it will never be. The second aim has been to identify the features of the occupational group and its characteristic work which truly distinguish them from others, and also to point to further questions of interest for future enquiry. It remains only to summarize these defining characteristics of the occupation. Those discussed in the paper are listed in Table 5.

Table 5. *Principal Characteristics of Professional Teaching*

Practitioner group	Clients and client relations	Work performance
1 Large size	1 Low status clients	1 Based on low expertise
2 Large proportion of female members	2 Clients confronted in large groups	2 Knowledge not created
3 Low social class	3 Compulsory relations	3 Holistic orientation
4 High rate of turnover	4 Protracted relations	4 Use of simple language
5 Loose organization	5 Emotionally charged relations	5 Performance hard to evaluate
	6 Multiple clientele	6 Isolation

The question must be raised whether this configuration is unique or whether

1 Lortie, *op. cit.* pp. 12-15.

there are other occupations that approximately share it. Unquestionably, nursing is the most nearly comparable occupation. Its group characteristics are similar. Nurses also transmit rather than create knowledge and perform their operations on captive, often intractable clients. Their language to patients has frequently to be simplified, though there is no evidence that this carries over into their speech outside the ward; indeed they share the technical language of the medical profession. They do develop liking for individual patients, and without doubt friendly relations are directly helpful to them in enlisting the cooperation of patients; and their work, being concerned with life and death, has a high emotional charge. Yet they are not as concerned as are teachers with the whole person. Though their knowledge base is weak in itself it is backed up by the highly technical and mysterious expertise of the medical profession. Finally, the autonomy of the nurse, who is continually overseen at work and who can be seen at times by patients to be of lowly status, is far less than that of the teacher. There are further similarities in client relations: the infirm, and especially the mental patient and the long-stay geriatric patient, are of low status. The element of compulsion may at times be yet greater than for school children and it is always present to some degree. So too, though for a minority of patients only, is the long span of the relationship. The open ward is closer to the public class-room than are other professional settings. Clearly there are dissimilarities and similarities that merit much more extensive treatment than is possible here.

FORESEEABLE DEVELOPMENTS

Of all trends that may in the future affect the teaching occupation there are two developments being promoted by a number of forces. The first is internal to the school, the conversion of the teacher's role from that of instructor into that of facilitator and resource person. The much commented upon clash of values between the generations results in the teacher as he or she ages and gains exper-ience knowing less well rather than better what to expect of his charges.[1] This must reduce the authoritative component in the teacher's approach, especially if, with a change in the age of majority, secondary school students become adults and no doubt also parents. Traditional authority could not be sustained in face of such developments. Further factors that are leading the teacher to become more of a facilitator are greater use of technology and of sub-professional person-nel in schools,[2] both causing teachers to become more specialized and supporting moves toward greater use of variable-sized groups as against the standard full-

1 See Margaret Mead, *The School in American Culture* (Cambridge, Mass., 1955), p. 31.
2 For a discussion of the introduction of sub-professionals, both paid and volunteer, into schools in the United States, and of the implications of their use see Timothy Leggatt, 'The Use of Nonprofessionals in Large-City Systems', in David Street (ed.), *Innovation in Mass Education* (New York, 1969), pp. 177-200.

sized class of traditional practice. The second major foreseeable change is in relations with the environment of the school as schools reach out into the community to provide a greater service for adults as well as for children and as parents become more involved in school affairs. Research in the future should be into these developments and, more generally, into the nature and processes of innovation: into the responsiveness of schools to growing external pressures and into redefinitions of the teacher's role as a result of external pressure, modifications of the teacher-pupil relationship and new modes of class-room organisation.

6 Critical Notes on Sociological Studies of Professional Socialization

VIRGINIA OLESON and ELVI W. WHITTAKER

6

CRITICAL NOTES ON SOCIOLOGICAL STUDIES OF PROFESSIONAL SOCIALIZATION

VIRGINIA OLESEN and ELVI W. WHITTAKER

One of the areas in contemporary sociology that strains the limits and worth of available concepts is the study of the sociology of the professions. For these very reasons this area presents the possibilities for the critical scrutiny of familiar concepts and alternatives for the development of new conceptual tools. The question of conceptual adequacy and innovation is greatly at issue in a sub-set of this general area, concerning the matter of socialization into the professions and professional life, or more plainly stated, the matter of how and in what fashion persons who are drawn to or elect to enter the professions are indeed drawn to or elected and how they and the profession subsequently fare as they attain and are accorded membership.

In the pages which follow we shall address ourselves to conceptual adequacy in studies of professional socialization, utilizing materials drawn from a number of enquiries, including our own, and from investigators in several societies. The latter resource should suggest a means of achieving conclusions which transcend the case of the United States from which the main core of our material arises. That we cannot fully transcend the cultural and therefore intellectual limits placed on us by reason of our own position and origins is taken for granted; that we should try to do so is more than an escape from intellectual isolation, provincialism and imperialism, indeed, it is mandatory if the central issue of this paper, conceptual adequacy in studies of professional socialization, is to be thoroughly explored.

The issue of conceptual adequacy in sociology is itself not without certain thorny aspects which emerge from the history of the discipline and the differing views of the nature, contours and purposes of sociology, irrespective of the society or the sector in which the sociologist is working. On the one hand these aspects are vertical in nature, referring to the historical transmission of concepts from the social theorists, philosophers, and early heroic figures in the field, transmission which carries implications of adequacy. On the other hand these aspects have horizontal attributes, for sociology, in company with other social sciences characteristically has utilized 'received concepts' from other disciplines, a type of cross-disciplinary borrowing which, like all such cross-cultural exchange, can lead not only to new applications of the concepts in question, but new notions of conceptual adequacy.[1] Not infrequently, as the earlier debate around measurement in American sociology revealed, concepts are deemed adequate with reference to the physical sciences, a mode of comparison rooted in two assumptions: first, that sociological concepts have the same degree of refinement as those in these other sciences and, second, that the human materials available to sociological enquiry are of the same order as those in physics.[2] Moreover, the degree to which those who call themselves sociologists regard themselves and their kind as ideological or non-ideological, e.g. the extent to which sociology is or is not strictly scientific, shapes their views as to whether concepts are adequate to the scientific or critical tasks which they believe lie before the discipline.[3]

These general comments not withstanding, most sociologists, irrespective of national origins, university affiliations, schools and intellectual parentage, or informal friendship ties aspire to and strive for a certain orderliness in their work and thought which in general generates a more or less commonly shared idea of the propriety of rigorousness. Not only the believers in the most rigid standards, but also those who espouse fluid conceptual apparatuses in which concepts emerge from data-gathering enterprises and are constantly refined in the course of such enterprises would be able to discuss conceptual adequacy along the lines classically understood among members of the sociological community, even if they did not agree.[4] It is appropriate therefore, as a way of spanning various positions on conceptual adequacy, to devote some discussion to these commonly understood themes. Such a discussion, however, must take account of the particular and peculiar parentage from which the study of professional socialization springs.

THE AREA OF PROFESSIONAL SOCIALIZATION

PROFESSIONALIZATION

Three streams of sociological thought and research merge in the study of professional socialization, each with its own traditions, conceptual problems and boundaries which both cordon off and insulate the particular sub-sector. These streams are the study of occupations, the analysis of individual change and the scrutiny of social institutions.

---

1 Neil Smelser, 'Sociology and the other Social Sciences', in Paul F. Lazarsfeld, William H. Sewell, Harold Wilensky (eds.), *The Uses of Sociology* (New York, 1967), pp. 3-44.
2 Alfred Schutz, 'Concept and Theory Formation in the Social Sciences', Maurice Natanson (ed.), *Collected Papers of Alfred Schutz*, vol. I, *The Problem of Social Reality* (The Hague, 1962), pp. 48-66.
3 Nathan Glazer, 'The Ideological Uses of Sociology', in Lazarsfeld, *et al., op. cit.* pp. 63-77.
4 Barney G. Glaser and Anselm L. Strauss, *The Discovery of Grounded Theory* (Chicago, 1967).

First, the study of occupations, their histories and place in society necessarily draws the analyst's attention to the functioning of occupations in society and the nature of the occupational structure *vis-à-vis* the social structure. Moreover, the study of occupations brings the student of professional socialization to questions of social change which shifts occupations and their incumbents vertically or horizontally in the society, splintering, eliminating, corroding or enhancing old occupations, whilst evolving new ones. A critical legacy of this sub-sector has been discussion around the category of 'profession' itself. This debate flowed from Carr-Saunders' classic statement of the attributes of 'profession' and continues unabated three decades later, manifested in attempts such as those wherein the idea of an 'order', as in religious orders is used to refine 'profession',[1] which then becomes *profession ordonnée*. Very much as the shift of certain occupations from mere occupations into professions from the beginning served to accommodate the needs of industrial England and the United States, so the definition of 'profession' has served the sociologist.[2] It reflected public definitions and regard for the occupations so designated and therefore pointed to a significant social reality. It bracketed the growing complexity in this sector of occupational studies and lent compactness to a field rife with ambiguities and complexities. Concern with the clarity of the concept itself, the very heart of the on-going discussion, led to such refinements as Carr-Saunders' own distinctions among the professions, new professions, near-professions, and would-be professions.[3] These distinctions, in company with others such as that between professions and semi-professions, allow for a taxonomy of occupations and differentiation among various occupations along the dimensions of what is thought to constitute a profession.[4] Not only is such a taxonomy useful for understanding broad changes which propel or retard occupations from entry into the category of the professions, but it highlights structural elements that have correlates in the socialization process. For example, in the United States medicine, nursing and librarianship differ greatly with respect to the dates when first training and university schools were established and the time of the first national professional association, yet a theme common to matters of socialization in these three occupations is the tension between the demands of the professional association or practitioners and of educators on standards of selection and education in training and in university schools.[5] In spite of the utility of these

1   A. M. Carr-Saunders and P. A. Wilson, *The Professions* (Oxford, 1933). Jean-René Tréanton, 'Le concept de carrière', *Revue Française de Sociologie,* 1, 1 (janvier-mars 1960), 78-80.
2   W. J. Reader, *Professional Men – The Rise of the Professional Classes in Nineteenth Century England* (London, 1966).
3   A. M. Carr-Saunders, 'Metropolitan Conditions and Traditional Professional Relationships', in R. M. Fisher (ed.), *The Metropolis in Modern Life* (Garden City, 1955), p. 281.
4   Amitai Etzioni (ed.), *The Semi-Professions and Their Organization* (New York, 1969); Carr-Saunders, *op. cit.* p. 336.
5   Patricia L. Kendall, *The Relationship Between Medical Educators and Medical Practitioners:*

G

attempts to clarify the parent concept, the much laboured question of what is or is not a profession has led the sociologist (and indeed many professionals themselves) into thickets from which there is no clear exit, for pursuits of an elusive final truth in this matter have tended to overlook major discrepancies between the symbol of 'profession' and the everyday human realities on which it rests. In the words of one analyst, 'Yet to some people, both those within the professions in question and laymen, it is not so clear that medicine and law are necessarily morally praiseworthy and plumbing not'.[1]

The issues in the taxonomy of occupations which can meaningfully or usefully be conceptualized as 'professions' and the attributes along which such conceptualization can proceed are tied to the larger questions generated by the interplay of social/technological change on the one hand and of occupational arrangements and structure on the other. For all the esteem accorded them, the established professions simply do not stand still, but, being in process themselves (even as are occupations deemed more lowly) splinter, extend their domains, and take into themselves new attributes which only they possess.[2] Coupled with these shifts in the old professions are those alterations subsumed in the process of professionalization, that is, the set of thrusts, self-generated or imposed by technological advancement, shifts in cultural roles, etc., that propel occupations and their incumbents toward an approximation of a professional model and that enhance or deter the occupation's thrust in that direction.[3] In that the professions, however extensive or limited one wishes to make the category, are themselves in process and in so far as other occupations are thrusting or being thrust toward professional standing, important alterations occur in core tasks, in the locus of training, in the organization of the occupation itself and organizations which seek to control it. These alterations may be thought of as occurring in the characteristics of the occupation but they are also part and parcel of the structural and interactional elements at issue in the question of training newcomers and for that reason bear on conceptual adequacy in studies of professional socialization.

The bearing of professionalization on conceptual adequacy in socialization

Sources of Strain and Occasions for Cooperation (Evanston, 1965); 'ANA's first position on education for nursing', *American Journal of Nursing*, 65, 12 (December 1962), 106-11; 'Are library schools education for librarianship?' *Journal of Education for Librarianship*, 2, 1 (Summer 1961), 7.

1 Howard S. Becker, 'The nature of a profession', in The Sixty-first Yearbook of the National Society for the Study of Education, *Education for the Professions* (Chicago, 1962), p. 31; Robert W. Habenstein, 'Critique of "profession" as a sociological category', *The Sociological Quarterly*, 4, 4 (Autumn 1963), 291-300.

2 Everett C. Hughes, 'Professions in Transition', in Everett C. Hughes, *Men and Their Work* (Glencoe, 1958), 131-38; Rue Bucher and Anselm Strauss, 'Professions in Process', *American Journal of Sociology*, 66, 4 (January 1961), 325-34.

3 Harold Wilensky, 'The Professionalization of Everyone?' *American Journal of Sociology*, 70, 2 (September 1964), 137-58, D. J. Hickson and M. W. Thomas, 'Professionalization in Britain: a Preliminary Measurement', *Sociology*, 3, 1 (January 1969), 37-53.

studies will be more amply developed in a later section. In passing, two brief examples will serve our point. It is thought that a necessary first step for occupations which begin to professionalize is for the practitioners to do full-time what has to be done.[1] Presumably what is to be done full-time is that which must be taught newcomers, but the question immediately arises as to what exactly is done full-time and therefore what should be transmitted to students. Some observers claim that in contemporary British and American social work the very professionalization of case work has supplanted one type of knowledge for another and that the new knowledge is discrepant with what the fundamental tasks of social workers are.[2] What then is to be taught student social workers? In the analysis of socialization of student social workers what concepts will serve to help the analyst discern the assimilation of these variant role skills? In the second example two different levels of professionalization are at issue, first, attitudinal variables, such as the practitioners' sense of calling and self-regulation by colleagues, and second, structural variables, including full-time pursuit of the work to be done, establishment of training schools, formation of professional associations and development of codes of ethics. One analysis of professionalization indicates that the beliefs pointed to by attitudinal variables are not necessarily as well developed as the structural arrangements suggested by the structural variables within the same occupation, for instance, the case of nurses, librarians, teachers, social workers and engineers.[3] This variation between the practitioners' attitudes on the one hand and the structural charac-teristics on the other hand points to the all too human intransigency of practitio-ners. For those who would analyse professional socialization, however, this variation also generates a number of questions about concepts to be used. In the case of business, for instance, which in several societies shows tendencies to professionalize, at least in such specialized sectors as management or production control, what viewpoints concerning such components as self-regulation, a sense of calling, seeing other management or production control specialists as a reference group are transmitted to students in an array of diverse teaching situations?[4] Or in the case of the profession of certified public accountant in the United States which has attained licensing and certain educational requirements, but is now reaching out to develop viewpoints towards clients which morally justify the occupation as a profession, what sociological concepts are best suited for the investigator who wants to analyse students becoming CPA's?[5]

1 Wilensky, *op. cit.* p. 142.
2 Barbara Wootton, 'The Image of the Social Worker', *British Journal of Sociology,* 11, 4 (December 1960), 385.
3 Richard Hall, 'The Components of Professionalization', unpublished paper read at the American Sociological Association, August 1967.
4 Richard L. Kozelka, 'Business, the Emerging Profession', The Sixty-first Yearbook of the National Society for the Study of Education, *op. cit.* pp. 168-9.
5 Morris J. Daniels, 'Expansion of the CPA's Role: some Ideological Implications', unpub-lished paper, Department of Sociology, San Diego State College, San Diego, California.

SOCIALIZATION

Whether or not 'socialization' is the most useful or productive parent area in which to locate studies of students in the professions is a question which can well be posed at this juncture. Some sociologists, who study occupations, those most narrowly wedded to ideas of occupational role performance, those whose careers are tightly enmeshed with curricular and practical problems of educators in the professions and those who worry about manpower allocation would perhaps prefer to settle for or deal with 'training' as an alternative to 'socialization'. 'Training' holds out neat visions of an experimental learning theory model with a before-after design and for those reasons may seem virtuously simple to the sociologist floundering with understanding of broader complexities of role ambiguities and cultural transmission implicated in student learning of a profession. Moreover, sociologists may long for concepts like 'training' because 'socialization' itself is not without certain ambiguities, either in its various meanings or the uses to which it has been put.

Enculturation

In the forefront of these problems are those which arise when 'socialization' is seen as synonymous with 'enculturation', that is, the learning process through which man, as child and adult, acquires the norms, values and relevant roles in his culture.[1] With respect to the professions, this use of 'socialization' places the area which those studies which focus on events within the adult sector of the life-cycle. Professional socialization thus becomes only one of many strands with which the individual is dealing in becoming adult, among which are acquiring mature values, defining and acting out sex roles, learning norms which guide adult behaviour, shaping and sharpening understanding of social and life goals. Of necessity this definition requires that concepts be used which can embrace more than that of the single strand of acquiring an occupational role, and in addition which can accommodate analysis of reciprocities between the movement along the occupational path and personal developments elsewhere in the enculturation process.

Notably neglected in this respect have been clarifications of concepts which could refer to the reciprocities between adult sex-role learning, that is, the acquisition of cultural norms and expectations around the sex role, and the professional role. An example of this is the interesting, unanswered question which asks whether certain images of one's adult sex role influence one's selection of a profession, one's very socialization into the occupational role and, further, whether this very selection may possibly be part of the individual's interests in establishing, augmenting or embellishing a preferred type of sex role.

1 Mischa Titiev, 'Enculturation', in Julius Gould and William L. Kolb (eds.), *A Dictionary of the Social Sciences* (New York, 1964), p. 239, esp. no. 2.

Clearly, it is not unfeminine for women to select engineering in the Soviet Union, but is apparently in the United States.[1] These questions momentarily take us back to certain issues in professionalization, for one is led to ask how the reciprocities between acquisition of the adult sex role and the professional role flow back into certain shifts within and among professions. For instance, without being narrowly psychological or overlooking economic variables, one can ask what part such reciprocities play in the observed 'femininization' of such medical professions in France as physicians, dentists and pharmacists, both with respect to individual selection of the profession and subsequent choice of setting for practice.[2]

To return to concepts in socialization studies, we may note that the simple analysis of 'sex role' singles out the existence of that particular track in professional socialization. To be sure, this use, limited as it is, has produced findings that married male dental students in the United States reported that they believed marriage had helped them work harder in their professional studies, their reports backed up by the evidence which showed that their grade point averages were higher than those of unmarried men.[3] In so far as any concept must produce both findings and new questions to meet the criterion of productivity, 'sex role' in this instance would seem to be adequate. However, if one is to conceptualize professional socialization as part of enculturation, then this path is only one of several related to acquisition of the occupation and the concept does not precisely indicate either the other paths or the reciprocities between the area of sex role or other role or value acquisition and the occupation. Such reciprocities are rarely dealt with in professional socialization studies, and in studies of adult socialization, an impoverishment that detracts from the fact that in many cases the exploration of the central topic or strand, whatever that may be, is often carried out with commendable competence. As we shall note in a moment, we have in our work tried to utilize a more precise definition of 'sex role', but even this effort does not incorporate as much as it could of other strains and strands in professional socialization. This well may be, both in our analysis and in the instance of other investigators, because the very concept of 'inter-relationship in roles and values' is itself so ill understood.

For these reasons as well as for emergent problems in the analysis of our own date we found that it was necessary to alter the concept of sex role, redefine and clarify it and use instead 'lateral role' and 'lateral role socialization' to

---

1 Norton T. Dodge, *Women in the Soviet Economy* (Baltimore, 1966), esp. Table 57, p. 112.
2 Jean Dang-Ha-Doan Bui and D. R.-Lévy, 'Les femmes dans la médicine et les professions libérales', *Cahiers de Sociologie et de Démographie Médicales*, 4, 4 (octobre-décembre 1964), 123-36.
3 Rolland J. Derenne and Jane E. Fallon, 'Sociological Study of the Relation of Marriage to Scholastic Achievement in Dental School', *Journal of Dental Education*, 28, 4 (December 1964), 422-7.

refer not only to the trajectory in the sex role area, but other areas as well.[1] This illustration of 'lateral role' provides a small model in the matter of conceptual clarification: having used a concept, 'sex role', related to the definition of 'socialization' as 'enculturation', we found that with respect to the parent area the concept was not precise enough, and even more importantly in the on-going analysis of our data we found it necessary to re-shape and alter this to become more productive, more precise and clearer. 'Lateral role' in the hands of other investigators will undoubtedly go through similar transformations not only in the area of socialization, but in the analysis of roles in professional organizations. There available research strongly suggests, but has not fully conceptualized such reciprocities, for instance, the finding that French school masters seek greater vocational satisfaction because, unlike their female colleagues, they usually cannot elevate their social status through marriage, or the lack of occupational communities among women in the 'semi-professions'.[2]

A second observation on conceptual adequacy can be noted when professional socialization is seen as a sector of enculturation, this second observation being related to the types of cultural discontinuities and continuities, present or absent to varying degrees in *any* society, which are experienced by any individual moving through the enculturation process. To speak of the United States for the moment, although the general point can be referred to any society, it has been observed that severe cultural discontinuities exist between the failure of the United States parents to socialize children for responsibility and the later abrupt demands of the society for mature, responsible behaviour.[3] Assuming the plausibility of this observation for the moment, it is then necessary to ask whether or not professional socialization is a pressure point in the enculturation process at which demands of the society for responsibility and maturity are mediated through the roles and norms of the socializing institutions, e.g. the professions' special schools or university schools, and once and for all brought home to the individual. (We cannot pause here to consider in detail the implications of this suggestion for persons being socialized in the other societies and where occupations of many types are undergoing 'professionalization' in various degrees; we may, however, note that these connections between 'professionalization' and 'socialization' have profound implications for the nature and styles of adult behaviour in such societies, if, indeed, the central point here is tenable.) That such is at least the case in the United States

1 Virginia Olesen and Elvi W. Whittaker, *The Silent Dialogue, A Study in The Social Psychology of Professional Education* (San Francisco, 1968), esp. 'Lateral roles and student culture', pp. 209-12 and 'Lateral role accommodation', pp. 213-18.
2 Ida Berger, 'Instituteurs et institutrices, hommes et femmes dans une même profession', *Revue Française de Sociologie*, 1, 2 (avril-juin 1960), pp. 178-85; Richard L. Simpson and Ida Harper Simpson, 'Women and Bureaucracy in the Semi-professions', in Etzioni, *op. cit.* pp. 241-3.
3 Ruth Benedict, 'Continuities and Doscontinuities in Cultural Conditioning', *Psychiatry*, 1, 2 (May 1938), p. 164.

is strongly indicated in the literature of the professions themselves, most particularly their admonitions to their students for highly responsible and mature behaviours.[1] Moreover, sociological findings which use 'reality shock', a social-psychological concept referring to personal stresses occasioned by meeting unexpected sets of norms or expectations in professional school, suggest that in part demands are being placed on students for mature behaviour in excess of the level to which they are accustomed.[2] If this is in fact the case, then 'reality shock' would need to be clarified to include this dimension of enculturation. The substance of these comments is drawn from United States studies of professions and it is well to be cautious about the extent to which the specifics of the point concerning cultural discontinuities can be extended elsewhere. The general issue, however, of the continuities and discontinuities in cultural conditioning is one which sensitizes the student of professional socialization irrespective of the society in which the studies are located to areas in which some concepts can be sharpened and clarified.

This is a view of professional socialization which makes it a special case of what has been termed 'developmental socialization', a more specialized synonym for 'enculturation'.[3] While this perspective, as outlined in preceding paragraphs, does suggest a number of guide-lines for the adequacy of concepts, it also puts a number of limits on this task which are well to note in passing. For one matter there have been substantial historical inter-disciplinary influences on studies of adult and professional socialization by a variety of disciplines, most importantly, child psychology.[4] This heritage, while rich in its coverage and depth and in its own right more systematic than has yet been the case with professional socialization, nevertheless has visited upon the sociologist concerned with professional socialization concepts suffused with implicit models from childhood socialization.[5] A single illustration will suffice to point out the problems of conceptual adequacy engendered by this particular heritage. Running through some of the literature on professional socialization and manifested in the concept of 'student role' is the subtle and presumed similarity between the child being socialized by parents and the student by faculty. Such a conceptualization of 'student role' falls far short of clarity and parsimony. Certain student behaviours, to be sure, can be explained with this concept of 'student role' but

1 Olesen and Whittaker, *The Silent Dialogue,* esp. pp. 59-68.
2 Olesen and Whittaker, *ibid.* esp. pp. 139, 251-9.
3 Stanton Wheeler, 'The Structure of Formally Organized Socialization Settings', in Orville G. Brim, Jr., and Stanton Wheeler (eds.), *Socialization After Childhood* (New York, 1966), p. 68.
4 John A. Clausen, 'A Historical and Comparative View of Sociolaization Theory and Research', in John A. Clausen (ed.), *Socialization And Society* (Boston, 1968), pp. 19-72.
5 Both this theme and the subsequent one of the 'divestiture model' are discussed at length in Virginia Olesen and Elvi W. Whittaker, in 'Some Thoughts of Images of Man Implicit in Sociological Studies of Professional Socialization', paper presented at the Sixth World Congress of Sociology, Evian, France, September 1966.

in the interests of wider explanation (the criterion of parsimony) this concept must be clarified to incorporate themes of 'student role' as one in which influence is exerted by students on faculty and the institution as well as vice versa. One need not limit one's attention to professional socialization to realize the inadequacies of this concept of 'student role'; the contemporary world-wide thrust of student activists, their impact on universities and societies demonstrates this very clearly.[1] To be sure not all studies of childhood socialization fail to analyse mutual parent-child influence, but the images in those which have done this have filtered through to studies of professionalization and socialization only very dimly. Whether or not this subtle imagery of 'student' is influenced by what some observers have seen as 'coercive' themes in studies of childhood socialization done in the United States is therefore a question of some interest.[2] Our reading of the literature on professional socialization done by some of our international colleagues suggests that this conceptual contamination, envisioning student as child, is not limited to American studies, and it is indeed the case that a number of studies done in a variety of settings and countries carry the coercive theme to the point of conceptualizing 'student' as 'a product', etc.[3]

Hidden away in the use of professional socialization as a part of enculturation is another theme which bears on adequacy of concepts. This theme derives from the view of some American sociologists and a good many professional educators in all societies that important elements of society are tied to the smooth workings of the professions, among these the adequate dispersal of moral skills and services, specialized knowledge and so forth.[4] In this view professional socialization, of necessity, is seen as the process of shaping the individual to fit the needs of the profession and by implication of society. 'Professional socialization' thus becomes a type of equilibrium concept, 'the socialized professional' being regarded as socialized in terms of how the balances are worked out as the professions distribute service and knowledge.[5] In turn this means that subsidiary concepts, for example, values, are regarded as adequate in the light of sufficiency to sustain equilibrium or to produce what might be paraphrased as 'the oversocialized professional'.[6] Objections to this view have been stated in a review of childhood socialization studies and can be applied to the present discussion:

1 Stephen Spender, *The Year of the Young Rebels* (New York, 1969).
2 Paul-Henri Combart de Lauwe, 'The Interaction of Person and Society', *American Sociological Review*, 31, 2 (April 1966), 245.
3 Olesen and Whittaker, 'Some Thoughts on Images of Man . . .', discuss such studies.
4 Talcott Parsons, 'The Professions and Social Structure', in Talcott Parsons, *Essays in Sociological Theory* (rev. ed.) (Glencoe, 1958), pp. 34-49.
5 Personal communication from Norman Scotney, Technical Advisor, British Society for International Health Education.
6 Dennis H. Wrong, 'The Oversocialized Conception of Man in Modern Sociology', *American Sociological Review*, 26, 2 (April 1961), 183-93.

'Some authors have written as if socialization were the process for producing a standard product, with the motivations, skills and role repertoire that are required for meeting society's needs . . . It is true that enculturation and acquisition of social skills must be accomplished if social interaction is to go smoothly, but deviant behaviours are learned in the course of any individual's socialization experience.'[1]

If such objections are plausible, then the adequacy of concepts which are sufficient in analysing the socialization of professionals to allow 'smooth working', may very well not clearly comprehend situations where professionals seem ill or poorly socialized. The point here is a critical one, for it suggests a genesis of social change and how much or what type of socialization is implicated in social change with respect to flexibility or rigidity in a given sector of society, for example, the professions.[2]

This leads us back to 'professionalization'. Is it useful to think of concepts for studies of professional socialization as adequate when adequacy is implicitly suffused with ideas of sufficiency and conformity, particularly if the occupation is in transition, e.g. undergoing professionalization? Perhaps not. Rather, some new dimensions of adequacy related to shifts in students learning the profession, resistances within practitioners and movements within the occupation would be more appropriate. This would accommodate a finding such as that which shows that many French nursing instructors thought psychology should be an element in nursing education (an instance of a profession's search for specialized knowledge), but fewer students believed this, which was acceptable to even fewer hospital staff nurses who supervise students.[3] (Reportedly, student views on this matter became more favourable after *les jours du mai,* 1968.) What would provide more plausible criteria for conceptual adequacy in professional socialization, a theme which would consider the confluence between socialization and professionalization, would be consideration of the reciprocities between individual aspirations and occupational and institutional structure, reciprocities which, as has been pointed out, imply the transformation both of the aspirations and of the structures in which the aspirations are realized, to whatever degree.[4]

Acculturation

Professional socialization is not customarily thought to be synonymous with

1 John Clausen, 'Research on Socialization and Personality Development in the United States and France: Remarks on the Paper by Professor Chombart de Lauwe', *American Sociological Review,* 31, 2 (April 1966), 250.
2 Irving Rosow, 'Forms and Functions of Adult Socialization', *Social Forces,* 44, 1 (September 1965), 45.
3 Association Nationale Française des Infirmières et Infirmiers Diplomés d'État, *L'Encadrement des Élèves-Infirmières en Stage Hospitalier* (Paris, 1967), p. 63.
4 Paul-Henri Chombart de Lauwe, 'Dynamique des aspirations et changement des institutions', *Cahiers Internationaux de Sociologie,* 44 (1968), 62; William J. Goode, 'The Theoretical Limits of Professionalization', Etzioni, *op. cit.* p. 274.

G *

'acculturation', which is understood to be 'the process of culture change in which more or less continuous contact between two or more culturally distinct groups results in one group taking over elements of the culture of other groups'.[1] Nevertheless, throughout the literature on professional socialization runs a strong emphasis on the processes of personal and cultural reformulation which are implicated in acculturation, particularly with respect to students who are seen as being assimilated, very much like immigrants or primitives, into the world of the profession, even though it is also recognized in most studies that collectivities of students rarely constitute cultural groups in the same sense as do primitives or immigrants. Numerous studies speak of students being drawn away from the culture of laymen and induced instead into the specialized role skills, norms, professional values and ethical postures which are transmitted by, peculiar and fundamental to the practice of the profession, in short, the culture of the profession. Thus: 'The period of initiation into the role (of the physician) appears to be one wherein the two cultures, lay and professional, interact within the individual.'[2]

Whether in fact the repertoire of norms, values, role behaviours and moral imperatives attributed to a profession do in fact constitute a separate and distinct culture is a fair question which may be answered in part by pointing out that there are variations among professions. These constitute degrees of cultural distinctness on a variety of dimensions which in turn influence student acculturation. A more telling answer is that many students, not a few professionals and the lay public often hold that their profession is a distinct culture. Laymen sometimes state this very sharply, as by a Mexican stenographer: 'Like many law students he was already acting like a lawyer, taking on their mannerisms and personality ahead of time. I smiled at his presumption and said, "Pardon me, I'm just a plain stenographer." He seemed to get the idea and stopped pushing his lawyer's shingle into my face.'[3] From the standpoint of definitions held by those whose world the profession is, the view of professional socialization, e.g. as acculturation is itself meaningful.

This viewpoint is not without certain implicit problems that bear on adequacy of concepts, one of which derives from seeing professional socialization as acculturation, but very narrowly in that 'assimilation' is implied. When this is the case, it is all too easy to select concepts, 'moulding', for instance, which reflect the elements of simple acceptance of the students by the profession or the mere intake by students of professional values.[4] Moreover, this hidden theme

1 Felix M. Keesing, 'Acculturation', in Gould and Kolb, *op. cit.* pp. 6-7. Other definitions there point to exchanges in culture contact.
2 Everett C. Hughes, 'The Making of a Physician', in Everett C. Hughes, *Men and Their Work* (Glencoe, 1958), p. 120.
3 Consuelo Sanchez, quoted in Oscar Lewis, 'A Death in the Sanchez Family', *New York Review of Books,* 13, 4 (11 September 1969), 36.
4 Henri Longchambon, 'La formation des ingénieurs dans l'université', *Revue de l'Enseignement Supérieur,* 1, 1 (janvier-mars 1957), 11-16.

in professional socialization seen as acculturation carries some overtones of equilibrium, which, as has been discussed earlier in another context, imports certain limits on conceptual adequacy.

The broader view of professional socialization as acculturation, e.g. groups in contact and exchange, shapes certain themes in conceptual adequacy, one such being the individuals' shift from one culture to another and their adjustment to this. The concept of 'student culture' used in studies of medical and nursing students allows analysis of this shift and, in addition, raises questions concerning students' emergent relationships and the learners' impact on the course of their own learning and the institution itself.[1] 'Student culture' thus avoids the bracketing elements which intrude when professional socialization is thought of too narrowly as 'assimilation'. The exchanges implicated in the broad view of professional socialization as acculturation, namely the rejection, acceptance and amendment on both sides of what is being transmitted to the students and what they are returning to the professional culture necessitate concepts which allow for these reciprocities, if concepts are to be adequate. From this standpoint a concept such as 'situation' is adequate for it allows precise inspection of these reciprocities,[2] or 'relative deprivation' for it points to differential acculturation among students,[3] or 'culture shock'[4] (rather than the narrower 'reality shock') which calls attention to differences between the cultures in contact.

Having noted some implicit meanings derived from 'enculturation' and 'acculturation', we may turn briefly to the third area which exercises considerable influence on conceptual adequacy in studies of professional socialization, the area of institutions.

THE INSTITUTION

Entry into the professions through formal, institutional schooling is nowadays taken-for-granted, although for some professions elements of this phase of entry have been the case for some time, for example, the early Inns of Court requirement that one had to eat a stipulated number of dinners there in

1 Howard S. Becker, Blanche Geer, Everett C. Hughes and Anselm Strauss, *Boys In White, A Study of Student Culture in Medical School* (Chicago, 1961); Robert K. Merton, 'Some Preliminaries to a Sociology of Medical Education', in Robert K. Merton, George G. Reader and Patricia Kendall (eds.), *The Student Physician* (Cambridge, 1957), p. 42; Olesen and Whittaker, *The Silent Dialogue,* chapter VI, 'The art and practice of studentmanship', pp. 148-99 and chapter VII, 'Processes in becoming: legitimation and adjudication', pp. 200-44.
2 Rue Bucher, 'The Psychiatric Residency and Professional Socioalization', *Journal of Health and Human Behaviour,* 6, 4 (Winter 1965), 197-206.
3 Charles E. Bidwell, 'The Young Professional in the Army', *American Sociological Review,* 26, 1 (February 1961), 360-72.
4 Thomas R. Williams and Margaret Williams, 'Socialization of the Student Nurse', *Nursing Research,* 8, 1 (Winter 1959), 5-15.

company with barristers older and wiser, but not necessarily those with whom the apprentice was doing private reading.[1] In recent times most professional socialization has come into specialized institutions. Indeed, one of the very attributes of professionalization is the establishment of a specialized, formal training school, most usually within a university. It may be noted in passing, however, that certain elite socializing institutions, *les Grandes Écoles* in France, important theological schools such as Union Theological Seminary in New York, the prestigious military schools such as Sandhurst, West Point or St Cyr are not within a university sphere. This fact prompts some leaders in occupations undergoing professionalization to question the desirability of university affiliation and to consider seriously whether there are advantages in remaining separate from the university situation.[2] In any event socialization into a profession is largely experienced within an institutional setting, be it university school or specialized academy. Certain significant aspects of further professional socialization lie in the institutions where the professions are situated, e.g. hospitals, law firms, military organizations, social work agencies, engineering firms, clinics.[3] One such aspect is the tension between organizational constraint and professional practice, faced by American engineers, lawyers, librarians, teachers and social workers,[4] another the presence or absence of colleague contact, such as that encountered by individual general practitioners in Britain.[5] Some brief consideration of what the framework of institutional studies means for analysis of professional socialization, especially in the earlier phase, is therefore in order.

Certainly in the United States institutional studies have drawn heavily on the analysis of persons in prisons and mental hospitals where a major theme has been the imagery of 'divestiture'.[6] This theme has had relevance for concepts in studies of professional socialization in that it posits a model in which the socialization is seen as stripping away prior inadequacies or weaknesses of the individual, reinvesting the person with the special concerns or goals of the institution in question. As an aspect of professional socialization, 'divestiture' is an especially seductive theme because it follows the lines of the prior assumption that the professions are somewhat special and different, 'a calling', and that entry into the company of the elect of necessity demands forfeiting less desirable or

1 Reader, *op. cit.* p. 22.
2 Marie-Louise Badouaille, 'La situation actuelle et future de la profession d'infirmière en France', *International Nursing Review,* forthcoming.
3 Virginia Olesen, 'Some Notes on Post-institutional Socialization in the Health Occupations', paper presented at the First International Conference on Social Science and Medicine, Aberdeen, Scotland, September 1968.
4 Richard H. Hall, 'Some Organizational Considerations in the Professional-organization Relationship', *Administrative Science Quarterly,* 12, 3 (December 1967), 461-78; Andrew Billingsley, 'Bureaucratic and Professional Orientation Patterns in Social Casework', *Social Service Review,* 38, 4 (December 1964), 400-7.
5 David Mechanic,'The Changing Structure of Medical Practice', *Law and Contemporary Problems,* 32, 4 (Autumn 1967), 727.
6 Olesen and Whittaker, 'Some Thoughts on Images of Man...'.

mundane attributes.[1] With respect to adequacy of concepts for study of professional socialization, the influences of these studies and in particular the aspect of 'divestiture' turn investigators to concepts which presumably measure or reflect gains and losses within this period. The concept of attitude has been a particular favourite in this regard and has generated data that show how much 'divesting' and 'reinvesting' has occurred in the course of events.[2] A problem arises with this particular concept, one having to do with precision, because the 'divestiture' model leads investigators to assume that changes or lack of them are derived from the institutional experience, which is often assumed to be total, that is to say, one-way impact of the institution on the student rather than both ways. Lacking here are the implications of exchange or reciprocity between institution and students which were noted in the earlier discussions of socialization as 'acculturation' and 'enculturation'.

In so far, however, as institutions in professional education are key factors in the professionalization of occupations, they therefore constitute particularly significant arenas in which the social and technological forces at play on the occupation may be highlighted. In this respect the inheritance of the institutional studies sharpens the investigator's conceptual range, for it forces attention to concepts which will accommodate certain tensions among elements of the occupation, such as the strains between conservative and progressive faculty as the debates around changes in the occupations go forward, 'factionalism' being one such useful and relatively precise concept in this regard, not only for the description of faculty positions, but for the understanding of student attitudes.[3] In sum, the tradition of institutional studies brings to the analysis of professional socialization some implicit boundaries on conceptual adequacy, boundaries unseen but articulated in terms of the presumed time and structural limits on institutional experience. It also, however, brings awareness of the institution as an arena for the changes implicated in shifts of established professions and movements within those believed to be undergoing professionalization.

Up until this point the discussion has reviewed themes in adequacy of concepts in the light of three parent areas for studies of professional socialization, namely professions and professionalization, socialization and institutions. This, however, is but one way of reviewing conceptual adequacy. Another approach is a review of the usual understandings that constitute conceptual adequacy. Since the pursuit of sociology, whether defined as science, history or humanistic study, is a social endeavour which implicates its followers in communication with one another a review of commonly understood criteria for adequacy provides a bridge across which sociologists of different dispositions and specialties communicate.

1 Anne-Marie Le Léannec, *La Vocation Réligieuse Féminine* (Paris, 1965).
2 Robert M. Gray and W. R. Elton Newman, 'Anomia and Cynical Attitudes of Medical Students', *Proceedings, Utah Academy of Sciences, Arts and Letters*, 38 (1961), 68-73.
3 Olesen and Whittaker, *The Silent Dialogue*, pp. 111-18.

The observation that 'The appropriate conceptualization of the problem already prefigures its solution',[1] leads to the further concerns stated by a number of sociologists who believe the foremost task in the discipline is the statement of meaningful and relevant questions.[2] Conceptualization of problems and the questions which emerge therefrom are in part dependent on concepts both received from already accomplished work and that body of research and thought which sociologists generate during the course of their work. It is well therefore to review adequacy from a number of standpoints.

COMMONLY UNDERSTOOD CRITERIA FOR ADEQUATE CONCEPTS

A review of almost any basic text in sociology or sociological research procedure incorporates in its discussions of research and theory the ideas that concepts, while clear and precise, ought to readily release and guide empirical research activity, sensitize the investigator to new ideas or areas in an efficient, e.g. parsimonious way, and should lend themselves to the construction of useful theory, namely, a coherent set of propositions concerning the area or phenomenon under enquiry.[3] Theory here and throughout this discussion refers to 'theories of the middle range' which lie between the over-arching explanations of the social order and the low level hunches of everyday life.[4] It may be observed in passing that the discussion of conceptual adequacy in the area of professional socialization is particularly complex, for on the one hand the area represents the merging of a number of concerns in substantive studies, namely the studies of the given occupations implicated, and on the other it embraces several formal areas, the area of adult socialization, the problems of professionalization and the issue of institutions.[5] Some of the problems generated by such complexity have already been referred to and will return again in our subsequent discussion of the nature of professional socialization.

Locating concepts which are adequate for the construction of 'middle range theories' whether substantive or formal in this area is, at best, difficult, for at this time in the history of sociology there are no theories of professional socialization and few systematic efforts being made toward such construction.[6] There

1 Abraham Kaplan, *The Conduct of Inquiry: Methodology for Behavioural Science* (San Francisco, 1964), p. 53.
2 Among others, Robert K. Merton, 'Notes on problem-finding in Sociology', in Robert K. Merton, Leonard Broom, Leonard S. Cottrell, Jr. (eds.), *Sociology Today* (New York, 1959), pp. ix-xxxiv.
3 John T. Doby, 'Concepts and Theories', in John T. Doby (ed.), *An Introduction to Social Research* (2nd ed.) (New York, 1967), pp. 31-50.
4 Robert K. Merton, *Social Theory and Social Structure* (rev. ed.) (Glencoe, 1957, pp. 5-10.
5 Glaser and Strauss, *op. cit.* pp. 32-5.
6 One exception in this latter regard being Rue Bucher, 'Mechanisms of Professional Socialization', unpublished paper, Division of Sociology, Department of Psychiatry, University of Illinois Medical Center, 1968.

is, however, no lack of potentially adequate concepts which could be and in some instances have been usefully imported from other sectors to the study of professional socialization. Particularly useful in this respect have been concepts borrowed from theories of symbolic interaction, the concept of 'perspectives', for example, being fruitfully employed to analyse and probe the emergent views of medical students in their course through school;[1] 'dialogue' being utilized in the micro-analysis of exchanges between faculty and student nurses to trace emergent changes through emotional expressions;[2] 'self-other' being brought to differentiate faculty-student attributions in dental schools.[3] The slow work, however, of weaving these types of concepts, referential to emergent psycho-dynamic processes to questions of structure and the delineation of propositions for theory goes slowly and much remains to be done.[4] Another type of borrowing has been that found in the utilitization of concepts from other areas, for example, 'anticipatory socialization' to build formal theories within which the general framework of professional socialization would be but one case, for example, work on theories of occupational choice.[5]

There is no good reason why students of professional socialization should not feel free to borrow as they wish from other disciplines or areas, where concepts may seem useful, at least to the extent of sensitizing them to aspects of their own subject which may have previously seemed self-evident, were thought to be unworthy of analysis or perhaps had not even come to the investigator's attention. Even such concepts as the 'organic' view of society, in bad odour since the time of Schaeffle, could undoubtedly tease out new perspectives on professional socialization, e.g. 'ingestion' and 'disposal' of recruits into professional systems. Used carefully as analogies to open up new areas of thinking, such borrowed concepts can be quite adequate in the sense of producing new questions for research. However, there is always the danger that the borrower forgets that he is utilizing an analogy and begins to think of professional socialization in terms of what he has borrowed, e.g. the organic view of society, instead of its own contours, such as those we have already discussed and those to which we shall turn shortly. Moreover, there is the risk of taking concepts from one realm, e.g. the phenomenological and shifting them into other realms where they do not fit

1 Becker, *et al., op. cit.*
2 Virginia Olesen and Elvi Whittaker, 'Adjudication of Student Awareness in Professional Socialization: the Language of Laughter and Silences', *The Sociological Quarterly*, 7, 3 (Summer 1966), 381-96.
3 Enrico Quarantelli, 'School Learned Adjustments to Negative Self-images in High Status Occupational Roles: the Dental Student Example', *Journal of Educational Sociology*, 35, 4 (December 1961), 165-71.
4 In a recent essay Becker has begun to integrate some related concepts such as 'commitment', 'self', 'situational adjustment', and 'involvement'. Howard S. Becker, 'The Self and Adult Socialization', in Edward Norbeck, Douglass Price-Williams, William M. McCord (eds.), *The Study of Personality, An Interdisciplinary Appraisal* (New York, 1968), pp. 194-208.
5 Peter W. Musgrave, 'Towards a Sociological Theory of Occupational Choice', *The Sociological Review*, 15, 1 (March 1967), 33-46.

the phenomena under analysis.

The question of conceptual clarity is a long-standing problem and by no means unique to the area of professional socialization,[1] which, indeed, has inherited the vagueness which characterizes many concepts borrowed from other areas. The widely differing uses to which borrowed concepts have been put in studies of professional socialization have not clarified concepts, and have muddied understanding of professional socialization. Two examples will suffice: the use of 'social origins' or 'social background' and 'attitude'. The problem with the use of 'social origins' or 'social background' has been that these ideas seem plausibly to carry implications of broad themes of family-life style, value, outlooks and so forth, but in many instances they have been narrowly predicated on explicit or implicit reference to 'social class' based solely on father's occupation.[2] Infrequently one finds the analysis of 'social origins' or 'social background' which include other, conceivably relevant factors such as mother's education, sibling order, family religious affiliation or parent activities in the local community.[3] Two issues emerge from this particular problem in lack of conceptual clarity, the first related to the intertwining of problems of professionalization and professional socialization to which we referred earlier, the second referential to the specific analysis of socialization. In the first instance, the question of social background is of some significance because of the connections between the rise of certain social classes which has accompanied shifts in occupations moving to professional levels, an example being the case of the rising English middle classes in the nineteenth century being attracted to occupations becoming professions.[4] It is important, therefore, to have a precise picture of the social origins of students in order to understand the shifts undergone by both the occupation and those who aspire to it. A recent analysis of Canadian medical students is a model in this regard.[5] To take this point one step further the interplay of students and those whose institutional responsibility it is to impart the professional culture may itself be shaded by fundamental differences

1 Merton, *op. cit.* pp. 114-17; Herbert Blumer, 'The Problem of the Concept in Social Psychology', *American Journal of Sociology,* 45, 5 (March 1940), 707-19.
2 Pierre Bourdieu, Jean-Claude Passeron, Monique de Saint Martin, B. Quésanne, *Les Étudiants en Médicine* (Paris, 1964, 1966); S. H. Croog, William Caudill and Jean L. Blumen, 'Career Decisions of Student Nurses in Japan', *Journal of Nursing Education,* 5, 1 (January 1966), 3 *et passim.*
3 Ronald. L. Pavalko, 'Social Backgrounds and Occupational Perspectives of Dental Students', *Journal of Dental Education,* 28, 2 (June 1964), 253-60; Dennison J. Nash, 'Socialization of the Artist: the American Composer', *Social Forces,* 35, 4 (May 1957), 307-13; Oxford Area Nursing Training Committee, *From Student to Nurse* (Oxford, 1961); Le Léannac, *op. cit.* p. 18; Olesen and Whittaker, *The Silent Dialogue,* 'Student-parent consensus', pp. 87-90.
4 Reader, *op. cit.* p. 43.
5 David B. Fish and C. Farmer, 'Some Social Characteristics of Students in Canadian Medical Schools, 1955-1966', unpublished paper presented at the First International Conference on Social Science and Medicine, Aberdeen, Scotland, September 1968.

between social background of instructors whose entry into the occupation represented a different point in the professionalization of the occupation and that of students whose entry comes at a much later juncture. The strains between certain United States nursing faculty from rural or working class origins and students from urban and middle class background is a case in point.[1] Finally, it may be observed that if the analysis of professional socialization in any way posits a relationship between the student social origins and the course of events in the various phases of socialization, then a precise statement of 'social origins' is certainly in order.[2] For example, such added precision in 'social origins' in analysing United States dental students would clarify understanding of these students' overriding concerns with monetary gain and personal prestige, their role relationships in professional school with certain types of patients, and their reluctance to specialize.[3] To know that substantial percentages (some studies show as high as 70 per cent) come from families where their fathers are in 'skilled occupations' furnishes but a small clue, one which could be enhanced by greater specificity of 'social origins', perhaps to include parent educational level and viewpoints.[4] By no means is this discussion meant to imply that in our view social origins are overriding factors in the socialization of students in the professions, but it would be desirable for the reasons just examined to make this concept clearer with respect to its empirical referents, irrespective of the place given to the concept in one's theoretical scheme or the definition one makes of the overall area of professional socialization.

'Attitude', having both psychological and sociological parentage, not unexpectedly has been invested with several meanings and used in a variety of ways. In one set of studies, the use seems to reflect individual definitions, responses to values, for example, findings that dental students hold unfavourable opinions about certain patients (a response to the human value of the patient); results that indicate medical school faculty have democratic, liberal or appreciative views which create teaching climate (a response to the social value of education); and that medical students develop certain ideas about classmates who are seen as capable (a response to the students' value of cooperativeness); and medical

1 Olesen and Whittaker, *The Silent Dialogue*, p. 86.
2 For example, the precise statement of Mickey C. Smith, 'Birth Order and Integenerational Occupational Mobility among Pharmacy Students', *American Journal of Pharmaceutical Education*, 32, 2 (May 1968), 279-89; John Colombotos', 'Social Origins and Ideology of Physicians: a Study of the Effects of Early Socialization', *Journal of Health and Social Behaviour*, 10, 1 (March 1969), 16-29.
3 Douglas M. More and Nathan Kohn, Jr., 'Some Motives for Entering Dentistry', *American Journal of Sociology*, 66, 1 (July 1960), 48-53; Enrico Quarantelli, 'The Dental Student Image of the Dentist-Patient Relationship', *American Journal of Public Health*, 51, 9 (September 1961), 312-19; Enrico Quarantelli, 'Attitudes of Dental Students toward Specialization and Research', *Journal of the American College of Dentists*, 27, 2 (June 1960), 101-7.
4 One which includes these: Claude Lévy-Leboyer, 'Note sur la mobilité professionelle', *Travail Humain*, 24, 1-2 (janvier-juin 1961), 51-64.

students' shift from idealism to cynicism (a response to the value of medical practice).[1] This use of attitude differs slightly from the application in other studies where the use shades away from an indication of response to values and into a definition where 'attitude' takes on the meaning of 'value'. For instance, adherence of young female students in chemical technical schools in France to traditional female role values or the rejection and acceptance of the value of career by student nurses.[2] Yet a third use pulls 'attitude' in the direction of the meaning of 'norm', for instance the finding that medical interns shift their behavioural proscriptions on interaction with hospital nurses and physicians to include both more egalitarian behaviour and behaviour strictly proscribed by their status in the hospital structure.[3] (In spite of the slipperiness of 'attitude' in this particular study, the research nevertheless deals explicitly with a significant problem noted earlier in these pages, namely the simultaneous analysis of professional socialization and the changing structure of professions and institutions in which professional practice is situated.)

To be sure, each of these studies of attitudes reveals a sector, or a snapshot of the internal realm of persons studied and these glimpses, while segmental and sometimes confused, are not entirely to be faulted, since the internal sectors of professional socialization merit the attention given to objective factors. Where the troubles begin, however, as must be obvious from the foregoing discussion, is in a comparison across these studies, particularly if the assumption is to be made, as it has been classically, that attitudes do somehow relate to behaviour. The issue is even more acute if we once again bring together the questions of professionalization and professional socialization. It has been suggested that attitudinal attributes are less central to professionalization than are structural components.[4] Yet certain occupations remain incompletely professionalized, pharmacy in the United States for one, in part because its students and practitioners tend to adhere to a business-oriented view of the occupation, rather than the humanitarian or service-directed one deemed to be characteristic of the ways in which professionals view their work.   In the case of American pharmacy or similar

1 Robert H. Stiff and Grant T. Phipps, 'Attitudes of Dental Students toward Chronically Ill, Aged and Disabled Persons', *Journal of Dental Education,* 28, 2 (June 1964), 149-54; Edwin F. Rosinski and George E. Miller, 'A Study of Medical School Faculty Attitudes', *Journal of Medical Education,* 37, 2 (February 1962), 112-23; R. V. Platou, L. Reissman, S. H. Sledge and D. H. Malone, 'Medical Students' Attitudes Toward Teachers and Patients', *Journal of Medical Education,* 35, 9 (September 1960), 857-64; Gray and Newman, *op. cit.*
2 Yves Legoux, 'Attitudes de jeunes filles devant une profession technique', *Sociologie du Travail,* 4, 3 (juillet-septembre 1962), 243-61; J. S. Zaccaria and Genevieve Reynolds, 'Nursing Students' Attitudes Toward their Careers: a Challenge for Nursing Education', *Journal of Nursing Education,* 5, 3 (August 1966), 31-4.
3 Melvin Seeman and John W. Evans, 'Apprenticeship and Attitude Change', *American Journal of Sociology,* 67, 4 (January 1962), 365-78.
4 Hall, 'The Components of Professionalization'.
5 Norman K. Denzin, with the assistance of Curtis J. Mettlin, 'Incomplete Professionalization: the Case of Pharmacy', *Social Forces,* 46, 3 (March 1968), pp. 375-81.

situations which might be observed elsewhere one would want to ask what precisely is transmitted to students – attitudes in the sense of opinions on business and service, beliefs and/or values which go more deeply, or norms which presumably would guide not only viewpoint, but behaviour. Clarification of 'attitude' would help to understand this question. It may well be that professional socialization in pharmacy implicates opinions, but not values – on this particular matter. It may also be that in any type of professional socialization there are differential emphases among faculty as to transmitting attitudes or values with respect, not simply to the ideals of service, autonomy, specific knowledge and so forth, but with respect to the issue of professionalization itself. The endless debates among social workers, nurses and librarians as to 'is this occupation a profession' and the frequent appearance of this question in courses taught students on the history of the particular profession suggests that it may well be professionalization which is being taught, not simply the ideals of service, etc.

We may note in passing that 'attitude' is also an inadequate concept from the standpoint of efficiency or parsimony, namely, of how much can be explained with this rather than other concepts. Since it comprehends primarily individual variables, hence only one sector of the complexities, it is of limited utility in explaining, for example, one of the critical phenomenon in the institutional phase of professional socialization, namely, the fact that some students who start do not complete their professional education for a variety of reasons. In a certain sense these students, too, are socialized, but the trajectory of the process for them differs in its outcome from that for those who see their studies through to the end. 'Attitude' is an inefficient concept with which to understand these differences in institutional careers, for not only does it refer to the individual rather than to the individual and the structure, but all too often those who depart display attitudes that are no different from those who finish their schooling. Perhaps part of the reason for the inadequacy of the concept in this regard is that whilst 'attitude' refers to the individual, it does assume, but often this is never made explicit, that there is something around which the attitude is formed or toward which it is directed. Hence there is an implicit structure in the nature of 'attitude' and this structure and its influence for the individuals studied are not carefully considered. Those who use 'attitude' seem to trust blindly and latently to the unrecognized possibility that the delineation of an attitude somehow sketches or enlightens one about the structure. This one-to-one connection does not sit comfortably and perhaps is the reason that those who use 'attitude' often choose to ignore structure in the hope that the confluence and interaction will be supplied by the reader to his own satisfaction. Further, as we have indicated in the brief note of students who do not complete professional education, 'attitudes' cannot provide acceptable glimpses at structure for they are used in ways which ignore the peripheral, latent and secondary influences, all of which constitute more dynamic elements than can be realized with the snap-shot quality of 'attitude'.

To continue our discussion of parsimony, our own concept of 'social insulation', which we originated to mean the degree to which those who did not finish were differentiated from their fellows by age, marital status, living situation and personal affiliation, was of equally limited parsimony, for it, too, neglected structural aspects and the relationship of these to individual attitudes.[1] Moreover, while it served to categorize such students, by no means did it fully explain how the process of departure commenced and proceeded, any more than efforts to rely on concepts such as 'personality' or 'aptitude' succeed in explaining facts behind student departure.[2] Greater conceptual efficiency in analysis of this particular sector of professional socialization can be achieved with concepts which link psycho-structural elements, for instance, self-role perception.[3]

To continue the discussion of adequacy in another direction, the ease with which a concept leads investigators to the choice of indicators, variables or operations necessary to select the indicators confronts the sociologist with some particularly acute problems. The concepts of 'socialization' and 'being socialized' represent examples of these difficulties. Should the fact of graduation or completion of formal studies be taken as the indicator of 'socialization'? If so, how does one account for the fact that so many married nurses depart their field after their studies?[4] How does one understand engineers who opt for jobs with more salary and less possibility for autonomy, one of the central attributes of being professional?[5] How does one explain librarians who waver in their professional authority on controversial materials?[6] How does one analyse 'socialized' (in the sense of having graduated) physicians and nurses who become drug addicts?[7] Clearly the indicator of graduation does not reveal all there is to know about what is implicated in socialization, even institutional socialization. The problem may be found at every level in the analysis of professional socialization, for example, 'success' or 'failure'. If grade point average is selected as the indicator of a certain type of institutional success, then one must confront the uncomfortable social fact that students who earn the highest grades in professional

1 Olesen and Whittaker, *The Silent Dialogue*, 'The drop-outs', pp. 294-7.
2 Claude Lévy-Leboyer, with the assistance of Charles Gadbois, *Les Infirmières en France*, vol. II, *Les Élèves Infirmières: Recrutement, Sélection, Adaptation*, esp. pp. 48-50.
3 Anne E. Kibrick, 'Drop Outs in Schools of Nursing: the Effect of Self and Role Perception', *Nursing Research*, 12, 3 (Summer 1963), 140-9.
4 Among many studies, Lévy-Leboyer, *op. cit.* vol. III, *Les Infirmières Diplomées: Satisfactions et Déceptions; Les Causes de l'Abandon.*
5 Marc Maurice, 'Professionalisme et syndicalisme', *Sociologie du Travail*, 10, 3 (juillet-septembre 1968), 243-56.
6 Marjorie Fiske Lowenthal, *Book Selection and Censorship* (Berkeley, 1959), esp. table 13, p. 125 and table 18, p. 127.
7 Basil J. Sherlock, 'Deviance in Professional Careers: the Process of Narcotics Addiction among Physicians and Nurses'. Unpublished paper presented at the Pacific Sociological Association, Salt Lake City, Utah, April 1965.

schools are not always seen as 'the best lawyer', 'the best doctor', 'the best social worker'.[1] Clearly, other elements are at work with respect to the concept of success.

When one considers the problem of finding variables or indicators for concepts such as 'recruitment to a profession', one begins to become aware that a single indicator is often not sufficient to suggest or point to the area denoted by such a concept. In the instance of 'recruitment to a profession', one realizes that such indicators as the age at which young people become interested in the occupation is of significance, particularly as early studies become more important to entry into the professional school,[2] and particularly as the recruits approach or pass through the turbulence of late adolescence which some investigators have found to bear on selection of occupation, and smooth entry into it.[3] Family background, particularly if the parents are practitioners of the occupation to which the son or daughter aspires,[4] interests in and knowledge of occupations,[5] the relationships with peers[6] also are relevant variables in the 'recruitment to the occupation'.

The discussion in the foregoing pages has been focused on attributes of concepts which lead sociologists studying this area to regard them as adequate or not. This discussion has allowed us to point up some critical instances of where the processes of professional socialization and professionalization merge to blur old concepts and generate the necessity for new ones. Implicity, however, this part of the discussion has turned on examination of concepts useful for studies in professional socialization in terms of a 'definitive concept', the concept which 'refers precisely to what is common to a class of objects by the aid of a clear definition in terms of attributes or fixed bench marks'.[7] There are few of these in the quiver of concepts available to the sociologist working in this particular area. It is, nevertheless, of significance to stand other, less well defined concepts up against these standards, not as a way of once again illuminating some of the conceptual problems in sociology, but by way of discussion and communication across wide sectors or the many types of sociologists interested

1   Our own shortcomings on this very point are documented in Olesen and Whittaker, *The Silent Dialogue*, pp. 206-7.
2   Natalie Rogoff, 'The Decision to Study Medicine', in Merton, Reader and Kendall, *op. cit.* pp. 109-29.
3   Elizabeth Douvan, personal communication; Jean-Daniel Réynaud and Alain Touraine, 'Deux notes à propos d'une enquête sur les étudiants en médicine', *Cahiers Internationaux de Sociologie*, Nouvelle Série, Troisième Année, vol. 20 (1956), 124-8.
4   John P. Lovell, 'The Professional Socialization of the West Point Cadet', in Morris Janowitz (ed), *The New Military* (New York, 1964), pp. 119-57.
5   Lois K. Cohen and Edward M. Knott, 'Interest of High School Girls in Dental Auxiliary Careers', *Journal of Dental Education*, 31, 1 (March 1967), 20-7; Joseph Fichter, *Religion As An Occupation* (South Bend, 1961).
6   Olesen and Whittaker, *The Silent Dialogue*, 'Friends as ratifiers', pp. 99-102.
7   Herbert Blumer, 'What is Wrong with Social Theory?' *American Sociological Review*, 19, 1 (February 1954), 7.

in professional socialization, e.g. sociological social psychologists, organizational experts, students of social structure and so forth. It also suggests that this is a way of noting crescive changes in concepts which in the hands of the humans engaged in the social enterprise called sociology are shaped and bent.[1] Moreover, like all of sociology itself and like sociologists themselves concepts ought to be 'public' if not 'replicable' and it does no harm occasionally to review them along some sort of standardized baselines in order to introduce change to them or to the baselines.

Yet the ultimate question remains of utility, construction of theory, utilizing of concepts in a widely shifting area such as professional socialization. In addressing ourselves to this final question we shall first review some factors in the sociology of sociological knowledge with respect particularly to our own position. We shall then enunciate certain observed attributes of professional socialization which lead us to the position that the matter of theory construction in this area is best served by utilization of emergent concepts closely tied to the empirical nature of the events in professional socialization, and being closely tied to that empirical nature, are therefore closely related to the natural social world from which the sociologist ought not to become separated. This does not infer that a raw empiricism is desirable, free of philosophy or the abstraction and conceptualization which lift sociology from a welter of facts and descriptions onto the level of interpretation, criticism, and quite properly, diagnosis.[2] It is a viewpoint, however, which differs substantially from that which advocates analysis of concepts solely in terms of logical requirements of theory.[3] It is a viewpoint which has been vividly stated:

'. . . this illustrates the fate of each branch of social science: that while it refines and purifies its theoretical core, its logic, it can never free itself from the human mess. Wallowing there, each purist will find himself in the company of others who, although they seek to create a different pure product of logic, must extract it from this same mess.'[4]

Not only are concepts referential to 'this human mess', but, as has been aptly observed about sociologists themselves, '. . . sociology is a human science, and as such is intimately connected to human foibles'.[5] Selection of concepts, the ideas guiding adequacy of concepts and theories, and positions on topics such as professional socialization are elements which emerge from and are shaped by the

1 Two analyses of crescive changes in 'role': William R. Catton, Jr., 'The Development of Sociological Thought', in Robert L. Faris (ed.), *Handbook of Modern Sociology* (Chicago, 1964), esp. pp. 935-43; Anne-Marie Rocheblave-Spenlé, *La Notion de Rôle en Psychologie Sociale* (Paris, 1962).

2 W. G. Runciman, 'The Nature of Social Science', in W. G. Runciman, *Social Science and Political Theory* (2nd ed.) (Cambridge, 1969), p. 17.

3 John Rex, *Key Problems of Sociological Theory* (London, 1961), p. 176.

4 Hughes, *op. cit.* 'Mistakes at work', p. 100.

5 Irving Louis Horowitz, 'Mainliners and Marginals', in Irving Louis Horowitz, *Professing Sociology: Studies in the Life Cycle of Social Science* (Chicago, 1968), p. 216.

sociologists' sector of 'the human mess' and are thus a part of social enterprise which is sociological social science. This point may be briefly developed before we discuss what we have observed about the natural social world of professional socialization and the bearing of these observations on conceptual adequacy.

MORAL DENSITY AND CONCEPTUAL ADEQUACY

We may begin by observing the commonplace, namely, that the social organization in which the sociologist is located, either to teach, to do research or to construct theory, in part shapes and articulates the circumstances in which both concepts and ideas of conceptual adequacy wax and wane. The lone sociologist whose academic position is on the faculty of a professional school (a situation probably more common in Britain and the United States than elsewhere) will perhaps experience constraints unknown to the sociologist who is a member of a university department. Knowledgeable faculty in the professional school, perhaps schooled in sociology, may wish to have their say about the utilization of concepts, and indeed, about the outcome of studies, if only as interested colleagues and not as partisans.[1] On the other hand, the lone sociologist in the professional school may be of such high social value to the profession, the faculty and students that any concepts he selects, even those which fail on counts of adequacy already discussed or those to be discussed, may be freely chosen and utilized, including utilization in the always sensitive reporting period.[2]

Significant though these situational factors are, it is of 'moral density' within sociological sub-sectors that we speak here.[3] 'Moral density' refers to the interconnections and interrelationships among sociologists, including systems of recruitment and socialization, universities of origin, locale and departmental positions, relationships with major and minor personages in the field, congenial (or perhaps not so congenial) access to and reciprocities with colleagues, places on key sociological or leading intellectual publications. Moral density, however, not only encompasses only these relational and structural factors, but it touches as well on the important matter of images, both of the field of sociology and of the individual sociologist. In this sense it points to the significant issue of how and where one develops a sense of self as a sociologist and how that sense of self is sustained. Comprehending as it does these varied levels in the sociological community, moral density is a useful theme with which to consider adequacy of

1 On experience with sophisticated faculty see, Olesen and Whittaker, *The Silent Dialogue*, p. 26.
2 Howard S. Becker, 'Problems in the Publication of Field Studies', in Arthur Vidich, Joseph Bensman and Maurice Stein (eds.), *Reflections on Community Studies* (New York, 1964), pp. 267-84.
3 Pierre Bourdieu and Jean-Claude Passeron, 'Sociology and Philosophy in France since 1945: Death and Resurrection of a Philosophy without Subject', *Social Research*, 34, 1 (Spring 1967), 203.

sociological concepts, for one begins to be aware (if one were not already so) that adequacy of concepts for study in professional socialization goes far beyond abstract baselines, structural factors that shape acceptance or rejection of the baselines and reaches right to the identity of the sociologist utilizing the concepts.

Perhaps most discernible in French and British sociology, but only less so in the United States, Japan and the U.S.S.R., moral density in sociology would appear to differ in degree across national boundaries. It would also seem that there are different moral densities within a national sociological community and these variations sensitize the analyst of concepts to major themes surrounding adequacy.[1] For instance, a consensus exists among some investigators of professional socialization on the utility and adequacy of concepts derived from symbolic interaction theory, e.g. 'self-other', 'perspectives', 'social act'.[2] These concepts have chiefly been used by first, second and third generation University of Chicago sociologists and by those whose kinship ties are less direct, but nevertheless sufficient to bind them, if only symbolically. The long emphasis in American sociology on the verification of theory may be seen as another example of where participants in yet a different moral density exerted a long and continuing influence on the very baselines of conceptual adequacy.[3]

Ossified though they may seem sometimes, sociological moral densities and their participants, very much as is true of those whom they study in the professions, are in flux. Large-scale shifts in society, of which both professions and sociology are part, yield social movements which play not only upon the professions, but upon academic sociology as well. If we can think of the processes of professionalization as a major social movement, then this bids fair, certainly in the United States, Britain and France, to give rise to sub-specialization within the sociological community, on this subject.[4] (We put aside the difficult question of the influence, if any, of sociological moral densities on professionalization, noting only that in some professions, notably American nursing and social work, participants in certain sociological and psychological moral densities have had parts in the professionalization process.)[5]

If professionalization and professional socialization as subjects for study are captured by participants in specific moral densities, then analysis of concepts and conceptual adequacy may well be bracketed by the moral and relational worlds of the participants in this specialized sub-sector. However, as we have noted elsewhere in this essay, the analysis of professionalization can have a refreshing effect on the understanding of empirical realities implicated in professional socialization. For example, it draws attention to changes in

1 Horowitz, *op. cit.*
2 Olesen and Whittaker, *The Silent Dialogue;* Becker *et al., op. cit.;* Quarantelli, *op. cit.*
3 Glaser and Strauss, *op. cit.* pp. 12-18.
4 For some contours see the bibliography on this matter, drawn up by Catherine Cajdos, Denise Walbert, Alfred Willener, *Sociologie du Travail*, 10, 3 (juillet-septembre 1968), 319-24.
5 Olesen and Whittaker, *The Silent Dialogue*, p. 77.

empirical matters which constitute the natural social world of those involved in professional socialization, namely conflicts between faculty people who teach 'new professional' themes versus those who impart 'traditional skills', or frictions between students who hold old-fashioned images of the profession and teachers who think in avant-garde terms. On the other hand, the scrutiny of professional socialization brings an equally refreshing input to the empirical issues in professionalization, for instance, the discord between new professionals and old-timers, or the sources of variations between attitudinal and structural elements in occupations undergoing professionalization. The recognition of reciprocal empirical materials in these two processes, professional socialization and professionalization, would seem to necessitate that sociologists transcend membership in their particular moral density in order to delineate relevant lines of conceptual adequacy.

We turn now to consider those factors in the natural social world of professional socialization, some of which are influenced by processes of professionalization, which are the foundations for empirically adequate concepts in the study of this area.

PROFESSIONAL SOCIALIZATION AND CONCEPTUAL ADEQUACY

The demands on an empirical science which would attend to the subject matter to be interpreted, require that the sociologist be concerned on the one hand with full understanding of subjective issues in the behaviour and lives studied and on the other hand that the investigator conform to the objective demands dictated by participation and membership in the social science community.[1] Implicated in this is the responsibility that the sociologist clarify for fellow social scientists the nature of the social being he has studied and whose social reality he will interpret, or, at the very least that he make clear what he has assumed about this social being, if only for purposes of transaction with those being studied. Of necessity this opens consideration of the most profound assumptions concerning the nature of social man and social reality and forces the sociologist to confront dim philosophical sectors of his own discipline, which, at least in America, have slid into memory for many sociologists.[2] Since these prerequisites apply to us no less than to our fellow sociologists, here we shall briefly state the position which we assume, which shapes our notions of participants and participation in professional socialization and which specifies the model of the actor at issue in the discussion of conceptual adequacy to follow. That position outlines an inter-

---

1 Here as in much else throughout this sector of the essay our position and thinking is shaped in ways often too subtle to footnote by the thinking of Alfred Schutz, in this particular instance, Natanson, *op. cit.,* 'The Scientific Model of the Social World', pp. 40-4.
2 Bourdieu and Passeron, *op. cit.* p. 212.

subjective view of persons in professional socialization as persons engaged in conscious, choice-making and intentional behaviours directed to and with others, living, dead or fictional, with whom they are implicated.[1] Our arrival at this particular position is detailed elsewhere and need not be reviewed here, except to note in passing that our comments in the previous section relevant to position in the sociological community and participation in various 'moral densities' apply as fully to us as to others whose work we have drawn on, critically or otherwise in these pages.[2] This means that we, too, are subject to the very criteria which we set forth, both in the preceding pages and those subsequent in this discussion.

In creating a view of the actor in professional socialization which assumes the qualities indicated above we have constructed a 'puppet show' whose activities, at least within the view we will outline, come very close to the activities and statements of the students, faculty, and members of the professions who participate in professional socialization. Our construction of the 'stage' on which the 'puppets' are acting, in this instance the institution, the professional and the socialization experience or process is one in which the 'puppets' are seen to have a hand in the very materials of the 'play', utilizing some 'props' furnished to them creating others out of the 'fabrics' and 'grease paint' imported to the 'stage' on which the 'play' will proceed, the very 'lines' of the 'script' in part written by the 'puppets' and in part enscribed by off-stage 'puppets' whose 'lines' themselves are buffeted and changed as newcomers compete for a place near the 'stage' and old timers learn new 'lines'. The seduction of metaphor could lead us on, but we shall return to more customary language for our discussion of adequate concepts, hoping that the nature and type of 'puppet' or construction which we have made is sufficiently clear so that the themes on which we base our criteria for adequacy in concepts with which to understand and interpret professional socialization will themselves be clear, as well as logical and precise with respect to this fundamental construction. Three major themes inform our criteria of adequacy for professional socialization: (1) Does the concept point to acts, behaviours or meanings which would be understandable to persons in real life using their own ways of understanding everyday life? (2) Does the concept incorporate understanding of the inner or subjective aspects of existence along with interpretation of objective factors? (3) Does the concept accommodate understanding dynamic factors in the subject being considered?

MEANINGFUL TO PERSONS IN EVERYDAY LIFE

The question of whether a concept points to acts, behaviours and meanings under-

---

1 Olesen and Whittaker, 'Some Thoughts on Images of Man...'.
2 Olesen and Whittaker, *The Silent Dialogue,* esp. Preface and 'Shifts and biases in researcher perspective', pp. 47-9. This work also details the longitudinal field work study of institutional professional socialization from which we draw materials cited here.

standable to persons in everyday life has been termed 'the criterion of adequacy',[1] a term which we have avoided in this discussion, since we have been using adequacy in a larger sense throughout these pages, namely the summation of all the various criteria discussed, e.g. efficiency, theory building and so forth. The criterion of 'adequacy' in this more limited sense has been more precisely stated as meaning that 'each term in such a scientific model of action [the puppet show] must be constructed in such a way that a human act performed within the real world by an individual actor as indicated by the typical construct would be understandable to the actor himself as well as to his fellow men in terms of commonsense interpretations of everyday life'.[2] In other words, is the concept compatible with the patterns of thought and folk explanation which people use in their everyday commerce with one another — is it in short, meaningful within the empirical reality under scrutiny? This has been stated more precisely:

'His data [those of the sociologist] are the already constituted meanings of active participants in the social world. It is to these already meaningful data that his scientific concepts must ultimately refer: to the meaningful acts of individual men and women, to their everyday experiences of one another, to their understanding of one another's meanings, and to their initiation of new meaningful behaviour of their own. So we see that the data of the social sciences have, while still in the pre-scientific stage, those elements of meaning and intelligible structure which later appear in more or less explicit form with a claim to categorical validity in the interpretive science itself.'[3]

The significance of this point may be referred to our earlier discussion on the matter of 'professionalization' as a useful concept in studies of professional socialization. Used to denote abstract qualities of 'professions' or 'occupations', themselves abstractions, 'professionalization' is in this sense not adequate, irrespective of what attributes are selected, e.g. rigorous admission criteria, establishment of a professional organization, and so on. Used, however, to point to the actions of persons in the occupation under scrutiny who define themselves as pushing for a situation they see as 'professional', who claim, as for example French graphologists do, that they wish to be 'professional' but that they do not wish to be controlled by the state since they themselves have rigorous requirements for admission, the concept in this sense is 'adequate' for it points to what is meaningful for the actors.[4] In the first case the concept denotes only the meaning of the sociologist; in the second it speaks to the intersubjectivity of and meaningfulness for persons involved.[5]

1 Alfred Schutz, 'Concept and Theory Formation in the Social Sciences', in Natanson, *op. cit.*
2 Schutz, *ibid.* p. 54.
3 Alfred Schutz, *The Phenomenology of the Social World* (Evanston, 1967), p. 8.
4 Personal communication on graphologists from Jean-Daniel Réynaud, Directeur, Institut des Sciences Sociales de Travail, Université de Paris.
5 A source which recognizes the second meaning: Kenneth Prandy, *Professional Employees, A Study of Scientists and Engineers* (London, 1965).

Concepts such as 'competition' and 'cooperation' which describe student willingness to share notes from classes, how many hours to study, when to support a fellow student in trouble with the faculty or with other students constitute examples of 'adequate concepts', for they are quickly understood by faculty or students, or, indeed, parents and the understandings easily and quickly transmitted to the sociologist, who is building theory or doing research on professional socialization.[1] Being close, however, to the everyday world of understandings shared by the students and faculty, these concepts, although adequate are also risky by virtue of the very fact that they are close to the everyday world, indeed the everyday world shared by the sociologist. But the task for the sociologist in using these concepts differs from that of faculty or students. For the sociologist the concepts of 'competition' and 'cooperation', though reflective of the empirical reality just indicated and the shared meanings of faculty and students, must be systematically used to scrutinize empirical reality rather than merely to live it, and must be subjected to the rigours of logic and theoretical relevance noted earlier. 'Competition', then must be understood as one of a trinity of concepts including 'cooperation' and 'conflict' to denote classes of relationships among occupants of specific roles (students, peers and faculty), where the intentions of the relationships were directed to allocation of institutional sanctions (grades, instructor approval).[2] To accept the constructs of everyday life as scientific for sociological purposes is to invite the possibility of confusion and ambiguity, even though the concepts may serve well in the everyday setting. For example, to accept the statement suggested by the students that 'competition' was the extent to which students studied for examinations would have led our analysis to overlook very divergent behaviours, for example, the ways in which students conducted themselves in seminar discussion, which we came to learn were also part of 'competition', not only through repeated observations but through scrutinizing 'competition' in the scientific manner suggested above.

Another example will illustrate the twin requirements that a concept retain the capacity to point to meaningful acts and action within the everyday world of those whose behaviour is being explained and at the same time be lifted to an abstract and logical level where it becomes part of systematic sociological discourse and is not mixed uncritically with everyday concepts. Sensitized by findings from students of United States medical students which showed that such students develop different 'perspectives' (meaning definitions of future goals and how to attain them) as they pass through medical school, we were concerned with similar definitions among the student nurses we were studying.[3] Moreover, because of our own immersion in their everyday world, our study

---

1 Becker, *et al., op. cit.*
2 Olesen and Whittaker, *The Silent Dialogue,* pp. 188-99.
3 Becker, *et al., op. cit.*

being an observation study, we had learned that students we were studying had highly developed formulae for finding out how to behave on the wards, how to manage persons including peers, staff, faculty and the research team, how to learn instructor styles and very importantly, how to act on the information once received.[1] In short, their everyday world included effective and subtle equations for finding their way through mundane situations which were part and parcel of their university education in nursing. A folk phrase, 'psyching out', spawned from the richness of American college student rhetoric, was in use among these students to denote these rich repertoires of formulae for the assessment of ways to survive and succeed in the professional school, most especially with respect to relationships with faculty. We retained the phrase 'psyching out' for our analysis of and subsequent write-up of student socialization for reasons which, in retrospect, had to do with the efficiency of the phrase and its utility in communicating to readers who would include not only sociologists but students and faculty in the professions as well. Our use of 'psyching out', however, implied more than that which was subsumed in the everyday student construct, for it actually referred to the more abstract (for our analysis) construct of 'situational learning', which in the course of some comparative analysis of students, we had learned goes on in a good many professional (and trade) schools, not just those educating doctors and nurses.[2] The penalty which we paid by retaining the student rhetoric is illustrative of one problem analysts can encounter when they indiscriminately borrow language from the everyday world. Because the term itself was meaningful to the students and sprang from their rhetoric, these very origins served to encapsulate our analytic use of 'psyching out' as 'situational learning'. We tended to overlook analysis of these processes among faculty, even though we were aware that something akin to 'psyching out' was in play among instructors, too.

In passing we may note this criticism from a slightly different standpoint — the uncritical use of 'psyching out' in this instance did not accord fully with the model of professional socialization which we had set ourselves. To be sure it was compatible with an assumption of an acting, choice-asking student, but in so far as the concept led us to concentrate less on the faculty role, our use was not consonant with those sectors of our model which posited an acting, choice-making faculty also implicated in inter-subjective processes with students.

In concluding we may ask about the extent to which abstract sociological constructs are part of the everyday student and faculty discourse in professional

1 Olesen and Whitaker, *The Silent Dialogue*, 'Ambiguousness, tenuous trust and psyching out', pp. 150-66.
2 Charles D. Orth, *Social Structure and Learning Climate: The First Year at the Harvard Business College* (Boston, 1963); Blanche Geer, Jack Hass, Charles Vi Vona, Stephen J. Miller, Clyde Woods and Howard S. Becker, 'Learning the Ropes, Situational Learning in Four Occupational Training Programs', in Irwin Deutscher and Elizabeth J. Thompson (eds.), *Among The People, Studies of the Urban Poor* (New York, 1968), pp. 209-33.

schools? No one who has examined the educational journals in various professions and would-be professions in a number of different societies can fail to find ample evidence that concepts such as prestige, career, identity, role, socialization, and attitude, have become part of the professional school language, used alike by students, faculty, practitioners, families and friends of students.[1] The observation, 'Who can think, talk, or write today without explicit or implicit use of terms such as mores, folkways, social structure, culture, role, self-conceptions and social status?'[2] nicely applies to the modern professional school. The spread of these concepts into the professional schools points to inter-connections between academic disciplines and the professions and to public communication, as well, which popularizes these constructs.

A further question, the extent to which this penetration of any sociological construct defines and shapes the everyday world with which the sociologist seeks to make his constructs compatible is less easily answered. If the chorus of complaints about the lack of clarity in various concepts is to be believed, then it is unlikely to expect that persons in professional schools have been able to settle on a given and clear understanding of these constructions, for, indeed, sociologists themselves are far from such consensus. (Ironically, professional schools tend to concrete thinking in their curricula.) If that were in fact the case, then the sociologist could utilize the construct directly in his questions and scrutiny for there would be − which there is definitely not − perfect correspondence and compatibility between the sociological construct and the interpretations of persons in everyday life. Perhaps in this instance sociology is its own worst enemy, for its own practitioners and those invidiously (and sometimes unfairly) denoted as 'popularizers' are busy diffusing their own vaguenesses to the very persons they would understand and in so doing muddy the already unclear constructs. Yet, the public quality of any science requires open discussion. For the time being sociologists can assume only that there is not yet a perfect relationship between the interpretations of everyday life and scientific constructions in sociology. The tension which remains because of the lack of correspondence requires close attention to adequacy as discussed in this section of the paper. In closing these comments we may note once again that the thrusts of professionalizing an occupation may exacerbate these very problems, for the demand that professional training be institutionalized and understood, which

1 Ralph R. Show, 'The Library's Role in Society Today?' *Journal for Education of Librarianship*, 2, 4 (Spring 1962), 178-82; D. Tallon, 'Les carrières ouvertes aux étudiants des facultés de droit et des sciences économiques', *Revue de l'Enseignement Supérieur*, 1, 1 (décembre-janvier 1963), 82-91; Paul W. Pruyser, 'The Impact of the Psychological Disciplines on the Training of Clergy', *Pastoral Psychology*, 19, 187 (October 1968), 21-32; Barbara K. Varley, 'Sociolization in Social Work Education', *Social Work*, 8, 3 (July 1963), 102-9.
2 John R. Seeley, 'Crestwood Heights: Intellectual and Libidinal Dimensions of Research', in Arthur J. Vidich, Joseph Bensman and Maurice Stein (eds.), *Reflections on Community Studies* (New York, 1964), p. 159.

implicates social science in the process pulls into the everyday language of the profession and the professional training school some of the very concepts most cherished by sociologists who would study the processes of professional socialization.

Our discussion of adequacy in the pages immediately preceding flows from a position which we take on the nature of concepts in sociology. The themes to be examined now with respect to adequacy find their source elsewhere, in these instances, in the type of assumptions we prefer to make about the processes and events subsumed in professional socialization. These are closely and logically related to the model of social life and behaviour which we indicated earlier, as indeed they must be, but they are also referential to a view of professional socialization which is informed by our earlier discussion of professionalization and its implications for the socialization processes, most especially in the sector embraced by the formal, institutional phase.

BRIDGING THE OBJECTIVE AND SUBJECTIVE

The first of these criteria speaks to the issue of how well concepts handle the subjective aspects of professional socialization in conjunction with objective factors. The issue is implicit in the very concept of 'professional' which implies, at least in our definition of it, a more or less commonly understood set of occupational values and technical role behaviours transmitted both through a formal institution and informal contacts and assimilated and acted on, partially or fully, formally and informally, by individuals whose subsequent behaviour is formally and informally evaluated in terms of these values and formal role behaviours. Indeed, if we accept the previous comments on conceptual adequacy in the sense of being referential to the empirical or everyday world we are constrained to look into the subjective aspects of the socialization process. Evidence from a number of quarters points to this: student nurses demonstrate varied patterns of acceptance for themselves of professional image, studies of dental and divinity students show that they personally do not agree with faculty values, enquiries show that junior and senior medical students differ among themselves as to whether they think of themselves in various institutionally-approved ways, for example, as 'scientists', 'professionals' or 'humanitarians'.[1] We may note in passing, however, that a number of assumptions held over from the influence of institutional studies on those being done in professional socialization tends to lead investigators away

---

1 Olesen and Whittaker, *The Silent Dialogue*, 'Professional values', pp. 123-30; Enrico Quarantelli, Margaret Helfrich and Daniel Yutzy, 'Faculty and Student Perceptions in a Professional School', *Sociology and Social Research*, 49, 1 (October 1964), 32-45; H. Richard Niebuhr, Daniel Day Williams, and James M. Gustafson, *The Advancement of Theological Education*, (New York, 1957); Leonard Reissman, Ralph V. Platou, S. H. Sledge and D.H. Malone. 'The motivation and socialization of medical students', *Journal of Health and Human Behaviour*, 1, 3 (Fall 1960), 174-82.

from subjective aspects of this particular process.[1]

What types of concepts then serve to meet this criterion of adequacy and to bridge the phenomenological aspects with those of structure and environment? One characteristic of such concepts is that they allow the investigator to bridge these aspects of the process with some sense of the reciprocities implicit in the exchange of definitions by students, faculty or professionals experiencing the more or less codified definitions of others. Those codified definitions in this instance are elements of structure, for example, how many courses, and what types of grades, how long an internship, what legal rules govern ethical practice, how much does schooling and establishment of practice cost and so forth. One such concept which has been utilized successfully in the study of the mental hospital is that of 'negotiated order', referring to the exchange of individual definitions that both respond to, and alter structural arrangements.[2] 'Negotiated socialization' as a parallel concept for studies of professional socialization has not been utilized, but several concepts which come very close have been adequate. We must note in passing that the sociologist must utilize more than the concept of 'self' or 'identity' in bridging the phenomenological and structural, for to dwell solely on the inner aspects of socialization is to over-look the necessary objective sectors. One concept, 'studentmanship', which does bridge these aspects of professional socialization may be cited.

Earlier we discussed the concept of 'psyching out', or phrased more abstractly, 'situational learning', as we had used it in our work. Clearly, this concept alone, although rich with subjective implications was not one which could bridge the experience of socialization from the view of the students, what was in the structure or what was attributed to them by others, whether in the form of institutional norms and sanctions transmitted by faculty or folk norms concerning illness, health, everyday affairs transmitted to them by their friends, patients, other professional staff, family and so forth. Clearly, not only some concept referential to 'situational adjustment' was called for — both by the logic of the earlier concept and by the ongoing analysis of the data. We found such a concept in 'fronting', which accommodated the sets of gestures, statements and behaviours exchanged between students and others. These 'fronts' are predicated on the evaluations accumulated through 'situational learning'. The concept serves to lift the analysis from the subjective to the interpersonal, since the 'fronts', being social products, came into the public parts of the socialization process and hence were the foundations for the responses of others implicated in the situations found in various parts of the process. But 'fronting' or to put it more formally, 'presentation of self' was useful only in denoting the phenomenological aspects of evaluating situations and did not necessarily integrate these with

1 Olesen and Whittaker, 'Some Thoughts on Images of Man...'.
2 Anselm Strauss, Leonard Schatzman, Rue Bucher, Danuta Ehrlich and Melvin Sabshin, *Psychiatric Ideologies and Institutions* (New York. 1964).

the structural parts. For that we needed a more embracing concept which not only could denote 'psyching out', the phenomenological, 'fronting', the inter-actional, but could also refer to the structure with implications of certain institutional realities found in the arrangements of sanctions and power. For this we generated the concept of studentmanship, similar in its meanings to student culture, but more attuned, we reasoned, to the integration of the subtle shadings between and among the phenomenological, interactional and structural, and more powerful in that it referred to the constant shifts of meanings, emergent norms and actions which, as we were to find out, both enhanced and deterred the institutional parts of the socialization process. In its structural sense, studentmanship articulated and created a 'shadow structure' of the institutions and its norms, power arrangements and sanctions, a shadow structure highly con-gruent at significant points with certain institutional factors, e.g. university codes concerning grades and grade points necessary for continued study and graduation, professional ethics concerning treatment of patients and conformity, rules con-cerning housing arrangements, knowledge of the formal stratification system in the professional school. Also a part of this shadow structure, however, were important points of departure from official sectors of the structure, for example, student reluctance to accept curricular emphasis on certain avant-garde themes in the profession, and attendant sets of norms within the shadow structure that were equally as stringent and binding upon students as certain formal institutional demands.

The structural aspects of studentmanship at points congruent with formal realities and divergent at others, stood literally *in loco parentis*, as it were, for the official structure and whatever structure faculty and professional staff defined. We stress the point that this shadow structure in studentmanship, the result of endless cycles of 'psyching out', 'fronting', and interacting among and between students, was created by the students to blend their world with that of the institution and profession. We emphasize this, because often bridging concepts are utilized as intervening variables between structure and person, somehow functioning to explain the filtering and mediating of the influences of structure when seen as an 'independent' variable. The intervening variable would be appropriate in a model where the sociologist assumed that the social actor in social life was moulded and shaped by his environment, for example, a model where student is seen as a product.[1] Whether or not we wish to accept such an alternative model as useful or adequate is not relevant to this point in the dis-cussion. What is relevant is that 'studentmanship' is consonant with our assumptions in that it denotes the students' creation for themselves of norms, sanctions, understandings, manoeuvres, definitions and evaluative strategies, in part predicated on institutional realities, but to large measure emergent from the onward flow of 'psyching', 'fronting', leading to consensus around personal

1   Olesen and Whittaker, 'Some Thoughts on Images of Man...'.

H

definitions salient to other sectors of life, as well as, for example, events in lateral role paths, e.g. the sex role and so forth. The phenomenological and interactional ingredients of 'studentmanship' were drawn from every sector of the 'multiple realities' in which students were implicated.[1] Clearly such a conceptualization demands a parallel concept with which to accommodate understanding of incumbents of powerful roles in the institutional structure, namely, faculty. In this instance we were not turned away from other parts of the empirical reality as we had been in the earlier instance of 'psyching out'. We conceptualized a parallel concept for faculty who themselves create and act on shadow structure of the institution and pass on their definitions of that creation to students.

Our discussion here does not deny that the sociologist, attending to the definitions of students, faculty and others, cannot characterize certain institutions devoted to professional socialization as 'tightly controlled', 'loosely structured', and that these characterizations of participants' definitions are not useful in understanding what is subsequently created by faculty or students. On the contrary, they are almost mandatory if sociological analysis of professional socialization is to avoid the charge of excessive pragmatism which has been properly levied against American studies of higher education, of which professional education is an important sector, and if the analyst is to attend to the lessons of history.[2] The lessons of history in this case refer specifically to the careers of the occupations designated as professions, at least those where students are being scrutinized in studies of professional socialization. It is important to account for, among other factors, the state of the profession with respect, not only to the types of training being necessary or adequate, but the nature and locale of such education, for example, the militaristic early hospital schools of nursing in the United States, the loose personal understandings of apprenticeship systems in English law and medicine and similar arrangements in American law, medicine and engineering.[3] Clearly, these structures, characterized in different ways which reflect the stage of the processes of becoming a profession, are significant, not as forces impinging on the identities or relationships students draw to them, for that statement would be inconsistent with the model which we have assumed. Rather, these are circumstances, which like a good many other factors in the varied sectors of the private worlds of the students, faculty and practitioners are ingredients for definitions of the situations com-

1   Alfred Schutz, 'On Multiple Realities', in Natanson, *op. cit.* pp. 207-59.
2   Olesen and Whittaker, *The Silent Dialogue*, 'Faculty Commonsense World', pp. 138-40. Joseph Sumpf, 'Aperçu sur la sociologie de l'éducation aux États-Unis, l'étude des effets', *Revue Française de Sociologie*, 6, 2 (avril-juin 1965), 203-14.
3   Olesen and Whittaker, *The Silent Dialogue*, chapter III, 'The Nursing World and the Collegiate School', esp. pp. 64-68; Reader, *op. cit.* p. 43; Daniel H. Calhoun, *Professional Lives in America, Structure and Aspiration, 1750-1850* (Cambridge, 1965) and Daniel H. Calhoun, *The American Civil Engineer, Origins and Conflict* (Cambridge, 1960).

municated to others and acted on by the individual, and eventually incorporated into a bridging concept which spans the inner and subjective parts of the process with these structural elements.

The analysis of 'studentmanship' speaks to the problems of analysing on-going matters in the course of the institutional part of professional socialization. These years or months are but part of the long-range processes which constitute professional socialization, processes in play before students arrive in school and which continue after they have or have not graduated into the practice of the occupation. Here the problem is to bridge the private world of the student with the structural one of the profession, either as found in the professional school or in locales of practice beyond schooling. 'Anticipatory socialization', meaning the prior rehearsal by an individual with respect to views to self, images of profession and behaviours in the future role either as student professional or full professional is an adequate concept to bridge subjective and objective factors, if it in turn is linked to the concept of 'reference group', those persons situated in the structure to which the individual is aspiring.[1] Both 'anticipatory socialization' and 'reference group' served us well in this regard for they denoted more or less effectively the expectations which students had held that later coalesced into role behaviours and norms around performance. However, our data analysis also guided us to two themes, 'differentiation' and 'induction', that we found necessary to conceptualize in order to denote what students reported had happened to them in the flow of events prior to the institution. Some facets of the prior rehearsal apparently served to cut students off from their usual social worlds and former selves, while other facets seemingly bound the student into the future professional role and the structure of the professional school. Other investigators who have faced the problem of analyses of facets of self and structure in professional socialization with respect to long range socialization have found the concept of 'professionalism' adequate to this task.[2] Their analysis of student actresses takes as a starting point a university drama department's institutional imperatives, e.g. producing successful plays (both financially and artistically) and links these through student and faculty interaction centred on aspects of 'professionalism' to student statements of emergent views of themselves as actresses and to various sets of behaviours among and between students and faculty which serve to keep the socialization process on an even footing.[3] Through the use of 'professionalism' they bridge analysis of emergent student

1 The fundamental discussion of 'reference group' and 'anticipatory socialization' may be found in Merton, *op. cit.* chapter VIII, 'Contributions to the theory of reference group behavior' (with Alice S. Rossi), esp. pp. 265-75; and 'Continuities in the theory of reference groups and social structure', pp. 281-384.

2 On the definition of 'professionalism' see Howard M. Vollmer and Donald L. Mills (eds.), *Professionalization*, Editors, introduction, p. vii.

3 H. L. Hearn, Peter K. Manning, Robert W. Habenstein, 'Identity and Institutional Imperatives: the Socialization of the Student Actress', *The Sociological Quarterly*, 9, 1 (Winter 1968), 47-63.

identity, as seen through the students' own views, and the structural, institutional imperatives experienced both by students and faculty, e.g. production of artistically meritorious, but financially successful plays whilst teaching and educating students.

ACCOMMODATION OF DYNAMIC MATERIALS

We come now to our third theme regarding adequacy of concepts, namely, whether constructs accommodate dynamic materials in professionalization, since the very term 'socialization' implies movement and change in the parties reciprocally implicated in the process, most specifically rearrangements and alteration in role behaviours and perceptions and definitions of individuals coming into the profession. Implicit in this latter section of the understandings around 'socialization' is that these behaviours, definitions and perceptions will be viewed as objectively acceptable to practitioners or those whose judgements define the individual as 'being socialized'. This latter aspect is critical since it would be possible to conceptualize, indeed even meet in real life a student in professional school who had indeed altered his definitions of his profession, but who in the eyes of the evaluators could not be thought of as 'professional'.

This critical point leads us back momentarily to the discussion in the preceding pages on the necessity to bridge subjective and objective facets of the process, but it also takes us forward to the crucial factor of time and the relationships between the inner and subjective modes of time, official calendar time, articulated by the institution, to cite but one point of divergence in the problem of time.[1] This means that where matters of change or socialization are at issue, the views of change within the subjective world of the students may differ quite substantially from that of the official calendar, or of individual faculty or of others. For example, patients act toward student physicians as if the students were already the professional people they (the students) do not believe themselves to be.[2] Transformations or socialization within the inner world of the student cannot therefore be considered or assumed to be isomorphic to those regularized by the official clock or calendar, hence the possibility of an 'unsocialized graduate', and hence the necessity to generate concepts which in speaking of process allow for the discrepancies (student defining self in advance or behind calendar time) and congruence (student defining self exactly in terms of calendar time) possible. Our own answer to this, the emergent concept of 'identity errors', referring to the first two types of discrepancies when manifested in behaviour, e.g. a student who indicated that she knew too much or too little

1 Alfred Schutz, *The Phenomenology of the Social World*, p. 12.
2 Mary Jean Huntington, 'The Development of a Professional Self-image', in Merton, *et. al.*, *op. cit.* pp. 179-87.

with reference to faculty, is not entirely adequate to this task.[1] It permitted us to integrate these disparate aspects of time, and to analyse some of the inter- actional and behavioural consequences of their expression, but the introduction of the term 'error' to stand as a synonym for discrepancy biases the use of the concept in a direction favouring institutional, rather than subjective definitions. To know more than faculty think one should, may indeed not be an 'error', but it is certainly a discrepancy.

Another solution to this problem of adequacy is to utilize concepts which denote the self-definitions of professionals or students in terms of larger systems of official and calendar time or historical time, for example research which closely ties the professional policeman's statements about himself in this role with the shifts and changes within the profession of policeman.[2] The risk here is that the categories of official time, used as concepts to denote phenomeno- logical changes, may not in fact denote those changes. Careful analysis is necessary to generate these categories from the statements of the students or professionals involved, as, for instance in an analysis of 'doctrinal conversion'.[3] We can see the hazards of 'stage' analysis in professional socialization for the stages may be the constructs of the sociologist's view of official time, quite divorced from that of the subjective world of the students, who may not in fact be assimilating techniques when they should be, but instead are working through value systems and so forth.[4]

Thus when one speaks of the dynamic materials in professional socialization one refers to these disjunctive questions in the matter of time. We must note here that these statements are not intended to fault static, snap-shot analysis of the materials denoted by certain concepts at any given point in time, assuming, of course, that the materials are empirically relevant and denote aspects of the everyday world of the students. These snap-shots are valuable for the fine-grained details and contours they, much as photos in old family albums, give. What can be utilized, however, to surmount the problems of divergent time flow with respect to dynamic analysis are transitional concepts such as 'status transition', or

---

1 An extended analysis with this concept may be found in Virginia Olesen and Elvi Whittaker, 'Adjudication of Student Awareness...'
2 James Leo Walsh, 'The Professional Cop', Unpublished paper presented at the American Sociological Association, San Francisco, September 1969.
3 Fred Davis, 'Professional Socialization as Subjective Experience: the Process of Doctrinal Conversion among Student Nurses', in Howard S. Becker, Blanche Geer, David Riesman and Robert Weiss, *Institutions and the Person, Essays in Honour of Everett Hughes* (Chicago, 1968), pp. 235-51.
4 Ida H. Simpson, 'Patterns of Socialization into Professions: the Case of Student Nurses', *Sociological Inquiry*, 37, 1 (Winter 1967), 47-54.
5 We use this very snap-shot method in our own work. See Olesen and Whittaker, *The Silent Dialogue*, table 11, 'Fronting: students who agreed strongly or in the main with aspects of presenting the self', p. 174. Items in the table were generated from student statements.

'cycles of depression and elation'.[1]

To conclude our discussion on adequacy, we may note again that the usual ideals of conceptual adequacy, clarity, utility in theory construction, parsimony and so forth are useful means of communication among sociologists of different persuasions. To these we added three dimensions of adequacy, one predicated on Schutz's notion of 'adequacy' or empirical relevance and two which spring from assumptions about the nature of professional socialization as a social psychological process. We may terminate our thoughts with some observations on the idea of adequacy itself.

SPECULATIONS ON CONCEPTUAL ADEQUACY QUA ADEQUACY

When we have discussed in these pages ideas of 'conceptual adequacy', we have referred to a construct which by virtue of being a mental product originated by sociologists at certain times and places is also subject to changing influences running through the history of sociology, shifts in scientific fashions, movements through sectors of 'moral densities', infusions of social reality via unrest in the social order, world problems and so forth. The term 'conceptual adequacy' is therefore like all human ideas prey to the moulding forces of history (although it, too, can serve as the thrust into new areas of endeavour), just as other concepts such as 'childhood', and 'progress' and 'adolescence' have been moulded by history.[2] And, indeed, concepts such as 'equilibrium' have helped to mould history, at least history of thought and method in the social sciences.[3]

Much, therefore, that is relevant to the question of adequacy itself has to do with the question of the field of sociology itself, how its members define the field with respect to other endeavours,[4] and, how they look upon it with respect to its scientific and humanistic aspects.[5] At the time of writing sociology is characterized by highly differing degrees of pluralism in the many societies where there are sociologists pursuing their discipline, for sociology in Western Europe, Japan and the U.S.A. seems to be more pluralistic than that in the U.S.S.R.[6] In

1 Fred Davis and Virginia Olesen, 'Initiation into a Woman's Profession: Identity Problems in the Status Transition of Coed to Student Nurse', *Sociometry*, 26, 1 (March 1963), 89-101; Olesen and Whittaker, *The Silent Dialogue*, 'Cycles of depression and elation', pp. 251-9.
2 Philippe Aries, *Centuries Of Childhood* (New York, 1962); J. B. Bury, *The Idea of Progress* (New York, 1955); Peter Musgrove, *Youth and the Social Order* (London 1964).
3 Cynthia Eagle Russett, *The Concept of Equilibrium in American Social Thought* (New Haven, 1966).
4 Smelser, in Lazarsfeld *et al., op. cit.*
5 Edward Shils, 'The Calling of Sociology', in Talcott Parsons, Edward Shils, Kaspar, D. Naegele and Jesse R. Pitts (eds.), *Theories of Society,* vol. II, pp. 1405-48.
6 Collection L'Evolution de la vie Sociale, *Aspects de la Sociologie Française* (Paris, 1966); Paul Halmos (ed.), *Japanese Sociological Studies, The Sociological Review,* Monograph No. 10, 1966; George Fischer, 'Sociology', in George Fischer (ed.), *Science and Ideology in Soviet Society* (New York, 1967), pp. 1-45.

this connection it may be observed that highly pluralistic disciplines do not readily develop tightly constructed baselines of adequacy or concepts around which there is a high degree of consensus, since the very pluralism imports a certain flexibility and suppleness that allows a variety of baselines and concepts to emerge, indeed, invites their emergence. We may speculate that future development of concepts for use in studies of professional socialization and of baselines for understanding conceptual adequacy will be shaped by this supple pluralism and its less welcome fellow travellers ambiguity and lack of clarity.

In the instance, however, of studies of professional socialization, as we have noted at several points throughout the essay, the very empirical materials, those matters of substance and definition seen through the everyday world of the persons implicated in the socialization process, are informed by the over-arching changes implicated in professionalization. The question of professionalization cannot be ignored by the student of professional socialization and indeed must be considered as a constraining and influencing element on the very issue of conceptual adequacy for analysis, theory construction and research in this area. The very substance of what is transmitted in the socializing process, the roles implicated, the definitions exchanged, the students recruited are shaped by professionalization, which we here extend to mean the broad changes in the occupation, as well as those thrusting it to professional status. We would be remiss, however, and false to our own model of the social actor indicated earlier if we left matters there, for this last sentence strongly suggests that we see professionalization impinging on students and faculty. We must go on to observe that if the student of professional socialization seeks to attend to processes of professionalization, this admonition may be turned on its head, for the student of professionalization may well attend to what studies of professional socialization have to say about the processes which bring newcomers to the occupation, newcomers whose arrival, presence and definitions are influential on the course of professionalization as they come to create the very culture of the profession. Conceptual adequacy in studies of professional socialization along the lines we have discussed in these pages and along patterns which are yet to emerge will enhance the analysis of professional socialization and in the long run nourish the systematic scrutiny of the reciprocities between these major streams of change, professionalization and professional socialization, as well as institutional and personal change.

INDEX

226

For EU product safety concerns, contact us at Calle de José Abascal, 56–1°,
28003 Madrid, Spain or eugpsr@cambridge.org.

www.ingramcontent.com/pod-product-compliance
Ingram Content Group UK Ltd.
Pitfield, Milton Keynes, MK11 3LW, UK
UKHW010043140625
459647UK00012BA/1574